Competition Policy Analysis

As markets become increasingly integrated and globalized, competition policy is facing new challenges. In order to meet these challenges, competition policy authorities have had to adjust their policy instruments, analytical approaches and enforcement behaviour. In such a context, this book examines the methods and tools of competition policy analysis, and contributes a wealth of new research to the contemporary debate.

Contributions from leading international experts explore both theoretical and methodological issues of practical relevance for the new competition policy order and give examples of practical policy adjustments. The book focuses on key topics such as the relationship between competition policy and sector-specific regulatory policies under deregulation and market orientation, and undertakes a critical review of traditional approaches.

Presenting new theoretical approaches and a range of international case studies, *Competition Policy Analysis* represents an essential text for those with a professional or academic interest in competition policy.

Einar Hope is Professor of Energy Economics at the Norwegian School of Economics and Business Administration, Bergen. He was Director General of the Norwegian Competition Authority 1995–99, and has been actively involved in work on regulatory reforms in Norway and other countries. He is the author of *Competition and Trade Policies* (Routledge, 1998).

Routledge Studies in the Modern World Economy

Competition Policy Analysis

Edited by
Einar Hope

London and New York

First published 2000
by Routledge
11 New Fetter Lane, London EC4P 4EE

Simultaneously published in the USA and Canada
by Routledge
29 West 35th Street, New York, NY 10001

Routledge is an imprint of the Taylor & Francis Group

Typeset in Times by
Keystroke, Jacaranda Lodge, Wolverhampton
Printed and bound in Great Britain by
St Edmundsbury Press,
Bury St Edmunds, Suffolk

British Library Cataloguing in Publication Data
A catalogue record for this book is available from the British Library

Library of Congress Cataloging in Publication Data
Hope, Einar, 1937–
    Competition policy analysis / Einar Hope.
        p. cm.
    Includes bibliographical references and index.
    ISBN 0–415–22653–8 (alk. paper)
    1. Industrial policy. 2. Competition. 3. Industrial policy—Case
studies. 4. Competition—Case studies. I. Title.
HD2757 .H67 2000
338.9—dc21

                                                    99–059062

ISBN 0–415–22653–8

Contents

EINAR HOPE

AGNAR SANDMO

FRÉDÉRIC JENNY

Figures

Tables

List of contributors

Timothy Besley is a Professor at the London School of Economics.

Nils-Henrik M. von der Fehr is a Professor at the University of Oslo.

Allan Fels is Chairman of the Australian Competition and Consumer Commission.

Svend Hylleberg is a Professor at the University of Aarhus.

Einar Hope is a Professor at the Norwegian School of Economics and Business Administration, Bergen and former Director General of the Norwegian Competition Authority.

Frédéric Jenny is Vice President of the Conceil de la Concurrence in France and a Professor at ESSEC, Paris.

Stephen Martin is a Professor and Director of the Centre for Industrial Economic Research at the University of Copenhagen.

Victor D. Norman is a Professor at the Norwegian School of Economics and Business Administration, Bergen.

Per Baltzer Overgaard is a Professor at the University of Copenhagen.

Anders Chr. S. Ryssdal, Dr. juris., is a partner in the firm of Wiersholm, Mellbye & Beck, Oslo.

Kjell G. Salvanes is a Professor at the Norwegian School of Economics and Business Administration, Bergen.

Agnar Sandmo is a Professor at the Norwegian School of Economics and Business Administration, Bergen.

Paul Seabright is a Professor at the University of Cambridge.

Carl Shapiro is a Professor at the Haas School of Business, University of California, Berkeley.

Margaret E. Slade is a Professor at the University of British Columbia, Vancouver

Lars Sørgard is a Professor at the Norwegian School of Economics and Business Administration, Bergen.

Frode Steen is an Associate Professor at the Norwegian School of Economics and Business Administration, Bergen.

Preface

This book documents the proceedings of the second Oslo Competition Policy Conference on 'The Foundations of Competition Policy Analysis', held in Oslo on 21–22 September 1998, and organized by the Norwegian Competition Authority (NCA). The first conference in this series, initiated and organized by the NCA, was held in June 1996 on 'Competition Policies for an Integrated World Economy'. The proceedings of that conference are published in the Routledge Studies in the Modern World Economy series: Einar Hope and Per Maeleng (eds): *Competition and Trade Policies: Coherence or Conflict?*, Routledge, 1998.

These conferences are intended as a meeting place for practitioners of competition policy in competition authorities and representatives of the academic and research communities and the business community, and as a forum for discussing important competition policy questions. The focus for the 1998 conference was on methodological and analytical issues in competition policy and cases in practice and thus contributed, hopefully, to improving such analyses by competition authorities.

The Norwegian Competition Authority is grateful to the Norwegian Ministry of Labour and Government Administration, the Norwegian Ministry of Industry and Trade, and the Norwegian Ministry of Foreign Affairs, respectively, for financial support to the conference. A number of my colleagues at the Authority rendered invaluable assistance in connection with the conference arrangements and in the editing process of the proceedings. I would particularly like to mention Unni Bache, Ingrid Braatejorde, Morten Berg, Lasse Ekeberg, and Knut Wettermark. Unni and Ingrid did a fantastic job when they had to contact some 150 conference participants from around the world at the very last minute when the conference, which was originally scheduled for mid-June, had to be cancelled because of an unexpected air traffic controllers' strike in Norway. They managed to contact all representatives in time! The cancellation had the unfortunate effect that two contributors, Professors John Kay and John Sutton, were unable to present their papers when the conference was rescheduled for September.

I would also like to thank Simon Whitmore of Routledge for stimulating cooperation during the editing and production process. I hope that the book will contribute to focusing on and improving the analytical foundations of competition policy analysis so that decisions by competition authorities can be based on sound principles and with the best analytical tools available.

Einar Hope
Director General
Oslo
February 1999

Introduction

Einar Hope

Antitrust cases can often be quite complex and competition authorities typically face a difficult task in analysing the cases and trying to reach well-founded decisions on the basis of all available, relevant information and evidence. They have to combine descriptive information and statistical data of markets and firms with legal, institutional and technical information into a coherent framework of analysis for decision-making within a fairly limited time. The cases are also as a rule becoming more complex to analyse and handle because of developments in market and competition conditions, e.g. market integration, convergence, and internationalization of markets. In addition, firms are drawing increasingly on advice from experts who are well versed in modern economic and legal analysis of competition, when cases are brought against them by competition authorities.

It is therefore important for competition authorities regularly to evaluate their principles and methods of analysis and update them with new methodological and analytical insights which can improve the case handling and decision-making processes. The intention of the conference, upon which this book is based, was primarily to make a contribution to one dimension of this issue, i.e. with regard to principles and methods for the *economic* analysis of competition. Legal and institutional issues are also covered, but the emphasis is on economic analysis.

In 1996 the Norwegian Competition Authority initiated a study on principles and methods of competition policy analysis as a background to developing an analytical, operational framework which could be used by the Authority to improve its approach to the analysis of practical issues and cases. It was also explicitly stated that the suggested framework and approach should be illustrated with specific examples to document its applicability and usefulness in practice. Four experts were appointed to undertake the study: Professor Victor D. Norman (chairman) of the Norwegian School of Economics and Business Administration (International trade, imperfect competition), Professor Nils-Henrik Mørch von der Fehr of the University of Oslo (Industrial organization, regulation), Professor Torger Reve of the Norwegian School of Economics and Business Administration (Organization theory, strategic analysis) and lawyer, Dr Anders Christian Stray Ryssdal of the Oslo-based law firm Wiersholm, Mellbye & Bech. The experts submitted their report in February 1998.[1]

Given this study, it was natural to use it as a platform to organize a 'foundations' conference on competition policy analysis, i.e. to focus on some basic principles, methods and analytical approaches. The experts were invited to present elements of their study, which is in Norwegian, to an international audience, together with some other leading experts invited to take up specific methodological or analytical issues. The book thus contains a core of papers around the Norwegian study, plus a number of additional studies illustrating a diversity of approaches to the common theme: competition policy analysis.

In the first chapter, Agnar Sandmo discusses the aims of competition policy from a welfare economics perspective, drawing in particular on the theory of the second best. If some parts of the market economy are explicitly excluded from the scope of competition policy, e.g. the labour market, is there, then, a justification for efficient markets in the rest of the economy? And can goals of efficiency and equity be as clearly separated as seems to be indicated by the prevalent tendency in the new competition laws of defining efficiency as the only goal, such as e.g., the Norwegian Competition Act of 1993? Adopting the vocabulary of Krugman,[2] he distinguishes between the narrow and broad arguments for competition policy and concludes on rather the same note as Krugman that '[promotion of competition] is a pretty good if not perfect policy, while an effort to deviate from it in a sophisticated way will probably end up doing more harm than good' (Krugman, 1993, p. 364).

The aims and objectives of competition policy are also very much in focus in Frédéric Jenny's chapter. As chairman for a number of years of the OECD Committee on Competition Law and Policy as well as chairman of the WTO Working Group on Trade and Competition, in addition to his position as Vice Chairman of the French Competition Authority, he is centrally placed with regard to international work on competition policy formation and application of competition laws in an international context. In his chapter he is particularly concerned with the influence of economic theory and reasoning on competition policy analysis and on defining the goal structure of the policy. Considerable credit is given to economic analysis in influencing and improving the analytical foundations of competition law and policy, but he also points to a number of shortcomings and deviations when theory is confronted with the complex realities of the world in practical law enforcement. The general rule seems to be that policy-makers pursue, explicitly or implicitly, a multi-objective function rather than the single economic efficiency objective when forming and enforcing the competition policy. Jenny gives examples and discusses the implications of such policy behaviour.

The next three chapters are based on the study mentioned above for the Norwegian Competition Authority by the four experts. Victor D. Norman introduces the study and describes the suggested three-step incentive-oriented approach to competition policy analysis by the group. For the purpose of the conference this necessarily had to be done in a summary fashion. Application of the approach to three selected sectors: telecommunications, electricity, and media (broadcasting and television) is not included. Nils-Henrik M. von der Fehr discusses the division of labour and responsibility between a general competition authority and sector-specific authorities under deregulation and market orientation of industries that previously have been subject to heavy-handed regulation, while Anders Chr. Stray Ryssdal gives a lawyer's perspective on some aspects and legal procedures concerning the enforcement of competition policy.

Taking into consideration that the study is documented in Norwegian, a more detailed account of it than contained in the above mentioned chapters ought to be given here in the Introduction to give an international audience the full flavour and implications of the suggested analytical approach. Fortunately, this has to some extent at least been done by two Danish colleagues, Professors Svend Hylleberg and Per Baltzer Overgaard in Chapter 6. The article was originally written for the journal *Konkurranse* of the NCA and is reproduced here with the permission of the journal. The authors give an overview and a critical evaluation of the study and also of the accompanying reports to the study by K. Bjorvatn and L. Sørgard on methods of competition policy analysis and on vertical relations, respectively.

Australia has recently undertaken a major revision of its competition law and policy. Allan Fels, Chairman of the Australian Competition and Consumer Commission, reviews the law reform and discusses the practical implementation of it in Chapter 7. The Australian competition policy experiment is, in my opinion, particularly interesting as it takes account of ongoing market and regulatory developments and tries to be ahead of those developments by adjusting the policy regime rather than lagging behind with law and policy revisions, as is typically the case in most countries. The underlying idea has been to develop a *comprehensive* competition policy that includes all government policies that affect the state of competition in any sector of the economy. An important aspect of the reform is the integration of competition policy with sector-specific economic regulation, previously the responsibility of sector-specific regulatory bodies, into a comprehensive policy framework and administered by a single independent statutory body, the ACCC. This promotes consistent application of competition regulation across all sectors of the economy. The chapter contains a case study of the new policy regime in relation to the telecommunications industry.

Carl Shapiro in Chapter 8 focuses on some important competition policy issues in the transition of the economy to an information-based economy. His contention is that in such a transition the economics of networks takes on greater importance in comparison with traditional economies of scale. The chapter explores the implications of the shift towards an information- and network-based economy for the three traditional branches of competition policy, i.e. mergers, inter-firm cooperation or collusion, and unilateral conduct by dominant firms. Shapiro maintains that we possess the economic tools to fashion sound competition policy in the information economy and those tools are indeed being used to develop and refine such policy. This is illustrated with examples from the United States, including the famous Microsoft case.

The following two chapters take up issues within areas of competition and regulatory policies that have been discussed a lot in the literature and in practice, i.e vertical relations and deregulation of regulated industries. Margaret Slade looks at exclusive retailing agreements and discusses some of the theories that attempt to explain why different types of retail organizational forms are chosen. She also examines public policy towards the relationship between manufacturers and their exclusive retailers, especially with regard to the United States and the United Kingdom. Finally, she assesses three cases of government regulation of manufacturer–retailer relationships, drawn from the gasoline, automobile and beer markets, and all involving the prohibition of certain types of upstream/ downstream contracts. Her conclusion from the analysis is that a thorough review of public policy towards such relationships is long overdue.

Kjell Gunnar Salvanes, Frode Steen, and Lars Sørgard analyse competition and regulatory aspects in the deregulation of the airline industry, with special reference to the deregulation of the Norwegian airline industry since 1994. The domestic Norwegian market has been a duopoly since deregulation. The authors observe collusion on prices in the business segment of the market and find that this has triggered intense rivalry between the duopolists for capacity. They also find that flight departures are located closer in time in the business segment than on routes that have continued to be served by a monopolist. Finally, they discuss the competition policy lessons that can be drawn from the analysis and how policy measures can be applied to destabilize price collusion within such markets.

How should a competition authority, facing budget constraints, prioritize different tasks and behave in order to obtain the full effects of a deterrence-based competition policy? This is the question posed by Stephen Martin in Chapter 11. More specifically, the chapter develops a model of resource allocation by a competition authority that monitors market performance in several industries by setting threshold prices for each industry. Observed prices above the threshold level trigger an investigation that leads, with known probability, to prosecution, conviction, and a fine. The implications of market size, demand elasticity, and seller concentration for enforcement decisions are examined.

Competition aspects of state aids to industry are increasingly coming under scrutiny by competition policy-makers and officials. In the final chapter, Timothy Besley and Paul Seabright look at possible distortive effects on competition and policy implications of such aids. They review the relevant literature on state aids and competition and develop a framework to analyse competition effects of state aids which they think can reconcile the different approaches in the literature. Then the framework is applied in a critical analysis of the actual practice of the European Commission as revealed in decisions of the last few years. The authors find that this practice has a number of strengths and weaknesses. On the positive side they emphasize, for example, that the Commission is often sceptical of arguments and judgements from member countries about the need for state aids and can thus have a restraining influence on the use of this instrument, while they are in general critical of the Commission's analysis of state aid cases and in identifying the circumstances that constitute genuinely defensible grounds for compulsory state aid control.

Notes

1 Victor D. Norman *et al.* (1998), *Ikke for å vinne? Analyse av konkurranseforhold og konkurransepolitikk.* (*Not to Win? Analysing Competition and Competition Policy*), SNF-report 8/98. See also the accompanying reports to the study by Kjetil Bjorvatn (1998), *Metoder for analyse av konkurranseforhold.* (*Methods for Analysing Competition*), SNF-report 9/98. and Lars Sørgard (1998), *Vertikale relasjoner: Finnes det enkle, konkurransepolitiske regler?* (*Vertical Relations: Are There Simple Competition Policy Solutions?*), SNF-report 10/98.
2 P. Krugman (1993) 'The narrow and broad arguments for free trade', *American Economic Review* 83, May, 362–366.

1 Towards a competitive society?

The promotion of competition as a goal of economic policy

Agnar Sandmo

Introduction

The aim of competition policy is usually taken to be the achievement of efficient resource allocation through the promotion of effective competition. In fact, this is more or less a literal translation of the official objectives of the Norwegian Competition Authority according to the Competition Act of 1994. It is of considerable interest to note that it was not always like that. The Price Act of 1953, which provided the legal foundation for the Authority's institutional predecessor, the Price Directorate, had among its aims the promotion of full employment, an efficient utilization of production possibilities and the achievement of an equitable distribution of income, and among its instruments the regulation of prices and dividends was accorded a degree of prominence at least equal to that of the promotion of competition. While the 1953 Act defined the objectives of the Price Directorate as being more or less equal to the goals of government policy in general, the new Act narrowed it down to the promotion of efficiency, while at the same time stating that the proper way to achieve this objective is to create conditions for effective competition.

It is probably fair to say that the new Act defines aims and objectives in a way which is much more congenial to economists who approach this area with a background in economic theory, but it also raises problems. Thus, by instructing the Competition Authority to abstract from distributional considerations, the new Act is based on some implicit assumptions about the separability of the goals of efficiency and equity which are not unproblematic. Moreover, by effectively excluding some parts of the market economy (e.g. agriculture and the labour market) from the scope of competition policy, the Act raises some fundamental questions about the justification for efficient markets in the rest of the economy. Basically, the question is whether the Competition Act represents a sensible policy of decentralization. In this chapter I propose to approach this question from the point of view of welfare economics, drawing in particular on the theory of the second best. Competition policy must fundamentally be judged in terms of its contribution to welfare, and the relationship between competition and welfare is one of the central concerns of welfare economics.

Before moving on to the substantial questions I should like to consider briefly the two central concepts used in the Norwegian Competition Act, namely, efficiency and competition. In a specific theoretical context the meaning of these terms is generally defined in a way which leaves little doubt about their precise content. However, theoretical concepts usually need a practical interpretation before they can be translated into the language of instruments and targets of economic policy.

Some history of thought

Economists are fond of quoting Adam Smith's pronouncement on the invisible hand, by which individual economic agents in pursuing their own interests are led to promote the interests of society as a whole. While it may be tempting to see in this statement an early version of the first fundamental theorem of welfare economics, this would be an idealization of the history of ideas.

First of all, the concept of the public interest or the interests of society as a whole is a complex one, and Smith never gave a precise definition of it. It is possible to read into his statements a concept of the public interest as *efficiency in production*, as we would now say. Clearly, his conclusion that competition leads capital to flow to sectors of production where its rate of return is highest, is consistent with a view of competition as ensuring productive efficiency. But to go beyond this to a more general definition of efficiency would have required theoretical concepts that Smith and the other early economists simply did not have. To define efficiency in an economy with many individuals with partly conflicting interests was not possible before the introduction of the notion of Pareto optimality, which again was built on the concepts of preferences and utility. Needless to say, it took another hundred years for these concepts to be developed in the theoretical literature.

Second, Smith never gave a reasonably precise definition of what he meant by competition. Stigler (1965, p. 234) comments that the concept of competition did not in fact receive systematic attention in the theoretical literature until the 1870s, and that earlier it was 'treated with the kindly casualness with which one treats of the intuitively obvious'. But it is clear that Smith identified competition with rivalry between independent agents, and that this rivalry would, at least in the long run, guide the flows of resources towards their most profitable uses.

Rivalry assumes at least two independent agents, i.e. the absence of monopoly, but the conditions for rivalry would be more likely to obtain, the larger the number of independent agents:

> If this capital [sufficient to trade in a town] is divided between two different grocers, their competition will tend to make both of them sell cheaper, than if it were in the hands of one only; and if it were divided among twenty, their competition would be just so much the greater, and the chance of their combining together, in order to raise the price, just so much less.
>
> (Smith, 1776 (1976), p. 361)

The formulation 'just so much the greater' probably should not be interpreted in a strict mathematical sense. In fact, the first mathematical formulation of a model of competition in the celebrated work of Cournot (1838) showed that such an interpretation would be incorrect. From his work one can easily derive an analytical expression for the degree of competition. For a monopolist the percentage mark-up of price over marginal cost will be equal to the inverse of the price elasticity of demand. In a Cournot duopoly equilibrium with identical cost functions it will be one half of the monopoly markup. With n oligopolists the mark-up will be $1/n$ times the inverse elasticity. As n increases, the equilibrium price approaches marginal cost, in which case 'the effects of competition have reached their limit'.[1] So the mark-up, the deviation of price from marginal cost, diminishes with the number of competitors, but at a diminishing rate.

Cournot's model was one of partial, not general equilibrium. The main step towards a model of general competitive equilibrium came in the 1870s with the work of Jevons, Menger and – above all – Walras (1874–77). When Pareto (1896–97) later laid the foundations for welfare economics, there is a direct line forward to the emphasis in contemporary theory on the two main theorems of welfare economics (first formulated by Arrow (1951) and Debreu (1951)) on the equivalence of competitive equilibrium and Pareto optimality. With Pareto optimality being the generally accepted standard of efficiency, it also became clear that the institutional framework that could be used to implement it was perfect competition, i.e. a market system in which no single agent was able to exercise market power.

Thanks to the precision of modern welfare economics it now also became clear to what extent one could set up an objective standard for the 'public interest' to be pursued by economic policy. Under 'first best' conditions, in which redistribution can be carried out by means of non-distortionary lump sum transfers, efficiency would always[2] be desirable as being in the public interest. However, when such transfers cannot be made, matters are more complicated, and a move towards greater efficiency would no longer necessarily be in the public interest in the sense of leading to unambiguously greater social welfare. The further implications of this conclusion will be discussed in more detail in the following.

This brief sketch of the history of economic thought on the connection between competition and efficiency over almost two hundred years shows a remarkable increase in the clarity and precision of the relevant theory. At the same time the theory also presents a competition authority with something of a puzzle. With perfect competition being necessary for efficiency, is *any* deviation from the competitive ideal a reason for interference? In order to answer this question one cannot rely solely on the formal theorems of welfare economics. All acts of policy interference are costly, and interference should therefore be based on a cost-benefit analysis. With limited resources on the part of the competition authority, priority should be given to interference in markets where the marginal efficiency gain, relative to the marginal cost of interference, is greatest. Such a conclusion fits well with the looser concept of competition in the work of Adam Smith and other classical writers: competition may be reasonably efficient even when it is not perfect. Most likely the prevention of monopoly is a more central task for the competition authority than the attempt to push the effect of perfect competition to its limit.

Another important distinction for competition policy is that between permanent and transient deviations of markets from the competitive ideal. Short-run variations in monopolistic mark-ups over the business cycle[3] should probably not be a major concern for competition policy. Nor should the high price charged by a successful innovator during the early life of a new product be an argument for policy interference; in fact, the expectation of profits is an important incentive for dynamic efficiency. It is the more permanent deviations from the standard of competitive efficieny that should be the focus of competition policy, and it is accordingly those that I have in mind in the following analysis.

The scope of competition policy

The deviation of monopolistic from competitive prices has in principle two effects. (A) By raising prices above *average costs*, thereby generating pure profits, monopolistic pricing leads to a redistribution of income in society, away from that which would materialize under perfect competition. (B) By raising prices above *marginal costs* a monopoly distorts the efficiency properties of the competitive equilibrium, the normal implication being that the use of the monopolized commodity in consumption or production becomes too low. This is illustrated in Figure 1.1, which assumes that the demand function is linear and

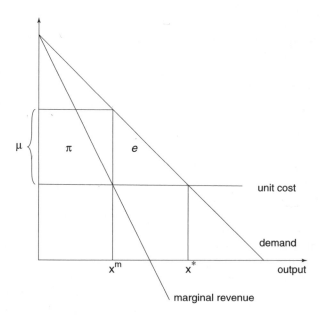

Figure 1.1 Monopoly profit and the social efficiency loss

that unit costs are constant. The monopolist's optimal output is x^m, which corresponds to the intersection of the marginal cost and marginal revenue curves, and this is to be contrasted with the competitive output of x^*. With μ being the monopolistic mark-up (the difference between price and unit cost), the monopolist's profit is $\pi = \mu x^m$, while the efficiency loss from monopolistic pricing is the triangular area $e = (1/2)\mu(x^*-x^m)$. In general, both monopoly profit and the effiency loss depend on the elasticity of demand as well as on the elasticity of supply (which in the case shown is infinite). It is perhaps worth noting that in the special case represented in Figure 1.1 it will always be the case that the efficiency loss is exactly equal to half the monopoly profit;[4] $e = (1/2)\pi$.

While private agents who try to create a monopoly (sometimes with the support of politicians) are motivated by (A), competition policy is mainly motivated by the efficiency losses implicit in (B). An interesting question is now whether competition policy should be designed with both objectives in mind, just like tax policy has to be designed with a view both to efficiency and justice. I take the standard answer to this question, just as in the formulation of the Norwegian Competition Act, to be no, implying that competition policy should be formulated solely with regard to efficiency. Whether the answer is a good one will be discussed further below.

To which sectors of the economy should competition policy be extended? The view from welfare economics is clear: to all of them! The aim to strive for is clearly to have price equal to marginal cost in all markets. In the markets for consumer goods and services the implication of this would be the equality between consumer prices and the marginal costs of production, while in factor markets the rule would have to be formulated as equality between the prices of factors of production, as facing consumers, and their marginal value products. Thus, the general principle would apply to markets for primary commodities like agriculture as well as to labour markets. As a matter of fact, these are both examples of sectors of the economy which are fairly well protected from competition policy, and I shall maintain later on that this is basically because of distributional considerations. It follows that competition policy must limit its scope to certain – although large – sectors of the economy. In the next section I discuss some problems that follow from this limitation, even when efficiency is taken as the sole aim of competition policy.

Another area which traditionally has been well protected from interference by competition policy is the public sector. Some decades ago the prevailing view was that competition was not an issue in the evaluation of the public sector's activities; in fact, in many cases it was maintained that private competition was harmful and should be forbidden. This has changed. It has increasingly come to be realized that actual governments are far from the picture of the night-watchman state which supplies a small set of public goods, including basic administrative infrastructure. To a large extent the public sector has become a supplier of prvate goods, like education, health, energy and communications, and in these areas private firms present government organizations with both real and potential competition. The prevailing opinion is now that this competitive pressure should be utilized to make the public sector more efficient. Increasingly, therefore, competition policy has had to concern itself with the interface between the private and public sectors of the economy.

Competition and efficiency

In its everyday work on implementation of competition policy, a competition authority must necessarily work on a market-by-market basis. Faced with monopolistic price-setting in a given sector, the aim of the authority should be to take measures which will lead to a reduction in price towards the competitive level.[5] This will promote effective competition. But will it lead to a more efficient allocation of resources? The answer to this question depends crucially on what is assumed about the nature of market equilibrium in the rest of the economy. To begin with, I shall focus especially on the conditions in the parts of the economy which lie outside the domain of the competition authority. If some sectors of the economy are taken as being protected from interference from competition policy, how then should competition policy be designed inside its own domain?

This is a classic problem in the welfare economics of the second best. Indeed, it is one of the central applications of the theory in the original formulation of that problem by Lipsey and Lancaster (1956–57).[6] What they showed was basically that partial or piecemeal reform which appears to move the economy in the direction of efficiency, may not in fact do so. In particular, suppose that there is one market where there is an exogenously given deviation of consumer price from marginal cost. This could be either because there is an institutional monopoly which cannot be removed or – perhaps more convincingly – a tax wedge which is motivated by overriding distributional concerns. Then it cannot in general be taken as desirable to have prices equal to marginal costs in other markets in the economy.

Why is this? There are two related explanations, one mathematical and one economic. To take the mathematical interpretation first, the classic conclusion about the efficiency properties of marginal cost prices can be seen as derived from the solution to a welfare maximization problem. In that problem the only constraint on the maximization of consumer welfare is production feasibility. If in addition it is assumed that there is one price which must be taken as different from the relevant marginal cost, this introduces an additional constraint into the problem. This constraint obviously prevents one of the first order conditions to be attained. But because of the interdependence of the variables in the overall maximization problem this also means that *all* the first order conditions will be affected by the additional constraint. Hence the conclusion.

This line of interpretation does not give us a good feel for the economics of the second-best problem. To achieve this, let us consider the problem within a specific model in which the structure is so simple that it can be analysed by purely verbal arguments. To be concrete, let us think of a model in which there are three goods – leisure, energy and a generalized consumption good which serves as the *numéraire*. For redistributive reasons there is a distortionary income tax, so that the consumer price of leisure, i.e. the after-tax wage rate, is below labour's marginal productivity. The assumption is that this price distortion is one that competition policy cannot touch. I shall also assume that the substitution effects on leisure demand are larger than the income effects, so that the consumption of leisure is too high relative to the first best, i.e. labour supply is too low.

Suppose now that it is found that the consumer price of energy is higher than its marginal cost and that energy use for this reason is too low.[7] This is within the domain of competition policy, and various measures are therefore considered which will lower the price of energy towards its marginal cost. The question is: when is such a measure welfare improving?

Focusing on the consumer side of the economy, assume first that energy and leisure are complements. A decrease in the price of energy will increase energy consumption, which is fine from the point of view of efficiency. However, because of the complementarity a fall in the price of energy will also lead to an increase in the demand for leisure. But the consumption of leisure was already too low in the initial situation; hence the efficiency loss from the distortion of the wage rate has become larger, and this has to be set against the efficiency gain in the energy market. There is no guarantee that there is an overall efficiency gain for the economy as a whole, although the price structure has apparently moved closer to the competitive ideal.

If instead we suppose that energy and leisure are substitutes, the conclusion will be a different one. A lower price of energy will now generate a lower demand for leisure, i.e. an increase in labour supply. The price reform in the energy market will counteract the distortion of the wage rate and lead to efficiency gains in both markets and therefore for the whole economy as well.

The point of this analysis has not been to make recommendations for competition policy in the energy market. I have named the commodities 'leisure and energy' rather than 'A and B' or 'apples and bananas' in part to convey the view that price reforms as a result of competition policy may be very important in terms of its consequences for the economy and certainly comparable in this respect to major changes of the tax system. I should also stress that I have simplified the analysis in some important respects from what one would do on the basis of a fully specified general equilibrium model; e.g. I have taken no account of the effect of a lower energy price on the *demand* for labour. But this is really beside the central point of the example, which has simply been to show the fundamental implication of second-best welfare analysis, namely, that piecemeal reforms do not necessarily lead to efficiency gains for the economy as a whole. We can identify additional theoretical restrictions which are sufficient to ensure that such gains will indeed emerge (Dixit, 1975), but these are very restrictive. Consider as an example Dixit's Theorem 7 (p. 118):

> Lowering the price of any one commodity towards its marginal cost will increase welfare if the commodity is complementary to all those with a

greater proportional distortion and substitute for all others including the *numéraire*.

In a particular case facing the competition authority conditions like this, to put it mildly, are unlikely to be satisfied. But note that the theorem is an example of a *sufficient* condition for welfare improvement; it does not imply that any other pattern of complementarity and substitutability will lead to a decrease of welfare. Basically, the signs and magnitudes of the spillover effects in other markets are an empirical issue that requires econometric measurement and informed judgement.

Similar second-best problems are also likely to arise within the domain of competition policy itself. Thus, consider an extension of the model in which there are two sectors within the domain of competition policy. Let us think of them as energy and public transportation. In both sectors the assumption is that the consumer price is too high because of monopolistic pricing, and the ambition of the competition authority is to bring both prices down to the level of marginal cost. However, it is not possible to take joint legal action against the two industries; they have to be tackled separately. This raises some problems of priorities. For example, if the energy market has to be tackled first, the optimal policy to pursue in the energy market will depend on the expected outcome of the reform process in the public transportation market. In general, the optimal competition policy in each of the two markets will depend on the outcome in the other market. If the competition authority should turn out to be unsuccessful in the energy market, so that a substantial excess of price over marginal cost should remain even after the policy interference, then the optimal outcome in the public transportation sector should reflect this. If energy and public transportation are complements, this would be a strong argument for pursuing the aim of marginal cost pricing in transportation. If, on the other hand, they are substitutes, this would suggest that it is optimal to leave a positive price-cost margin in the public transportation market as well.

This analysis suggests that competition policy becomes extremely complicated once we move away from the unrealistic world of first-best policy instruments. Regulators must always think in a general equilibrium perspective, which introduces a number of interdependencies among different areas of economic policy. Thus, in the example above the estimate of the efficient price of energy should be sensitive to the magnitude of the marginal tax rate on labour income. A way out of this difficulty is to institutionalize a decentralization of objectives by which the task of the competition authority is limited to that of achieving competitive conditions, with prices being equal to marginal costs. It is then left to other institutions of public policy, e.g. the ministry of finance, to decide on additional measures in order to internalize the externalities between different policy areas. To return to the leisure–energy example above: if a careful analysis shows that the optimal consumer price of energy is above marginal cost, the task of the competition authority should still be to ensure that the producer price equals marginal cost. It will then be the duty of the ministry of finance to propose a tax on energy use that is optimal relative to the income tax distortion.[8] This tax should be determined on the basis of the same kinds of considerations as were sketched above concerning the optimal deviation of the consumer price from marginal cost.

This division of responsibilities has a number of attractive features, allowing each policy authority to concentrate on doing what it knows best. Its appeal is strongest when in fact there exist a number of other policy tools that can be used to pursue other objectives. If, on the other hand, there are numerous political constraints on the differentiation of taxes, it becomes much harder to argue for a narrow view of the objectives of competition policy.

Obviously, the conclusion to be drawn from this exercise in the welfare economics of the second best is that there may be some difficult problems and challenges for the definition of competition policy as a separate area of economic policy. A one-to-one allocation of instruments to targets will only be optimal under particular assumptions on the availability of policy tools and the nature of political organization. What the implications of this are for the organization of competition policy will be considered in the final section.

Competition and income distribution

One difficulty for competition policy is clearly that some monopolies have been created with at least implicit public support in order to change the distribution of income in favour of the owners. This is perhaps most obvious in the case of the trade unions, which have always had strong political support, especially from social democratic parties. However, over time trade unions have won the respect, although not always the love, of liberal and conservative parties as well. Similarly, agricultural monopolies have been able to count on the political support of parties with a strong base among rural voters. There is now probably a political consensus in Norway as well as in other countries that trade unions and agricultural organizations are established features of the economic and political system. As such, they are more or less immune to interference from competition policy.[9] To gain a full understanding of why this is so, it would be necessary to widen the perspective of the analysis to take account of political factors as well; see the discussion in Dixit (1996). Here I shall limit myself to a discussion of the political and economic *legitimacy* of the claim of workers and farmers that their monopoly organizations can be defended on the grounds of fairness.

If there had been no trade unions and no agricultural monopolies, would the markets for labour and agricultural products then have been competitive? It seems highly likely that the answer is no. If there had been no employers' organizations, there would have been a strong asymmetry of power in labour markets in favour of the employers. There are two reasons for this. One is simply that there are many more workers than firms, so that the concentration of power is on the employers' side of the market. The other is that in many industries it is the workers who make the heavy investments in particular jobs in terms of investment in firm-specific human capital and choice of residence. Their individual bargaining positions *vis-à-vis* owners of mobile capital are therefore likely to be weak. In agricultural markets there would similarly have been a much higher degree of concentration on the buyers' side of the market (wholesale purchasers, supermarket chains, etc.), while the industrial mobility of farmers is obviously much less than among the buyers of their products. Trade unions and farmers' organizations can therefore be explained and defended as the development of 'countervailing power' (Galbraith, 1956) to redress the structural asymmetries in the balance of power under *laissez-faire*.[10] Obviously, the implication is not that this development will re-establish efficiency. The point is simply that the magnitude of the distortionary effects of farmers' organizations and trade unions on prices and wages should not be taken for granted but rather be seen as an object of empirical research and measurement.

The social acceptance of some types of monopolies does not imply that nothing is done to alleviate their possible adverse efficiency effects by means of public policy. A typical measure taken by a competition authority against 'normal' monopolies is to require the removal of barriers to entry. By introducing actual or potential competition this results in lower consumer prices and *lower* monopoly profits. Measures taken against agricultural monopolies, however, usually take the form of price subsidies to consumers. Although not usually regarded as an instrument of competition policy, such a subsidy lowers the consumer price towards marginal cost[11] while at the same time *increasing* monopoly profits.[12] The two types of policy will have the same effect on consumer prices and on efficiency but opposite effects on monopoly profits. The relative attractiveness of the two types of policy can easily be explained by their distributional effects. In the case of trade unions the situation is less transparent, although it can be argued that the adverse effects on unemployment of high wages have to some extent been counteracted by the government in the form of selective employment subsidies and creation of jobs in the public sector.

Many economists would argue that the creation and tolerance of monopolies is an expensive way to redistribute income, because the distortion of prices will have a cost in terms of efficiency. It would be preferable to achieve the same amount of redistribution through direct transfers to the groups that one wishes to support, because this can occur without creation of the substitution effects that impair efficiency. In other words, income redistribution ought to take the form of lump sum transfers, a point well known from the general theory of welfare economics.

But there are several difficulties with this type of recommendation. First of all, the design of truly lump sum transfers which do not create unintended incentive effects is no simple task. Second, even if it were possible to design the criteria for the allocation of transfer payments in a non-distortive manner, they would have to be financed by taxes, and taxes do result in price distortions and inefficiencies – just like monopoly mark-ups. It is then not a question of avoiding price distortions completely; rather, the issue is whether the tax or mark-up distortions have the more adverse efficiency effects.

There are those that would argue that there is no reason to favour some people through redistributional policies simply because they are in particular occupations; income support should be given to the poor, not to farmers (some of whom are rich) or to particular groups of workers (some of whom also enjoy high incomes). There is something to be said for this point of view, but it tends to ignore the asymmetries of bargaining strength discussed above. Perhaps what competition policy should strive for in these areas of the economy is to reduce the role of such asymmetries, so that competitive efficency could become a real alternative to institutional monopolies. However, there is probably no escape from the fact that some of the asymmetries, especially in the labour market, are of a deep structural nature, not easily removed by government policy.

An area of increasing importance for competition policy, at least potentially, concerns service production in areas like health, child care, care for the elderly and education. In many countries these have been areas where production has been dominated by public monopolies and where the guiding principle has been to make the same level of service available to all. The argument in favour of uniformity is a redistributional one, since it means that rationing of these basic goods among individuals will not be based on their ability to pay. But, on the other hand, the uniformity of service implies a loss in efficiency, both because it restricts the extent to which supply can be tailored to individual needs and desires, and because institutions that are sheltered from competition are likely to become inefficient. The trend in recent years has been towards increasing public institutions' degree of exposure to competition from private producers, and this trend is one that has been recommended by a number of economists; see e.g. Lindbeck *et al.* (1994). If the trend continues, it will move some important new areas into the domain of competition policy and present policy-makers with some difficult challenges. One of the main problems in the area is e.g. to ensure that competition between public and private producers takes place 'on equal terms'. This notion is undoubtedly appealing, but it is also important to ask on whose terms. If private and public agents are to compete under conventional market conditions, it may come to imply that the original redistributional justification for public production will no longer be able to count in the production of welfare services; there is then a small step to full privatization of the production of these services. If, on the other hand, the terms are defined so as to include standards of equal treatment, such as equal access, non-discriminatory pricing, etc., the regulatory constraints on private agents could easily become so restrictive that competitive incentives would lose much of their force. The role of competition policy in this area will not be an easy one to define.

Implications for the organization of competition policy

The arguments in the previous sections cast some doubt on the wisdom of organizing competition policy as a separate area of economic policy with its own institutions and policy tools. The general point is that a one-to-one allocation of instruments to targets is unlikely to result in an optimum. Different areas of economic policy should really be seen as parts of an integrated whole. Tax policy, trade policy and competition policy should, according to this view, be designed jointly in order to internalize the spillover externalities between them. Attempts to design competition policy with the single aim of achieving social efficiency through effective competition may in certain circumstances do more harm than good. This line of argument has far-reaching implications, leading one, for example, to doubt the wisdom of organizing a competition authority as an independent body outside the central government administration.

For my own part I am not entirely convinced by this conclusion. Having discussed some of the intricacies of policy interdependence, I still believe that one needs to distinguish, using the vocabulary of Krugman (1993),[13] between the narrow and broad arguments for competition policy. The narrow arguments are of the type that I have mainly discussed above. Although welfare economics tells us that competitive markets result in overall social efficiency, piecemeal reforms are not guaranteed to result in welfare improvements. This is first of all because there are other distortions in the economy that may interact negatively with reforms intended to stimulate competition, and, second, because of constraints on redistribution policy. Competition policy, according to this perspective, has to be much more sophisticated than, for example, indicated in the 1994 Norwegian Competition Act.

The broad arguments for competition policy are more political in nature. They recognize first that the design of policies to attain efficient resource allocation is a very difficult task which involves considerable costs. It has to be pursued along several dimensions like general tax policy, environmental policy, trade policy and competition policy – to name just a few. Each of these areas requires particular expertise both among politicians and bureaucrats. Reforms must be based on legislation, which takes time. A reform proposal which is contingent on the existing level of a distortion somewhere else in the economy will have to be revised when that level for some reason changes. The insights of policy-makers and administrators which such a policy requires are very demanding and may easily lead to mistakes. By pursuing the single aim of perfect competition, leaving other aspects of policy to others, the competition authority will probably make a few mistakes, but probably not as serious mistakes as it would do in the attempt to carry out more ambitious and sophisticated policies. To paraphrase Krugman: '[promotion of competition] is a pretty good if not perfect policy, while an effort to deviate from it in a sophisticated way will probably end up doing more harm than good' (1993, p. 364).

In addition to this argument, which emphasizes the transaction costs of policy design and reform, there is also an argument which is based more explicitly on the nature of the political process. Competition policy is an area where policy-makers inevitably face resistance from private agents who have a direct interest in preserving existing inefficiencies. If these agents could legitimately resist the actions of the competition authority on the grounds that the existing market structure had beneficial effects on the environment, the terms of trade, etc., then presumably similar arguments would have to be admitted in areas like environmental and trade policies. The result could then easily be that it would become impossible both to promote effective competition and improve the environment. A decentralization of policy, although not based on the most sophisticated of theoretical arguments, would be more likely to make the economy as a whole move in the general direction of greater efficiency.

This conclusion seems to indicate that my detour through the welfare economics of the second best was an unproductive effort, but I do not think so. It is by trying to understand the theoretical complexities of policy design that we are able to understand the nature and consequences of the simplifications on which policy must be based. Or in other words, to appreciate the broad arguments for competition policy, one has to understand the essence of the narrow arguments.

Notes

1 Cournot (1838), quoted in Stigler (1965, p. 243).
2 Actually, this requires the further assumption that the index of social welfare is of the Bergson-Samuelson individualistic variety.
3 Bils (1987) finds evidence of counter-cyclical mark-ups, i.e. mark-ups are lower during booms than during depressions, and this finding, although not universal, agrees with that of a number of other studies.
4 With a linear demand function the slope of the marginal revenue curve is twice that of the demand curve. Hence $x^* = 2x^m$, and the conclusion follows.
5 The analysis here is cast entirely in terms of prices. This is not meant to imply that other aspects of competition, such as quality or the degree of product variety, are irrelevant for welfare evaluation. I concentrate on prices mainly because it simplifies the exposition, but also because lower quality may under certain assumptions be interpreted as a higher price per 'quality unit'.
6 The relevant application is actually formulated by Lipsey and Lancaster as finding optimal price/output policies for nationalized industries when there are monopolies in the private sector whose existence must be taken as given. The nationalized industries in the Lipsey–Lancaster formulation correspond in the present discussion to the firms which are within the domain of competition policy.
7 Obviously, I am not trying to capture all aspects of reality which are relevant for the determination of the socially efficient price of energy. Energy use has environmental effects which call for a higher price of energy than its marginal cost of production in the usual narrow sense. Although I ignore this aspect of the problem, it could easily be incorporated in a more complete analysis.
8 For an example of a second-best tax analysis of this kind see Christiansen (1984).
9 I do not of course mean to imply that the market power of these institution cannot be influenced by economic policy; indeed, economic history is full of examples to the contrary. But competition policy in the more specific sense is usually taken to have no bearing on them.
10 This answer to the hypothetical question of the likely outcome of the removal of the monopolies gains some support from our knowledge that, historically, this is a reasonably realistic description of the situation in labour and agricultural markets before the formation of labour unions and agricultural cooperatives.
11 Indeed, a first-best optimal price subsidy per unit of output would be equal to the inverse of the price elasticity of demand.
12 Let p and x be price and quantity and s the consumer subsidy per unit. Monopoly profits are then $\pi = px(p-s)-c(x(p-s))$. Using the envelope theorem, we have that $\partial\pi/\partial s = -px'+c'x'=x>0$, where the last equality follows by substitution from the first-order condition for profit maximization.

13 Krugman's article discusses the case for free trade in the light of the insights provided by the so-called new trade theory, which has emphasized the importance of imperfect competition in international trade.

References

Arrow, K. J. (1951) 'An extension of the basic theorems of classical welfare economics', *Proceedings of the Second Berkeley Symposium on Mathematical Statistics and Probability*, Berkeley, CA: University of California Press, 507–532.

Bils, M. (1987) 'The cyclical behavior of marginal cost and price', *American Economic Review* 77, 838–855.

Christiansen, V. (1984) 'Which commodity taxes should supplement the income tax?', *Journal of Public Economics* 24, 195–220.

Cournot, A. (1838) *Recherches sur les principes mathématiques de la théorie des richesses*, Paris: M. Rivière & Cie. Translated as *Researches into the Mathematical Principles of Wealth*, New York: A. M. Kelly, 1960.

Debreu, G. (1951) 'The coefficient of resource utilization', *Econometrica* 19, 273–292.

Dixit, A. K. (1975) 'Welfare effects of tax and price changes', *Journal of Public Economics* 4, 103–123.

Dixit, A. K. (1996) *The Making of Economic Policy: A Transaction-Cost Politics Perspective*, Munich Lectures in Economics, Cambridge, MA: The MIT Press.

Galbraith, J. K. (1956) *American Capitalism: The Concept of Countervailing Power*, Boston: Houghton Mifflin.

Krugman, P. (1993) 'The narrow and broad arguments for free trade', *American Economic Review* 83 May, 362–366.

Lindbeck, A., Molander, P., Persson, T., Petersson, O., Sandmo, A., Swedenborg, B. and Thygesen, N. (1994) *Turning Sweden Around*, Cambridge, MA: The MIT Press.

Lipsey, R. G. and Lancaster, K. (1956–57) 'The general theory of second best', *Review of Economic Studies* 24, 11–32.

Pareto, V. (1896–97) *Cours d'économie politique*, Lausanne: Rouge.

Smith, A. (1776) *An Inquiry into the Nature and Causes of the Wealth of Nations*, Edinburgh. Glasgow edition by R. H. Campbell and A. S. Skinner (eds), Oxford: Oxford University Press, 1976.

Stigler, G. J. (1965) *Essays in the History of Economics*, Chicago and London: The University of Chicago Press.

Walras, L. (1874–77) *Eléments d'économie politique pure*, Lausanne: Corbaz. Translated by W. Jaffé as *Elements of Pure Economics*, Homewood, ILL: Irwin, 1954.

2 Competition law and policy*

Achievements and failures from an economic perspective

Frédéric Jenny

At the most basic level, micro-economic analysis tells us under which conditions a decentralized market mechanism would lead to Pareto efficiency in a static boundless and timeless world in which perfectly informed economic agents can be assumed to behave as if they maximized their resources and the utility they derive from these resources. What economic analysis suggests is that, barring externalities or market failures, competition will lead to efficiency. Applied micro-economic analysis (industrial organization) recognizes that market competition will not necessarily prevail spontaneously on all markets and tells us what both the structural and behavioral the determinants of competition are. Industrial organization thus provides us with useful information about how market structures and behaviors which could prevent competition should be monitored. Finally another branch of applied micro-economic theory, namely economic theory of crime, tells us something about the conditions which must be met to efficiently or optimally enforce laws, and something can be learned from this branch of economic analysis when one considers the enforcement of competition laws.

Competition law and policy have become widely used tools to monitor market mechanisms. More than a hundred countries now have a competition law, the deregulation movement has gathered momentum in a number of developed countries over the last fifteen years and has allowed competitive processes to emerge in many sectors which were previously monopolized or in which competitive forces were severely limited, the successive GATT negotiations have, over a period of fifty years, led to a lowering of tariff barriers allowing a greater level of international competition, etc. The multilateral community has also decided to take a look at the issue of trade and competition in the globalized markets.

At the outset, it must be emphasized that economists have played an important role in the above-mentioned developments. They have provided a strong rationale for market-oriented reforms and they tend to play an increasingly crucial role in the enforcement of competition policy as well as in the discussion and the establishment of rules in recently deregulated sectors.

It is fair to say that the populist view of competition policy which in many countries was the dominant view until the end of the 1970s has since given way to a generally more subtle interpretation of competition laws that is more in line with economic analysis.

In certain international fora, such as the OECD, a great deal of attention has been devoted to the (micro-)economic analysis of market mechanisms. This has led such organizations to promote competition policy and law and market-oriented reforms. The outreach programs of the OECD have greatly contributed to help countries which did not previously have a competition law (particularly in Eastern Europe, some Asian countries and Latin America) or wanted to improve their laws by adopting competition laws based on economic principles.

Among OECD member countries, the exchanges of views taking place in the Competition Law and Policy Committee have succeeded in presenting state-of-the-art economic reasoning on specific issues in terms understandable to less experienced competition policy enforcers. I do not think that it is too presumptuous to say that over the years this form of international cooperation has greatly increased the economic awareness of competition law officials. It has also contributed to the process of soft harmonization of national competition laws and policies. This harmonization has been characterized by a progressive alignment of competition laws and policies on the teachings of economic analysis.

The use by competition policy enforcers of concepts derived from economic analysis such as contestability of markets, essential facilities, supply side substituability, transaction costs, interbrand and intrabrand competition, bears witness to the growing influence of economic reasoning in their practice. Similarly, the generally greater caution with which mergers or vertical restrictions of competition or practices by firms having intellectual property rights are assessed than used to be the case is also indicative of a growing sensitivity of competition law or policy enforcers to economic reasoning.

Having said all this, I feel that if I decided to rest my case, we could all go home with the reassuring thought that there is a lot of evidence that economic analysis is more important than ever before in the enforcement of competition law and policy and that these policies have tended to replace alternative tools of regulation which were either misguided or not mindful enough of market forces. This rosy development (which by the way has significantly increased the economic opportunities of micro-economists themselves) must mean that competition policy and laws (and micro-economists) are more relevant today than they were in the past.

Yet, I feel it is my duty (and perhaps in my own self-interest if I want to have any chance of being invited in two years time to the third Oslo conference) to examine the relationship between economic reasoning and competition policy and law in a little more detail than I have done so far. Unfortunately, as a result, the picture will become less rosy as we proceed.

Some questionable assumptions

There are several ways to approach the topic of the achievements and failures of competition policy and law from an economic perspective. Let me single out two possible approaches: the first is to ask oneself whether competition policy as it is practised (in most countries) and competition laws as they are designed and implemented (in most countries) conform to the teachings of economic analysis.

The second is to ask oneself whether competition law and policy, as they are implemented, actually make a difference and contribute to achieving the goal of economic efficiency which underlies the economic model of competition.

In both approaches we start from the assumption that economic analysis is the relevant yardstick by which to assess the success or the failure of competition laws and policies either in their design or in their implementation, or, to put it in another way, that the goals of competition policies and laws should be that of promoting economic efficiency (as defined by micro-economic analysis) in a context of decentralization of decision-making. This implicit assumption merits discussion.

If the goals of competition policy and law are (at least to a certain extent) related to the teachings of economic analysis, an attempt to assess their achievements and failures from an economic perspective exposes us to the risk of making a second assumption. This second assumption is that any failure of competition policy and law to conform to the teachings of economic analysis (or to achieve the goal of economic efficiency) means that there is something wrong with either the design of the competition law and policy or with their implementation. Yet this is not necessarily the case. It might also mean that there is something wrong with economic analysis (either because economic analysis is insufficiently developed or because it is not relevant as a guide for designing or implementating competition policy and law).Therefore this second implicit assumption also needs to be discussed.

The legitimate goals of competition law and competition policy

Defining the legitimate goals of competition policy and competition law has been the subject of an intense debate in recent years. This debate arose from a more general discussion on the future of the multilateral trading system. While all the aspects of this debate may not be of interest to our present discussion, some undoubtedly are.

Clearly if the 'legitimate' goal of competition policies and competition laws is to promote economic efficiency as defined in micro-economic analysis, several consequences result. First, the design of competition laws should follow the teachings of economic analysis. Second, competition laws and policies of different countries should closely resemble one another. Third, competition laws and policies should be as universal as the applicability of micro-economic analysis. Fourth, economic expertise should play a large role in the implementation of such policies. Fifth, any contribution of competition policy and law to achieving economic efficiency should be considered to be an achievement of the competition law or policy and any divergence between what economic analysis suggests and what the competition law and policy achieves should be considered to be a failure of the competition law and policy.

If, on the other hand, competition policies and laws can be conceived to legitimately pursue other goals than economic efficiency or if they pursue a variety of goals, including economic efficiency, then competition policies and laws need not be patterned solely on the teachings of economic analysis, competition policies and laws need not be the same in all countries (if some of the other goals are non-economic but reflect social or political values), economic expertise may not be so useful to the enforcement of such laws and policies, and finally the whole exercise of assessing the success and failures of competition laws and policies from a strict economic perspective has at best limited value (although such an exercise can still tell us something about the cost of achieving non-economic goals).

What seems to emerge from a quick perusal of competition laws and policies is that if most have the 'ultimate goal' of fostering economic development (through a more efficient use of resources brought about by the competitive mechanism), they tend to pursue various other goals (sometimes qualified as intermediate goals) simultaneously. Furthermore, many public policy-makers in the competition area would tend to agree with Allan Fels, Head of the Australian Competition Authority, that it is these other (often non-economic) goals such as the promotion of fairness or pluralism, the sheltering of the political process from the influence of economically powerful interests, social cohesion through the protection of small and medium-sized enterprises, etc. which in many countries have 'tipped the balance of social consensus towards competition'. Gabriel Castaneda who contributed immensely in shaping the first Mexican competition law states: 'It would be wrong to claim extreme (economic) purity and virginity for antitrust analysis.'

We note, for example, that the explicit goals of EU competition law and policy are the promotion of competition and the integration of the European market. The latter is a socio-political goal rather than an economic goal. In the Japanese Antimonopoly Act, the promotion of competition is considered a means of achieving two underlying goals: the wholesome development of the national economy and economic democracy. To a certain extent, in Germany, the promotion of economic democracy is a more important goal of competition law than achieving an efficient allocation of resources. The goals of the Canadian competition law are not only to maintain free competition and to promote economic efficiency but also to achieve international competitiveness. Anna Fornalczyk, former head of the Polish Competition Authority states that 'even the most liberal-minded reformers in transition countries may be interested in the agency's price control function' etc.

Undoubtedly, the pursuit of goals other than economic efficiency implies a departure from what economists would consider to be an appropriate design or enforcement of competition law. Allowing a merger leading to a high degree of domestic concentration because such a merger could improve the international competitiveness of the firms involved, exempting cartels between small and medium-sized firms, refusing efficiency defenses for mergers or anti-competitive practices, treating certain forms of vertical restraints (such as the prevention of parallel imports in the case of exclusive distribution systems) as *per se* violations because they prevent market integration, controlling prices of firms holding a dominant position, prohibiting refusal to deal, prohibiting holding companies, etc. may, at least in some cases, lead to a reduction of competition and efficiency.

A classical economic argument is that competition laws ought not to be assigned goals other than the promotion of economic efficiency. In other words, economic reasoning posits that there are less costly ways to achieve other goals than tampering with the market mechanisms. However, if economists are probably justified in arguing that governments should look for less costly ways to redistribute income than creating price distorsions (or more appropriate ways to fight inflation than to control price), it is not so obvious that there are other less costly ways (than tampering with the market mechanism) to achieve some of the non-economic goals sometimes assigned to competition policy or law (such as the promotion of security, fairness, social cohesion or the protection of political democracy).

Overall, what may sometimes appear to the economist to be an 'economic failure' of competition policy regimes or competition laws and their enforcement may be in fact 'a failure of economists' to recognize the potentially legitimate desire of society to produce (at a cost) intangible public goods of a socio-political nature. For example, until economists have demonstrated that a collective sense of 'fairness' or 'social cohesion' can be socially produced at a cheaper cost than through 'fair competition laws' (which typically restrict competition) they may be misguided in criticizing such laws.

Relationship between competition law and policy and economic development

Whatever other (non-economic) goals competition laws and policies pursue, they all share the long-term (or ultimate) goal of promoting economic efficiency and development. However, the idea that competition fosters economic development is not universally accepted as is obvious from the fact that a number of countries (mostly developing countries) do not yet have a competition law and policy and in some cases resist the idea that they should.

This fact begs the question of whether, from an economic standpoint the promotion of market competition through competition policy and law can be said to foster long-term economic development or whether more modest competition policy and law are effective tools to improve the efficiency of already developed economies.

Unfortunately, the economic literature (whether theoretical or empirical) on this question is neither well developed nor conclusive. The basic analytical problem is that of assessing the trade-offs between static efficiency losses due to a lack of competition in the short term and dynamic efficiency gains.

As Patrick Rey has demonstrated in a recent paper, the economic literature in this area has focused on two related questions: the relationship between competition and innovation, assuming that firms are profit-maximizers, and (more recently) the question of the impact of competition on the objective function of firms.

As is well known, the question of the relationship between market power and innovation was originally addressed by Schumpeter in 1943. Monopolistic power may promote innovations by making it easier for firms to fund their R&D, because they face less market uncertainty and because the prospect of monopoly rent on their innovations is more attractive than would be the case in a competitive environment. This schumpeterian view of the world suggests that there is indeed a possible trade-off between short-term static considerations and long-term economic development (at least to the extent that innovation is considered to be the main source of economic development). Some empirical support for this hypothesis has been provided, notably by Scherer, who finds that oligopolistic structures may be more conducive to innovation than purely competitive structures.

The possibility of a trade-off between innovation and competition has led a large number of countries with competition laws to provide for exemptions or at least a more lenient treatment of anti-competitive practices or mergers which may have a direct bearing on specific R&D efforts. However, this relief is only a partial one and does not address the more general question of whether a generally lenient attitude toward competition will be conducive to a faster rate of economic development. For example, if the Schumpeterian view of the world has any validity, one may question the wisdom of the merger regulation adopted by the EU that declares mergers which create or strengthen dominant position in the European market to be incompatible with the Common Market.

A more recent way of thinking, however, has questioned the hidden assumption in Schumpeter's thesis that firms maximize profits whatever market environment they face. This part of the literature focuses on the fact that if firms adopt a managerial attitude, they may well choose to introduce innovations later than they would if they had a more entrepreneurial (profit-maximizing) attitude. If competition forces them to adopt a stricter profit-maximization attitude, the rate of innovation and hence of economic development may be faster in a competition regime. In such a case, competition and competition law or policy would therefore indirectly benefit economic development by forcing firms to adopt a profit-maximizing attitude.

Considered as a whole, the economic literature focusing on the microeconomic behavior of firms remains rather inconclusive on the issue of the relationship between competition policy and law and economic development. Furthermore, the empirical evidence used to measure the rate of innovation of firms in different market environment is also sometimes difficult to interpret or leads to contradictory results.

A casual observation of the recent financial crisis in Asia may, however, provide us with some macro-economic evidence of the relationship between competition and economic development. A number of Asian countries have based their rapid expansion on national champions or domestic firms faced with weak competitive constraints on their home market, sheltered from the discipline of the financial market (and therefore not constrained by profit-maximization in the neo-classical sense) and financed by bank loans. These firms were free (or even encouraged) to invest massively and to export (so as to provide employment which was good for political stability) and could count on the political support of the government of their home country to be able to find the funds necessary for their expansion. An exogenous shock has revealed the fragility of such a system. A downturn in the products export market has led a number of these firms to be unable to repay their loans, thereby leading banks and financial institutions which had bankrolled their economic expansion to lose their credit rating or to go bankrupt and the domestic currency to lose its value. In the course of the adjustment mechanism, unemployment has risen and political stability has been shaken.

It is too early to say whether this scenario will lead to a significant shift in attitude on the part of many developing countries with respect to competition policy. One can even doubt it from a 'political economy' perspective if we recognize that whereas efficiency and economic development are long-term benefits of competition, public officials or politicians are the world over interested in short-term benefits which they can turn into immediate political advantage. Put differently, even if we are convinced that the Asian story tells us something about the ultimate dangers (both political and economic) of ignoring market forces, the fact remains that for some decades before the crisis broke some of these countries were able to enjoy the benefits of rapid expansion.

In general, the lack of enthusiasm for competition law and policy in certain developing countries must be attributed to failures of economic analysis (and more specifically to the inability of economists to integrate micro-economic analysis and the economic theory of development to provide convincing arguments that competition law and policy are useful tools of economic development).

Economic theory and the legal instrument

Assuming that one of the main goals of competition law and policy is to enhance efficiency and that there is no conflict between short-term static objectives and long-term objectives, I would now like to turn to the question of whether economic analysis can provide useful guidance for the design and implementation of competition laws and start with a discussion of the nature of the general relationship between the instrument and its theoretical foundation.

Some of the main difficulties in this area come from the fact that the instrument used to bring about more competition is, in many cases a law (an antitrust law) and that the use of such an instrument to monitor markets creates specific problems with respect to economic analysis.

Two features of economic analysis are worth discussing here. First, economic analysis suggests that competition analysis is complex and requires a careful consideration of the market context in which the practices or the structural changes examined take place. Economic analysis suggests that in competition analysis there are relatively few practices which should be assessed under a *per se* rule and that a rule of reason analysis is warranted except possibly for the simplest and most obvious horizontal restraints. Certainly, abuses of dominant positions, oligopolistic behavior, mergers, vertical restraints should be assessed under a rule of reason approach.

Second, micro-economic analysis provides us with an abstract model of the relationship between individual behaviors of consumers and producers, market mechanisms and social welfare. However, economic analysis gives us very little insight about how economic agents actually behave: thus the validity of the general assumptions of profit maximization or utility maximization rests with the fact that they lead to predictions which are not contrary to the observed facts at the aggregate level. Therefore the assumption of (general) rationality leads to the prediction that monopolized markets will be characterized by a lower output and higher prices than if competition prevailed. Indeed, there is at least some empirical support for this idea. But as Gary Becker has shown, the posited objective function of economic agents may not be the only one leading (at the general level) to an accurate prediction; the facts observed could be equally consistent with another objective function (for example, everything else being equal, prices would be higher and quantities would be smaller in monopolistic industries even if entrepreneurs behaved randomly).

The speculative nature of economic analysis and its complexity make it a particularly inappropriate guide for the design and implementation of competition laws enforced through judicial or quasi-judicial processes. Apparent failures of competition authorities to promote competition are often denounced by economists. But at least in some cases such criticism is based on a lack of understanding on the part of economists as to what can be expected from a judicial instrument.

Regarding the question of the complexity of the elements to take into account to establish whether or not a particular practice is or is not anti-competitive, it must be recognized that there can be a trade-off between the correctness of a rule (and the benefits expected from its implementation) and the cost of enforcement of this rule. The cost of adjudication of particular cases can be quite significant when they are adjudicated by judicial or quasi-judicial proceedings in which rules of due process of law must be observed. Furthermore, the dissuasive nature of a law is partly associated with the predictability of the enforcement process of this law and this predictability (as perceived by economic agents) may itself be a function of its simplicity. Finally, complexity in the enforcement process and the difficulty of predicting the result of a law may also have the undesirable effect of deterring firms from engaging in perfectly legitimate practices.

A good illustration of the difficulties raised by the complexity of economic analysis when it comes to the design or enforcement of competition law is provided by the treatment of vertical restrictive arrangements in the context of the European Union. Economic analysis suggests that to assess the impact of vertical restraints on competition (such as resale price maintenance, exclusive or even selective distribution arrangements etc.), a great many considerations must be factored into the analysis. The first question is whether the practice was imposed by the retailers on the manufacturers as a condition for carrying their products (in which case there is *prima facie* evidence that the practice was anti-competitive) or whether it was the deliberate choice of the manufacturer to use the restraint. In the course of this assessement, the possibility that such a practice may be a facilitating device for the implementation of a horizontal anti-competitive agreement between manufacturers (which requires an investigation of the past behavior of the competitors of the firm whose practice is being examined) must be considered. Assuming that the practice is not the result of horizontal agreement between retailers nor a facilitating device to enforce an anti-competitive agreement between competing manufacturers, the issue is that of assessing the contradictory effects on interbrand and intrabrand competition from the practice as well as its effect on welfare. The welfare effect depends on a host of considerations related to the shift of the demand curve for the product of the manufacturer, the relative valuation of the services provided by the distributors to marginal and infra-marginal customers, the likely reaction of competing manufacturers (and, in particular, whether the adoption of the practice is likely to induce competing manufacturers to enter themselves into vertical restrictive agreements, thus leading to a situation in which too many services will be provided on the market).

Clearly, the cost of enforcing a rule of reason for such practices which is respectful of economic analysis is tremendous. What is more, at the Community level there are thousands of exclusive distribution agreements. This has led the EU Commission to adopt a simplified rule that such agreements *a priori* fall within the purview of Article 85 (i.e. are anti-competitive within the meaning of Article 85-1 but could benefit from a class exemption under Article 85-3 if they meet certain conditions). This system came under a lot of fire from economists who argued not only that the assumption that all exclusive distribution agreements are anti-competitive is unwarranted but also that the conditions for exemption were for the most part unrelated to any contribution to economic progress (or efficiency).

There is no question that for this category of practice the EU Commission's approach has been far removed from what one could consider a competition policy implementation soundly based on economic analysis. The desire to reduce the administrative cost of enforcement of the EU competition law with respect to vertical restrictive practices has led the Commission to make questionable economic judgments.

To bring its treatment of such practices more in line with economic analysis, the Commission has recently undertaken a reassessment of the way it handles vertical restrictive agreements in general and exclusive distribution agreements in particular. What the new system will be is as yet undecided but it is worth mentioning that it will not give full weight to economic analysis since it will remain based on a system of block exemptions based on the idea that exclusive distribution agreements are *prima facie* violations of the EU treaty Article 85. However, it should be mentioned that in the course of the discussions which have taken place about EU policy revision, the EU Commission has suggested that a market share screen might be applied since vertical restrictions emanating from firms having very small market shares are unlikely to entail severe detrimental effects to competition. It is also worth mentioning that this rather sound approach from an economic perspective met with considerable hostility from the European business community which argued that market share tests are themselves too complex to handle and not predictable enough. In other words, the business community clearly expressed its preference for a simpler (and possibly more restrictive approach) than what economists would recommend.

Besides the cost of implementing a complex rule, one should also mention the problem of the procedural difficulties faced by the party upon which the burden of proof falls, to obtain through the judicial process the evidence required to argue its case successfully. One of the reasons why private action can be used more extensively in some countries than in others to enforce competition law is that in some countries private plaintiffs seeking damages have the burden of proof and cannot use civil law procedures to get the evidence they need to establish the validity of their claim and the illegality of the practice they denounce. This is a rather severe limitation, given the necessity of intensive fact findings for the adjudication of competition cases on the basis of economic analysis. This is the main reason why in some jurisdictions most (or all) enforcement is done through administrative procedures. Indeed, administrative competition authorities typically have broad investigatory powers.

The second issue related to the use of economic reasoning for the design or enforcement of competition law is linked to the difficulty of relying on a general abstract model of the world, based on an assumption about the objective function of economic agents, as a standard of proof in legal proceedings.

From the standpoint of economic analysis, it is well known that firms can collude without actually meeting or explicitly agreeing to limit competition. For example, price signaling techniques can be used to establish tacit price collusion. In such cases the economic proof of tacit collusion often rests on the assumption that the firms involved, if they maximized profits independently of each other, would not engage if the particular practice examined (such as, for example, announcing future price changes or capacity expansion through the professional press). However, this standard of proof is often insufficient from the legal perspective because it is at best an indirect proof of the collusion using a general and abstract reasoning based on a hypothesis how firms would be likely to behave if they maximized profits in a competitive environment rather than as direct proof of the intent of the firms involved to distort competition. A good example of this type of difficulty is provided by the EU wood pulp paper case in which the evidence gathered by the EU Commission strongly suggested tacit collusion but for which the court dismissed the evidence as being insufficient. Another example is provided by cases of bid rigging on procurement markets when the indirect (economic) proof of the violation is based on the fact that the pattern of bids does not match what rational firms acting independently would have done.

The underlying difficulty in these type of cases is that of using the general presumption of profit maximization to infer the existence of a competition violation in a specific case. The economic model tells us that if firms maximize profits, then competition will have desirable properties. It also tells us that in a competitive environment in which at least some firms maximize profits, in the long run non-profit-maximizing firms tend to be eliminated. But the economic model does not tell us that in the short term all firms maximize profits even in a (realistically) competitive environment. As a matter of fact, there is a rather large body of economic literature on agency problems and on the conditions under which firms may actually have non-entrepreneurial objective functions. The only thing the economic model does tell us clearly is that assuming profit maximization in general leads to better predictions than competing hypotheses. Thus, in a specific case, basing the proof of a violation of competition on the premise that profit-maximizing firms in a competitive market would not engage in the practice examined may not be justified.

Finally, regarding the limitations of the legal instrument to reflect the teachings of economic analysis, I would like to address the question of gaps in coverage. It is quite obvious that there are gaps between what economic analysis would consider to be undesirable market outcomes and what is actually prohibited by most competition laws. For example, non-cooperative oligopolistic behavior can lead to anti-competitive outcomes and economic inefficiencies whereas in most countries oligopolistic behavior is not prohibited (even though in some jurisdictions such as in the EU there is an attempt to widen the scope of applicability of the prohibition of abuses of dominant position to cases of 'collective dominant positions', a rather ill-defined category). Such a gap is particularly bothersome as many markets tend to be characterized by oligopolistic structures. Of course, merger control can be used to prevent the emergence of oligopolistic structures or the tightening of an oligopoly (and has been used to that effect in the EU albeit in rare cases and somewhat questionably) but merger control is at best of limited use in this area since many oligopolies do not result from mergers but from more 'natural' causes such as the competitive process.

The reason for this unsatisfactory situation (from the economic standpoint) lies in the fact that, as the EU Court of Justice has suggested, from a legal standpoint one cannot fault a firm for trying to adapt itself independently and as intelligently as possible to its environment and to the expected conduct of other firms. In a non-cooperative oligopoly there is no attempt by any of the oligopolists to reduce or eliminate competition (even though competition is reduced as a result of the independent behavior of the oligopolists) and from the legal standpoint there can therefore be no fault. In the case of a cartel, on the contrary, each firm engages in a practice (whether limiting its output to a prearranged level or sticking to a prearranged price) after having deliberately agreed with its competitors that they will do likewise. It is the agreement or the 'meeting of the minds' to reduce competition which constitutes the fault.

This limitation of the legal instrument may explain why, for example, in some countries competition authorities or courts have been reluctant to find that pricing at a monopolistic level by a firm holding a dominant position is in itself an illegal practice. Indeed, monopolistic pricing can clearly be in the immediate and personal interest of the monopolist. Therefore from the legal point of view it is more difficult to consider that it constitutes a fault.

To conclude on this question, I would venture that some of the failures of competition authorities or courts fully to take into account the teachings of economic analysis result not so much from a misunderstanding of economic analysis but rather from the strict constraints involved in enforcing a law (in order to be respectful of the general legal principles applying in their country). This does, of course, beg the question of whether competition law is the right instrument to promote or preserve competition or whether other less constrained policy instruments would be more appropriate.

Economic analysis as a guide to competition law enforcement

If we now focus on the sub-set of issues for which there is consistency between the goals of antitrust laws and economic reasoning and for which the legal standards of proof do not preclude consistence with economic analysis, I would like to address the question of the extent to which economic concepts are useful to guide competition law enforcers.

To illustrate my point I will focus on the concept of market. Practically any competition case will start with the question of the definition of the relevant market. Competition authorities or courts either try to assess the cross-price elasticity of products or services which might be considered likely substitutes to define markets or, more frequently, because they do not have the data required for such analysis, resort to empirical tests such as the 5 per cent test to assess the contour of relevant markets. Over the last ten years many competition authorities have added a test of supply side substitutability in their search for the definition of relevant markets.

What is most striking about the market definition techniques used by competition authorities is that while they are reasonably closely linked to what standard micro-economic reasoning would suggest as a way of approaching the problem of market definition, they are widely considered to be questionable by the business community.

Business people tend to consider that markets are far too narrowly defined by competition authorities. It is clear that in many countries public officials in charge of industrial policy tend to have a broad vision of industries and markets and they therefore tend to see the definition of relevant markets provided by competition authorities as being unrealistically narrow.

The criticism addressed by the business community to competition authorities is not surprising since firms involved in a competition case (at least when they are defendants) have a strong incentive to pretend that they are competing with a host of other firms and that their proposed merger or their past practices could not therefore conceivably alter the competitive process.

Reciprocally, however, it must be acknowledged that antitrust authorities have a vested interest in defining markets narrowly in order to have the means to intervene. As an example of this second type of moral hazard let me say that during a recent roundtable on abuse of dominant positions in which a large number of OECD competition enforcers participated, after having examined the more or less sophisticated tools of analysis, an unnamed participant (who happens to be a leading industrial organization economist) put down his prepared notes and ventured (jokingly) that reality was a bit different from theory and that one could legitmately ask whether the thought process of competition enforcers was not the reverse of what economic analysis would suggest, i.e. that when a competition authority finds a practice (by a single firm) it wants to eliminate or sanction, then it decides that it has to be an abuse of dominant position or market power and therefore it defines the market accordingly.

The possibility of a modicum of moral hazard or strategic behavior either by the competition authority or the defendants should not distract us from addressing the issue of whether there is a unique definition of what a market is and of whether economic analysis provides enough guidance for competition policy enforcers when it comes to the definition of relevant markets.

In many jurisdictions the definition of relevant markets does not only surface in competition or antitrust laws but also in other areas of economic law such as, for example, trade or tax laws. In most countries trade or tax laws are administered by different agencies than competition laws and discrepancies in market definition between such agencies are routinely attributed to the fact that some of the agencies involved did not have a proper understanding of economic analysis.

However, in the EU, the Commission and the EU Court of Justice have to deal both with Article 85 and 86 cases and, for example, with Article 95 which provides in its first paragraph that 'No Member State shall impose, directly or indirectly, on the products of other Member States any internal taxation of any kind in excess of that imposed directly or indirectly on similar domestic products' and, in its second paragraph, that 'Furthermore no Member State shall impose on the products of other Member States any internal taxation of such a nature as to afford indirect protection to other products.' Although the wording of Article 95 does not include a reference to the concept of market, it is clear from the case law that the second paragraph of this Article applies to differences in taxation between products which although they are not similar are competing at least indirectly with each other.

For the purpose of enforcement of this article the EU Court of Justice has held in an number of decisions that all spirits (such as cognac, whisky, vodka, gin, ouzo, etc.) can compete with each other at least partially and that therefore a difference in the domestic taxation regime between the two types of spirits, one imported and one domestic, fell within the purview of Article 95 of the EU treaty if the domestic spirit was taxed less heavily than the imported spirit. This, however, has not deterred the Commission from finding in applying Article 85 that gin was a distinct sub-market within the global market for spirits and that whisky was a separate market from other spirits in general and from cognac in particular.

A common justification of the narrow interpretation of markets for the purpose of competition law enforcement (and the wider definition of markets for the purpose of trade law enforcement) is that competition laws aim to protect the competitive price mechanism whereas trade laws protect economic opportunities of importers. Such a justification is partially convincing. On the one hand, it is clear that the price mechanism in a given market will be undoubtedly influenced by the possibility of entry (as the theory of contestable markets shows) and by the fact that supply side substitutability and the protection of economic opportunities of entrants are considerations commonly used to assess the potential anti-competitive effects of mergers (irrespective of the fact that merger control is a part of competition law and that the definition of markets used for merger control is often quite narrow). On the other hand, the requirement of non-discrimination in taxation between imported and domestic products in Article 95 is at least partially based on the desire to promote price competition.

One of the difficulties encountered by competition authorities when using economic analysis, is that its comparative static approach implicitly considers that market definitions are stable and exogenous. It does not explicitly take into account the possibility that the perimeters of markets are endogenously determined by the strategies of firms and are not necessarily stable over time. The definition of cross-price elasticity is the relative variation of the quantity sold for a product divided by the relative price change of another product, everything else being constant. This a short-term definition. The benefits of competition are long-term. If one assumes that the world is stable, and in particular that the perimeters of market are invariant with the practice there is no conflict between an assessment of market definition using a short-term instrument and the assessment of the long-term potential effect of the practice or the structural change examined. However, in the real (dynamic) world this need not be so.

To take an example from the past, competition authorities have often considered that the market for film exhibition in movie theaters is separate from the market for television viewing of films. However, the available evidence in many countries is that as TV viewing became more widespread, the attendance at movie houses has tended to decline. It may be that firms in the movie industry anticipated this movement before antitrust authorities did. Likewise, antitrust authorities tend to consider that various forms of retail selling (such as mail order houses, traditional stores, large stores) operate in separate markets because they offer slightly different services to consumers and charge different prices. Yet it is clear that in many countries as large stores developed, traditional stores started losing customers and this reality led some of these countries to adopt tough laws to prevent the further development of large stores.

The problem is further complicated by the fact that firm strategies are often based on their expectations of what tomorrow's product definitions will be like rather than on what today's market looks like. Thus in industries whose technology changes rapidly or in which innovations (and the definition of products or services) are likely to affect the expected perceived needs of consumers, there can be an interdependence between the practices of the innovating firms and the definition of the market on which they operate. What may look like an unjustified and anti-competitive bundling of products or services (or of functions) if one looks at today's market definition may be an innovation which will change the standard functions of the product or service in question if one can anticipate tomorrow's market definition (or today's latent demand). This difficulty concerning the proper time reference for evaluating markets is at least partially at the heart of controversies about what is or is not an anti-competitive practice in the telecommunication or computer sectors.

In summary, it seems that contrary to what we would like to think, economic analysis (and in particular analysis of substitutability) does not provide us with a 'scientific' non-ambiguous tool to assess market contours for the purpose of economic law. On the one hand, the definition of markets depends to a certain extent on the objectives of the law for the purpose of which markets are assessed. On the other hand, even in the case of competition law, in an increasing number of situations, market definition contains an implicit judgment on the respective valuation of the short-term anti-competitive effects of the practice or structural change considered and their long-term effect.

Conclusion

Finally, even if it is clear that competition law is at least partially based on the teachings of economic analysis, we must realize that economic analysis provides only a general foundation for competition law and policy and that its ability to provide worthwhile guidance to competition authorities enforcing competition law should not be overemphasized.

* This chapter was originally published as part of the twenty-fifth annual proceedings of the Fordham Corporate Law Institute on International Antitrust Law & Policy in New York City, 1998, edited by Barry E. Hawk and published by Juris Publishing, Inc., Yonkers, New York.

3 Competition policy and market dynamics

Victor D. Norman

Introduction

One of the oldest controversies in competition analysis concerns the relationship between market structure and innovation. As usually posed, the question is whether monopoly is more conducive to innovation than competition. No-one has been able to give a clear-cut answer, probably because there is none. In a sense, however, the question is more interesting than the answer – not so much in its own right as in what it reveals about the traditional way of thinking about market structure. Most economists, and virtually all designers of competition policy, take market structure as their starting point – as something which is somehow, almost exogenously, given (although it may be affected by competition policy), and which produces results in terms of costs, prices, innovations, etc. Elementary microeconomics tells us that this is wrong. Market structure is inherently endogenous; determined by the behaviour of existing firms and by entry of new ones, simultaneously with costs, prices, product ranges, and investments in R&D and marketing. Exogenous variables (if any) are things like the fundamental characteristics of the products and the production processes, entry conditions, the initial preferences of the consumers, variables determined in other markets, and government policy. To ask if there will be more innovation with monopoly than with competition is no more meaningful than to ask whether price-cost margins will be higher if costs are high than if they are low.

This is true not only for the relationship between market structure and innovation – it is true more generally for the relationship between market structure, competition, and economic efficiency. We can, of course, easily construct cases in which a high degree of market concentration goes along with lack of competition and inefficient resource use. We can, however, equally well construct examples in which concentration is the result of aggressive competition, and where the result is efficiency. It is also possible to construct cases where concentration reflects monopoly, but where monopoly power is exploited in a way which is consistent with efficiency.

The question that should be asked is not, therefore, what the 'ideal' market structure might be, but what set of circumstances are conducive to static and dynamic efficiency and what implications that has for the design of competition policy and for the way in which the competition authorities should handle particular cases. Once the question is formulated in this way, it is immediately apparent that market structure by itself is of little interest. Circumstances will affect efficiency to the extent that they affect the behaviour of firms; and the behaviour of firms reflects profit opportunities and other incentives that firms face. It is through the effects on firm incentives, therefore, that exogenous variables affect efficiency. It follows that the focus of competition analysis should be on incentives and variables that affect those.

In a report to the Norwegian Competition Authority,[1] by Nils-Henrik Mørch von der Fehr, Torger Reve, Anders Chr. Stray Ryssdal and myself, we have sketched an incentive-oriented approach to competition analysis. In the first part of this chapter, I shall summarize that approach. While we claim some originality for the approach as such, most of the details are familiar from the more traditional way of approaching imperfectly competitive markets. We have also pointed out some implications of incentive-orientation for competition policy. These will be discussed in the second part of the chapter.

An incentive-oriented approach to competition analysis

Perhaps the most important question in competition analysis is what the object of analysis should be. Is it the market, the industry, or the individual firm we want to study? The obvious answer is the market. We are ultimately concerned with prices and quantities, and these are determined in the market. Although that is obviously correct, we argue that the focus ought to be on the individual firm. There are two reasons for this. One is purely pragmatic: the firm is a well-defined entity; the market is not, and there are good reasons to avoid the minefield of market definition. The other reason is substantive: we cannot understand the market unless we understand the agents in the market; and in imperfectly competitive markets, the 'interesting' agents are the firms.

We would also argue that it is natural in most contexts for competition analysis to take a firm or group of firms as the point of departure. US authorities are concerned about the behaviour of Microsoft towards its customers and competitors, and this concern has little to do with the question of what the appropriate definition of the market for computer software is. Norwegian authorities may have to make up their minds about a possible merger between the two largest banks. If so, they will be concerned about how the merged bank will behave and how that will affect the behaviour of other financial institutions. This may, of course, be phrased as a question of how the merger will affect financial markets. Ultimately, however, it is firm behaviour they are interested in.

Our approach, therefore, has the individual firm as object of study. The starting point is that firm behaviour is determined by incentives – by the profits and losses that follow from alternative courses of action, and by the consequences that profits and losses will have for the firm. It follows that competition is important only to the extent that it affects firm incentives. It does so in two ways. First, it reduces the profitability of monopoly-like practices. Second, it narrows the 'survival space' – the set of actions that are possible without endangering the future of the firm – and thus makes it more likely that the firm will innovate and produce efficiently.

We suggest that the second of these is perhaps a more fruitful point of departure for competition analysis than the first, i.e. that one should start by mapping the 'survival space' of the firm (or group of firms) under consideration. The way to do this is by asking whether the firm owns or controls something which gives rise to pure rents or potential monopoly profits. If it does, the firm may be able to survive even if it is inefficient. If not, its only feasible course is to minimize costs.

If the firm earns pure rents or has potential market power, the next question should be what the positive incentives are. Will the firm minimize costs even if it can survive without doing so? Is it in the firm's interest to exploit potential monopoly power? And if so, will it be done in a way which creates inefficiency? The answers to these questions depend in part on the characteristics of the firm's environment, and in part on the nature of the contracts that are possible between the firm and its customers.

We therefore recommend a three-stage approach, where the first stage maps any exclusive ownership or control that might give rise to pure rents or potential market power, the second stage considers how the firm's external environment affects incentives for profit maximization and exploitation of potential market power, and the third stage considers whether the customer relationship is such that efficient contracts may be possible.

Looking for exclusive ownership and control

Mapping the potential for pure rents and monopoly profits requires a careful assessment of technology, inputs, products, and customer relationships. One way of doing that is by first mapping the value chain – from primary inputs to final consumers – for the products of the firm, and then look specifically at three aspects: whether the firm owns or controls key inputs, whether it has a technological advantage (either because economies of scale give insiders an advantage or because it possesses unique know-how), and whether it has exclusive control over products, distribution channels, or customer groups.

Three points should be emphasized. The first concerns economies of scale. It is tempting to look for these at the level of the firm – i.e. to ask whether the technology is such that large firms have a natural advantage over smaller ones. Since most empirical estimates are of scale economies in the production of widely defined product groups (economies of scale in banking, in steel production, or whatever), there may be no alternative. Still, it is important to keep in mind that economies of scale relate to characteristics of production processes, and that firms are different from production functions. If one accepts the Coase–Williamson view of firms as means of internalizing transactions, it is likely that the activities of the firm will comprise a number of separate production processes, and these could have quite different scale characteristics.

The second point concerns market control. To assess to what extent the firm has control over products, distribution channels and customer groups, it may be necessary to define the relevant market and be useful to draw on traditional concentration measures deriving from market shares. This is, as already touched upon, a well-known minefield. We therefore strongly recommend a sharp focus on the firm and its products. The purpose is to assess the potential market power of the firm – specifically, to what extent the firm can raise prices without losing sales. Definitions of relevant markets and measures of market shares are only relevant to the extent that they make it easier to assess the price elasticities facing the firm. For that purpose, it usually does not matter whether one defines the relevant market narrowly but opens for high cross-price elasticities to neighbouring markets, or defines the market broadly but takes account of product differentiation within the market.

The third point which should be emphasized is the importance of customer relationships. There may be a tendency to ignore this, perhaps because it typically plays little role in formal models of imperfectly competitive markets. Empirically, however, an established customer base may be a more common source of potential market power than economies of scale or control over key inputs. The extensive use of consumer-loyalty programmes is one indication of that.

The firm's environment: looking for turbulence

The second main question is whether the firm will exploit its profit opportunities fully – whether it will minimize costs, and whether it will exploit potential monopoly power. The answer that is implicit in much thinking about competition is that firms automatically will exploit monopoly power, but that they will not minimize costs unless they are forced to do so. The logic behind this must be that firms are thought to choose the easy way out, and that exploitation of monopoly power is easier than cost cutting. That is too simple-minded a view. Firms are concerned about profits, even if it requires effort to reap them. Moreover, it is not obvious that cost cutting is always more painful than monopolistic behaviour.

A more realistic view is that there is a symmetry between cost inefficiency and monopoly practices because both involve an element of irreversibility, in the sense that there are costs associated with eliminating inefficiency and re-establishing confidence among customers who have been subject to monopoly pricing. Whether the firm chooses to exploit profit opportunities today should then depend on how current exploitation affects future opportunities. If the effect of current practices on future profit opportunities is small, it may be reasonable to assume that firms will choose the easy way out. If the effect is negative and large, there is less reason to expect the firm to choose cost-inefficient or monopoly practices.

A key question, therefore, is how current practices affect future opportunities. That is in turn largely a question of the firm's environment. The more stable and predictable the environment is, the less likely it is that current practices will have to be reversed in the future. It follows that uncertainty and turbulence may discipline the firm. The opposite is also possible, however, if the future is sufficiently uncertain, the firm may be tempted to cash in today, simply because it does not know whether there will be any profit opportunities in the future.

The degree and nature of turbulence in the firm's environment are therefore important. The ideal, from our point of view, is an environment which is sufficiently stable and predictable to make the firm believe in long-term survival, but at the same time sufficiently turbulent to scare it away from monopoly practices and cost inefficiency.

The list of factors which are relevant in this respect is straightforward. It consists largely of the potential threats that the firm faces. Entry conditions, customer loyalty, and the rate and nature of technological change are obviously important. In a small economy like the Norwegian one, existing and potential international competition is particularly important.

Again, a couple of points should be emphasized. The first is, once more, the need for a clear focus. The purpose of the analysis is not to carry out a broad survey of the industry, but to analyse to what extent the environment serves as a disciplining device on the firm. Thus, for example, when looking at entry conditions, the question that should be asked is what risk the firm takes if it tries to exploit a monopoly position. Could this trigger entry? Are the potential entrants a well-defined group which is known to the firm? If so, can the firm create artificial entry barriers, and will that be in the firm's interest?

The rate and nature of technical change provide another example. It is tempting to say that rapid technical change will discipline a firm which might be tempted to exploit monopoly power. As a general proposition, that is not true. The crucial question is whether technical change is exogenous to the firms in the industry or generated by the firms themselves. If there is rapid technical change, and the changes are a combination of exogenous and endogenous change, each firm will have to either innovate or perish. If changes are purely exogenous, on the other hand, they are unlikely to have much impact on the strategies pursued by individual firms. And if technical change is purely endogenous, equilibria both with and without innovation are possible.

The second point is that capital markets and the structure of ownership of the firm are more important, and should be given greater attention, than is customary in traditional competition analysis. The capital market is in many cases the strongest disciplining device for a firm, in the sense that the possibility of take-over bids is the chief mechanism forcing it to maximize profits. If the result is exploitation of monopoly power, this need not, of course, coincide with what the competition authorities want. If, as we do, one regards cost inefficiency as a greater problem than monopoly pricing, competition for ownership should nevertheless be desirable. In any case, it is clear that the ownership structure is important for the firm's incentives.

Turbulence is particularly important to prevent tacit collusion between firms. For tacit collusion to be a stable equilibrium, two conditions must be satisfied.

The first is that the industry and market must be sufficiently transparent to enable mutual surveillance. The second is that the relationship must be a long-term one, so that the short-term gain from defection is outweighed by the long-term loss that the defector will incur when the competitors retaliate. It follows that tacit collusion is more likely in an industry with a stable population of firms, stable demand conditions, and stable technology. It is particularly likely in a stable industry in which there is a well-defined market price or some other key variable which can serve as a focal point.

Contracts and information

Firms have nothing to gain from inefficiency as such. Even if a firm has market power and wants to exploit it, it does not necessarily follow that the outcome will be economically inefficient. The perfectly discriminating monopolist is the best example: he will capture all the surplus that would otherwise have accrued to the consumers, but the outcome will be economically efficient. Generally, a seller with market power will search for ways to exploit the market power efficiently, since an inefficient outcome means that some of the profit potential is wasted. Only if he is unable to design efficient contracts with his customers will he have to fall back on more stylized monopolistic practices with the inefficiencies that those entail.

The third question is therefore whether there is reason to believe that a monopoly outcome is inefficient. This is largely a question of whether efficient contracts between buyer and seller are possible. There could be formal or informal constraints on the types of contracts that are possible. Alternatively, efficient contracts could be impossible because of information asymmetries. Both possibilities must be checked.

In general, we should expect information asymmetries to be more severe in consumer markets than in intermediate-goods markets, and more severe for goods where the value of the good is small relative to the cost of obtaining information. Thus, for example, it is probably less of a problem for expensive consumer durables than for other consumer goods.

Some implications for competition policy

The firm-based, incentive-oriented approach to competition analysis has important implications for competition policy as well. The implications concern the ambitions of competition policy, the focus of competition authorities, and the policy instruments that should be used.

Ambitions

A naïve, but surprisingly common, view is that competition policy should ensure a high degree of competition in all sectors, at all levels, and at all times. It is almost self-evident that implementation of such a programme would require information that it is impossible for the competition authorities to have. What is worse, is that it would have disastrous effects on firm incentives. Firms would hesitate to introduce products that might capture a large share of the market; they would be afraid of the consequences if they were to gain too much of a cost advantage over their competitors; and they would continually waste resources trying to evade or avoid the ever-present 'competition police force'.

The basic premise of competition policy must be that detailed regulation of firms and markets is undesirable, and that detailed surveillance is impossible. It follows that we have to accept that firms try to obtain market power and some-times succeed, that they do so through behaviour which may be undesirable, and that it may not always be possible to distinguish between tacit collusion and desirable networks.

The ambition should be a self-regulating environment in which monopoly positions are unsustainable, non-price competition is unprofitable, and collusion is unstable. That is roughly the same as saying that the aim of competition pol-icy should be to affect firm incentives, to make cost efficiency and innovation more profitable relative to attempts at establishing market power.

This relates to the older discussion of regulation of conduct vs. structure and can easily be interpreted as an argument for the latter. That need not be the case, however. It could well be that regulation of structure in particular cases is more detrimental to incentives than regulation of conduct. The question of patents could be an example. It may well be that patent protection combined with price regulation gives better incentives for firms than elimination of patent protection. We should also remember that the existence of conduct regulation by itself can have positive incentive effects, just as patrolling police can have a positive effect on crime in the streets.

Focus and design

The implications for the focus and design of policy are even clearer. If we are correct, the most severe examples of cost inefficiency and monopolistic practices are to be found in markets where products and technology remain unchanged over time, and where there is a small number of well-established firms that know each other well. The type of industry which should be expected to perform best is characterized by rapid change in technology and products (particularly if there is a combination of exogenous and endogenous change), open entry and exit, and consequent uncertainty about who the future competitors are likely to be. In such industries we may see highly successful firms which, for a time, capture very high market shares and enjoy monopoly power, but such positions are often temporary, and few firms would dare rely on such a position.

The fundamental objective of competition policy should be to create, or at least contribute to, the latter type of industries and prevent the former. That has direct implications for the focus and design of policy. First, it says something about which sectors one should be concerned about. There is little reason to be concerned about markets and industries where exogenous factors change rapidly, entry of new firms occurs, and there is significant international competition. The industries one should worry about, are the stable ones – particularly if they also enjoy shelter from international competition. Since stable industries typically are anonymous as well, a corollary is that it is rarely necessary to worry much about firms and industries that we hear a lot about – it is the silent ones that attract our attention.

Second, the best policy instruments are those which create turbulence and thus uncertainty about who the future competitors are likely to be. This suggests that a policy of free trade, at least in small economies, may be the single most important ingredient in competition policy.

Third, the actions of the competition authorities should encourage innovation and change, not stability. This is a strong argument against traditional 'trust-busting'. The rationale for a policy of preventing mergers and breaking up large firms is that the ideal state is one of many firms, each with a small market share. Our view is that stable market shares are more disturbing than high ones. It is important for firm incentives that success is permitted, even if it implies high market shares. There is reason to be concerned only when high market shares become permanent. On the other hand, there could be every reason to be concerned even if market shares are low, if they are sufficiently stable for tacit collusion to be possible.

Note

1 N.-H. M. von der Fehr, V. Norman, T. Reve and A. Stray Ryssdal, *Ikke for å vinne? Analyse av konkurranseforhold og konkurransepolitikk*, SNF-report 8/98.

4 Who should be responsible for competition policy in regulated industries?

Nils-Henrik M. von der Fehr

Introduction[1]

The introduction of market-based competition in industries previously subject to heavy-handed regulation – examples include utilities such as electricity, gas and water, as well as transport, telecommunications and financial services – raises a number of new policy issues.[2] Among these is the question of where to place the responsibility for competition policy in these industries.

This question has two dimensions. The 'horizontal' dimension concerns the relationship between the competition authorities and other government agencies with similar, or overlapping, responsibilities; in particular, those agencies responsible for the regulation of specific industries. The industry regulators often have broad responsibilities, typically including competition policy considerations. It is therefore necessary to make clear the respective roles of the competition authority and the regulators.

Closely connected to this is the 'vertical' issue of delegation and the autonomy of the regulation and competition authorities. Acknowledging the necessary trade-offs between competition policy considerations, on the one hand, and other policy considerations, on the other, we shall ask to what extent is it possible – and, indeed, desirable – the competition authority be given discretionary decision power?

The question of how to allocate responsibilities for competition policy and regulation falls under the more general issue of the optimal organization of government. In particular, we may ask why the organization of government is separated in the first place. Ideally, an integrated administration should be able to achieve economies of scale and scope through better utilization of expertise and by facilitating the co-ordination of different tasks. The merit of creating separate agencies – each with some degree of discretionary decision power – must originate from some sort of government 'failure' or 'imperfection'.

A split along the vertical dimension implies that decision power is delegated to subordinate authorities. This means that decisions will involve fewer levels of the government hierarchy and may therefore be reached faster. The obvious drawback is that subordinate decision-makers may act in ways that are not consistent with overall political objectives.

A horizontal split implies that tasks and responsibilities are allocated between authorities with different jurisdictions. The allocation may be according to policy area or according to sector. For example, in Norway the Competition Authority (NCA) is provided with a limited set of tasks (namely, to improve economic efficiency by promoting 'effective' competition), while its jurisdiction covers many (but not all) sectors of the economy. A similar split applies to the authorities responsible for carrying out environmental policy and policies of health and work place safety. The jurisdiction of an industry regulator, however, is restricted to a specific sector of the economy, but often involves a wider set of tasks (including promoting competition).

There are consequently two questions that concern us in this chapter. First, to what extent should decisions be delegated to the competition authority and other regulatory agencies? And, second, how should the responsibility for regulation and competition policy be allocated between the competition authority and industry regulators?[3]

Before continuing with an analysis of these questions, we pause for a brief discussion of the concepts of competition policy and regulation.

Objectives, tasks and instruments

In principle, there is really no clear distinction between 'competition policy', on the one hand, and 'regulation', on the other. Consider first their objectives. In Norway, the Competition Law states that the aim of competition policy is to 'improve economic efficiency by promoting effective competition'. Elsewhere, the objective of competition policy may not have been defined with equal precision (varying from broad aims such as 'upholding the public good' to the more narrow goals of 'preventing anti-competitive conduct'), but in practice the interpretation appears to be much the same. Similarly, regulation policy often includes distribution objectives, such as providing 'universal service' and ensuring 'fair and non-discriminatory prices', but – following the recent wave of regulatory reforms – emphasis is generally put on efficiency, as opposed to equity concerns.

One might argue, therefore, that, at least in some fairly general sense, competition policy and regulation are different means towards the same end. However, this is not quite right. First, the two sets of policy instruments are to a large extent overlapping. For example, an important part of recent regulatory reforms has been the design of market structure by, for instance, imposing vertical separation between different lines of businesses (such as generation and transmission of electricity). The distinction between market structure regulation and merger policy is, of course, nominal. Also, restricting the use of particular forms of business contracts (such as exclusionary dealing arrangements, retail price maintenance and price discrimination) is central to competition policy, but is really just another form of price regulation.

Second, and more fundamentally, both policies are 'interventionist', restricting or directing the decisions of market participants. The idea that competition policy is dealing with 'market structure', whereas regulation is concerned with 'market conduct', tends to divert attention from this fact. This idea is rooted in the so-called Structure-Conduct-Performance (SCP) paradigm, in which market structure is seen as exogenous, ultimately determining the conduct of firms. However, the SCP paradigm has become increasingly unfashionable among economists over the past twenty years, due to the realization that 'structural' features (such as technology, product characteristics and the number and size distribution of firms) are constantly changing, subject to decisions made by market participants. In essence, therefore, just as regulation interferes with market conduct, so does competition policy.

Consequently, rather than focusing on the differences between regulation and competition policy, it may be more useful to stress their relatedness and similarities. Indeed, if by 'regulation' we mean measures to control or restrict the decisions of private agents, competition policy should clearly be considered under this heading. Or, alternatively, we could include under the term 'competition policy' traditional (monopoly) regulation, so as to mean any policy measure aiming to curb market power, either by promoting competition or, where effective competition cannot be established, by other more direct means.

Grouping policy instruments together in this way is also helpful from a practical point of view, in particular in those cases in which these instruments, which are otherwise seen as belonging to different policy agendas, are in fact substitutes. In some markets there may be a choice between facilitating effective competition through a strict merger policy – at the cost of forgoing economies of scale or scope – and accepting a technologically more efficient, but more concentrated, market structure, and relying instead on direct (price) regulation. An example can be found in electricity retailing, in which imperfect competition derives, to a large extent, from the vertical integration between retailing and distribution activities. Is it, in this case, more efficient to require full separation between monopoly activities and competitive activities, or should one accept vertical integration and instead, by imposing rules on price information, contracts and accounting, regulate the business?[4] The example illustrates that in some cases it may be necessary – or at least beneficial – to be able to consider a wide spectrum of policy instruments, some of which have traditionally been in the domain of competition authorities and some only available to regulators.

It may, in fact, be useful to consider an alternative distinction between what we might call 'economic' (or 'market') regulation and 'technical' regulation. Economic regulation would then include competition policy, as well as the (price) regulation of natural monopolies. By contrast, technical regulation means the qualitative regulation of products or production processes, such as imposing industry quality standards or introducing measures to promote health and safety. Unlike economic regulation, technical regulation will generally not be motivated by imperfect competition as such, but rather by other forms of market imperfections, notably incomplete or asymmetric information.

Clearly, technical regulation will in most cases have economic consequences. However, unlike economic regulation, technical regulation will generally not affect market power or the competitive rivalry between firms. In fact, in many cases technical regulation will merely mean facilitating the coordination between market participants; for example, imposing standards for air control or setting voltage levels in electricity networks. In other cases, technical regulation may impose costs on market participants without affecting competitive conditions, such as when setting standards for electricity supply security and transmission quality in telecommunications networks. Consequently, the undertaking of technical regulation does not necessarily require a comprehensive analysis of market performance.

The distinction between economic and technical regulation is evidently not always clear-cut. For example, the choice of technical standards for the interconnection of telecommunications networks, or the choice of metering system for electricity consumption, could potentially have profound effects on the development of competition. In such cases, the likely effects on market performance should obviously guide the choice of regulatory measures. Indeed, as a general rule, the economic impact should always be taken into account when deciding upon the appropriate regulatory policy. Nevertheless, in many circumstances the effects of technical regulations on market performance will be small or, at any rate, negligible relative to the main objectives that such measures are meant to achieve.

If by economic regulation in general, and competition policy in particular, we mean countering (the abuse of) market power, we may want to include a wide range of policy measures that can potentially affect market conduct and performance. At one end of the spectrum is 'market design', that is, establishing the basic framework that shapes market behaviour, including legislation and the creation of specific market institutions (such as an electricity 'pool'). At the other end are the day-to-day operations of market surveillance and the enforcement of rules and regulations. Some of these tasks have traditionally been allocated to a competition authority while others have rested with industry regulators, superior authorities or the courts. It is the purpose of the rest of this chapter to discuss how this diverse group of tasks should be allocated between various government bodies.

Organizational models

Obviously there is a wide range of possible ways to organize the competition and regulation authorities. Basically, however, and as has already been argued in the introduction, the choice is twofold. On the one hand, there is the question of to what extent decision power should be delegated to subordinate agencies, and, on the other, how tasks should be allocated between different agencies. In this section we outline some alternative organizational models which occupy different positions in this two-dimensional set. The following sections are devoted to a discussion of issues relevant to the choice between these models.

Delegation

Delegation involves a number of different elements; these include the ability of the subordinate authority to make final decisions in concrete cases, its discretion to prioritize between tasks and the extent to which there are specific rules governing the decision-making process.

For some tasks it is clearly not possible to delegate decision power to subordinate authorities. For example, market design issues often involve fundamental policy conflicts and cannot therefore be delegated to an agency with only narrow goals or limited responsibilities. For other tasks, however, such as market surveillance, rule enforcement and sanctions, there is, at least in principle, no difficulty in delegating authority.

While delegation may consequently be limited, it will nevertheless typically be the case that an agency is responsible for carrying out a number of different tasks. The question therefore arises as to how the agency should prioritize these tasks. To some extent prioritization may be imposed through rules laid down by superior authorities. In practice, however, delegation will always involve considerable freedom for the agency to follow its own priorities.

Delegation of decision power is normally accompanied by rules (in the form of instructions, manuals, etc.) to ensure that decisions are made in a proper manner. Such rules may, for example, apply to information requirements, procedures and rights of appeal. By imposing strict rules a superior authority can guarantee that decisions are made according to a specific standard of good government. However, strict rules may unnecessarily delay decisions and cause inflexibility as decision-makers are prohibited from relying on their own good judgement to adjust the outcome according to the particularities of the case.[5]

One way or another, decision power will always have to be delegated to lower levels of the government hierarchy. The question of vertical delegation therefore concerns the extent to which such delegation is optimal. We shall consider three alternatives:

1   *Independent agency*: in this alternative the agency would enjoy the same independence as the courts, in the sense that its decisions could not be appealed to superior government authorities, either administrative or political. This model requires specific rules about decision-making procedures, including the opportunity to appeal against decisions within the organization of the agency itself.
2   *Semi-independent agency*: in this case the agency is organized as a separate government entity, but its discretion is limited by the imposition of a right to offer its decisions to superior authorities for appeal.
3   *Integrated authority*: the third system is one in which competition policy tasks are not delegated to a specific government agency but are instead made the responsibility of a larger government body, such as a ministry.

The Norwegian Competition Authority (NCA) falls in the second category; it is organized as an independent government agency, but many of its decisions can be appealed against to the Ministry of Labour and Government Administration. The Ministry may also instruct the NCA with respect to which cases should, and which should not, be dealt with. A similar organization has been chosen for many of the industry regulators, although the regulators are subordinate to different ministries. For agriculture, forestry and the fisheries, however, competition policy is integrated with the other tasks of the relevant ministries.

The decision procedures of the NCA are regulated by law. General government procedural rules are of course relevant and, in addition, there are specific regulations laid down by the Competition Law. The NCA must deal with all applications for dispensations from the Competition Law. However, the NCA has considerable freedom to decide whether and how to intervene in cases of competitive malpractice and which merger cases to investigate. This implies, for instance, that the NCA can, to a large extent, choose whether to follow a policy of market surveillance and information activities, a policy of strict law enforcement, or a policy of market interference based on common law principles of fair trade and efficient use of resources. The Competition Law mandates all these obligations, but the NCA itself decides on the priority given to different tasks.

Nevertheless, the NCA's ability to choose its priorities is limited by the ministry's ability to instruct the NCA and the fact that the NCA regularly make strategic plans for its activity. The NCA can hardly expect its superiors to accept that very low priority is given to any of its tasks. Nevertheless, it is a fact that within certain limits the NCA has considerable freedom to choose what sort of competition policy to pursue.

Division of tasks

The question of how to divide the responsibility for competition policy between different parts of the government is mostly relevant for those industries – like electricity, telecommunications, air transport and financial services – where specific regulators have been established. The rationale for establishing designated industry regulators is partly particular market features that limit the opportunity for establishing effective competition, but also that specific expertise is required to understand the working of these industries.

The industry regulators have – explicitly or implicitly – a responsibility for promoting competition. In this respect their tasks overlap with those of the NCA. However, their main tasks concern the following:

- regulation of natural monopolies; examples include setting prices and technical standards for transmission and distribution of electricity and for access to telecommunications networks;
- taking measures against market failure due to imperfect or asymmetric information; examples include regulating air transport safety and the financial viability of credit market institutions.

The obligation of the regulators is primarily to correct the decisions of market participants where competitive forces are inadequate to ensure efficient utilization of resources. However, conflicts may arise between regulatory measures – for example, to further the security of air transport or the financial viability of credit market institutions – and regard for entry conditions and competition. In such cases it is necessary to make clear how competition policy concerns should be weighed against other regulatory concerns.

Tasks and sector responsibilities may overlap. For the competition policy tasks (or, more generally, tasks concerning economic regulation), we shall therefore consider three alternatives:

1 *Centralized competition authority*: in this case competition policy is entirely the responsibility of a single competition authority. The set of tasks of other government authorities, including industry regulators, is correspondingly limited. This organizational model consequently envisages a division of labour, with industry regulators leaving the responsibility for alleviating (abuses of) market power to the competition authority. In cases in which the remaining regulatory tasks become sufficiently few and small (for example, because the incidence of natural monopoly is relatively unimportant), it may be practical to transfer these tasks to the competition authority as well, in effect completely integrating the regulation and the competition authorities.

2 *Decentralized competition authority*: this alternative to the centralized model excludes certain sectors of the economy from the responsibility of the competition authority while including competition policy among the tasks of the industry regulators. Competition policy then becomes the responsibility of industry regulators where such exist, whereas the competition authority covers all other sectors. The delimiting of sectors must be done such as to avoid overlapping responsibilities.

3 *Competing competition authorities*: a third alternative would see the competition authority and the industry regulators share responsibility for competition policy. To the extent that this involves duplication of responsibilities, a division of labour can be achieved according to the instruments that the different authorities have at their disposal. This model warrants a system for appealing decisions to a superior authority when conflicts between regulation and competition authorities arise.

We find examples of both the second and the third models in Norway. First, the NCA's responsibility is restricted to commercial trade and industry, and furthermore does not include the (first-hand) sale of produce from agriculture, forestry and the fisheries. Second, there is overlapping responsibility in those sectors of the economy that have been provided with industry specific-regulators. In some cases the NCA has been able to reach agreements with the industry regulators that clarify the division of labour with respect to the tasks of competition policy.

Alternative organizational models

Along the two dimensions – the vertical and the horizontal – one can conceive of a number of alternative models of how to organize the competition authorities. Table 4.1 summarizes the alternatives considered.

Not all alternatives are equally relevant. It is difficult to see how a horizontal division of tasks between competing authorities could be achieved without some opportunity to appeal decisions to a superior authority being given; consequently, the alternative 'Independent–Competing' may be excluded *a priori*. It is also difficult to imagine a complete integration of the competition authorities within superior (ministerial) bodies, without there being some horizontal division of labour between ministries responsible for particular sectors of the economy; and so the alternative 'Integrated–Centralized' may therefore also be excluded.

It would appear difficult to rule out further alternatives on *a priori* grounds; indeed, and as we shall see below, each of the remaining models has arguments in its favour. Consequently, the choice of organizational model can only be made on the basis of a comparison of the relative merits of the different alternatives. In the next section we provide an overview of issues relevant to such a comparison.

Organizational challenges

A government administration does not operate in a vacuum. Nor does it react to incentives provided by a single principal, such as its administrative or political superiors. In practice, a wide range of factors influence the priorities of government agencies. For example, a competition authority operates in an environment in which positive and negative feedback originates from many sources, including superior authorities, the parliament, trade and industry, consumer interests and professional specialists of different backgrounds. Its priorities will consequently be affected by expectations and restrictions formulated by different individuals or groups.

Our point of departure is the observation that a government bureaucracy performs its tasks according to the convenience of the individual decision-maker. By suitably choosing the organizational structure, procedural rules and incentives it is possible to direct agents' (i.e. bureaucrats') decisions. The opportunities for optimising individual decisions are, however, limited by the following:

Table 4.1 Organizational models of the competition authorities

	Centralized	*Decentralized*	*Competing*
Independent	X	X	
Semi-independent	X	X	X
Integrated		X	X

- *communication costs*: communication between the different parts of the administration – and between administration and political superiors – is not without costs, and it is therefore neither possible nor desirable to make available, to analyse and to communicate all relevant information.
- *measurability of success criteria*: the tasks of the government are such that there are only limited opportunities for designing criteria that could form the basis for formalized incentive systems;
- *credibility and consistency*: the government is exposed to continual external pressures which create difficulties in establishing and sustaining a credible and consistent practice.

It is only under highly idealized conditions – when communication is free, success criteria are measurable and the government is able to commit to its preferred policy – that a completely centralized structure does as well as any other organizational form, and consequently the internal organization of government is not really an issue.[6] In practice, the choice of organization is of vital importance for the possibility of carrying through the desired policy.[7]

It should perhaps be pointed out that this view – that organizational design matters because of organizational imperfections – applies not only to government, but to any sort of organization. Moreover, the organizational imperfections considered above are not peculiar to government. However, although the organizational imperfections may be similar in character, they do differ in relative importance; in particular, government possesses certain features – notably the multiplicity of principals and objectives – that represent extraordinary organizational challenges.

We do not attempt a comprehensive analysis of these organizational challenges and their possible remedies in this chapter. On the contrary, we restrict attention to the much more limited task of assessing the relative performance of alternative administrative structures, asking the following question: 'In view of the different forms of organizational imperfections, how well do each of the designs outlined in the previous section perform?' This means that we shall not discuss (although sometimes briefly touch upon) issues such as appointments, statutes, procedural rules and (judicial and political) oversight – all of which are, in practice, of vital importance for the performance of government agencies, but nevertheless beyond the scope of our analysis.[8]

Costs of communication

Information is fragmented, spread among individuals and costly to communicate. It is, therefore, often desirable to delegate decisions to those who are closest to the relevant information. Delegation is particularly useful when it is important to reach decisions quickly. Competition policy cases are often made difficult by the fact that vital information is not easily accessible to government authorities. It may therefore take considerable time to reach a decision in any given case. Sometimes, the government may even decide not to react against illegal or undesirable acts because the handling of a case has taken such a long time that it is in practice difficult, if not outright impossible, to remedy the defects. In a recent case the NCA decided not to require Trio Ving AS to sell off the company Møller Undall Gruppen, even though it was felt that the acquisition had led to a significant restriction of competition in the relevant market (namely, the Norwegian market for keys and locks). The reason for this decision was that the NCA found that such a long time had passed since the acquisition – and consequent events – that it would be impossible to re-establish a company with strength comparable to that of the original Møller Undall.[9] Long decision lags may also imply that market participants refrain from bringing cases to the government authorities or complaining against decisions.

If communication is easier horizontally (between agencies at the same level of the government hierarchy, such as the competition authority and an industry regulator) than vertically (between an agency and its administrative or political superior), it may be efficient to delegate decisions to one of the subordinate authorities.[10] Rather than having each agency communicating with the superior authority – which would then base its decision on the incoming information – information is collected at one of the authorities, which also reaches the final decision. Such an organizational model might for example involve the competition authority transferring the results of its market analyses to the relevant industry regulator, who would then use these, together with other relevant information, to reach its conclusion.

A counter-argument to this proposition is that specialization reduces the cost of gathering and communicating information, and that possessing the right expertise makes it easier to find relevant information and analyse it. Any competition authority is dependent on considerable expertise to be able to understand the behaviour of market participants, in order, first of all, to distinguish between conduct which, respectively, promotes and undermines competition and, second, to predict how policy measures affect market conduct. In addition to the more traditional juridical and economic expertise, a competition authority must possess expertise in subjects such as business management, administration and strategy. The necessity of establishing and maintaining such extensive expertise implies that there are considerable economies of scale. Taken in isolation, this is an argument in favour of concentrating the responsibility for competition policy within one agency. Communication is also more effective between parties with similar qualifications. For an industry regulator to be able to understand and take advantage of the expertise of the competition authority, it would itself have to establish the necessary know-how. That would require duplication of efforts.

An alternative model, which does not require direct communication between the competition authority and industry regulators, would see decision power shared in such a way that decisions could only be reached by mutual consent. This would, for instance, imply that stopping a harmful merger between two financial service companies would be possible only if the regulator responsible for overseeing the financial viability of such institutions did not find the merger necessary in order to enhance the companies' financial strength. Similarly, the credit market regulator would not be able to impose regulations if the competition authority found these to introduce entry barriers that would undermine competition. An organization model based on decisions by mutual consent would therefore tend to conserve the status quo and limit market interference by the government.

Incentive problems

The tasks of government are such that it is difficult to design formal incentive systems. The government has many, partly inconsistent and imprecise, objectives and decisions must often be made on the basis of complex considerations. For external observers it can often be difficult to judge whether the decision process was sound and the final decision reasonable.

When there is a lot of 'noise' in the observation of success, a system of formal incentives is typically not efficient.[11] The risk of rewarding bad performances – and failing to reward good performances – becomes great. Formal incentive systems will also tend to distort efforts towards measurable results to the detriment of objectives that are not measurable, or perhaps difficult to measure.

Such distortions may occur even in cases in which incentive systems are not formal. For example, the financial markets regulator would most likely find any sign of an emerging bank crisis very disturbing. However, being subjected to criticism for not doing enough to promote competition may well be considered an unpleasant, but nevertheless relatively endurable experience. Because imperfect competition is difficult to assess, while a bank crisis will hardly go unnoticed, the regulator has incentives to sacrifice competition for the financial viability of incumbent firms, even in cases in which, from an overall policy point of view, it would be beneficial to give priority to competition.

It is consequently problematic to delegate decisions that necessarily involve trading off different concerns. With more than one agency it may nevertheless be possible to establish beneficial rivalry which can improve the basis for such decisions.[12] An agency that takes an interest in the result of a particular decision has incentives to provide information that favours its preferred outcome. Multiple authorities – with different goals, but to some extent overlapping responsibilities – may therefore, in sum, provide more information than would an integrated agency.

The sharing of tasks is not equally helpful when it is possible to suppress, or withhold, information. Then the result may be lack of decisiveness. In such cases one has to take into account that even though information has been provided which favours a particular decision, the agency which prefers this decision may have found – but without communicating it – information that is damaging to its favoured outcome.[13]

The combination of task division and clear responsibilities may nevertheless reduce opportunities for strategic manipulation of information. An agency with a single-dimensional objective has incentives to pass on any information consistent with the achievement of this goal, and suppress all other information. An agency with a multidimensional set of goals can play on a wider register. It will have incentives to provide information that supports its preferred priority within a set of objectives, but not to provide all relevant information, since this might lead the superior authority to prioritize differently. If, for example, the competition authority wanted to grant dispensation to a price cartel, the case would have to be presented in such a way as to explain why collusion would not, in this particular instance, be harmful to market performance. A regulator, with a wider set of responsibilities, could argue that there would be additional beneficial effects that would more than outweigh any detrimental impact on competition. Hence he could more easily argue his position.

Credibility and consistency

It is difficult to establish and maintain a consistent administrative practice. In particular cases it may be tempting to deviate from normal practice in view of specific circumstances. However, lack of steadfastness may be exploited.

Assume for example that a company is undertaking a predatory pricing and marketing campaign aimed at neutralizing a newly-established competitor, or even driving it out of the market. If the time needed for the competition authority to handle the case is sufficiently long, the entrant may be forced to exit the industry before a final decision has been made. Then it may well be difficult, or even impossible, to re-establish the competitive situation. When damage is done, government intervention has no purpose. Consequently, if market participants know, or believe, that the government will, in such cases, leave matters as they are, incentives to undermine competition become correspondingly greater.

The organization of government affects how decisions are made and, consequently, governmental credibility. By choosing a suitable organizational structure the government may be able to commit to certain decisions. Such commitments are of course costly *ex post* – because sometimes decisions must be made that are counter to what would be most desirable in a particular case viewed in isolation – but provide benefits *ex ante* because they reduce the exploitation by private agents of imperfect credibility.

Delegation can act as such a commitment, provided the subordinate agency is issued with clear rules to guide its decisions and that its opportunities for discretionary judgement are restricted.[14] It must also be impossible – or at least costly – for market participants to appeal the agency's decisions to a superior authority.

The sharing of tasks and responsibilities between different authorities could also enhance credibility.[15] In the above example – in which the gains from greater competition were insufficient to justify the costs of re-establishing a competitive market structure – an integrated agency would refrain from interfering. If the decision had been left instead to an agency with the sole responsibility of promoting competition, such an agency would have had to take action. The same result would emerge if tasks were shared between authorities, so long as the agency responsible for competition policy could act on its own judgement.[16] If action required mutual consent, however, no action would be taken.

External influences and regulatory capture

The administration of government is generally better informed about the implications of policy measures than are its political superiors. These measures may affect individuals or firms who have interests that are not necessarily well aligned with general policy objectives. Consequently, there often exists both opportunity and pressure for distorting decisions in favour of those affected.[17]

It is neither unusual nor unreasonable for bureaucrats to develop sympathies for those they deal with professionally. Identification with the interest of market participants does, however, mean that the administration may lose sight of the overall objectives of those public policies they are set to pursue. Instead of being the instrument of policy-makers, an agency may become a promoter of special interests.

It is more likely that such regulatory capture will occur if contact between the government agency and particular interest groups or individuals is frequent. Also, where an agency represents a single-interest 'clientele', the rules it generates are more likely to reflect the interest of that clientele than the rules of an agency that represents a competing-interest clientele. Indeed, over time, because of close contact and, possibly, sustained lobbying by one or a small number of firms with similar concerns, a sector-specific regulator may find it increasingly difficult to distinguish between the general public good and the interests of the regulated parties. Consequently, we would expect an industry regulator to be more susceptible to regulatory capture than an agency with a wider jurisdiction.

The sharing of tasks reduces the opportunities and the incentives for favouring special interest groups. If more than one agency is involved in the decision procedure, there will be more obstacles to reaching a decision that is not in line with overall priorities.[18] The individual agency has less influence over the final decision and consequently less incentive to argue in favour of particular interests.[19]

Principles of good (government) organization

The discussions in the previous section should have made it clear that different considerations conflict in the choice of organizational model for the regulation and competition authorities – no model solves all problems. Delegation allows for quick and efficient decision-making, but at the same time makes it difficult to ensure that decisions are consistent with overall political priorities. Division of labour between separate authorities allows for economies of specialization and the possibility of establishing well-defined objectives for each individual agency, but such a fragmented organizational structure does make it difficult to delegate decisions regarding issues that span the jurisdiction of many authorities.

Allowing agencies to share tasks provides a check against mismanagement and abuse of power, but requires costly duplication of efforts.

Notwithstanding the fact that no clear-cut answer may be found to the question of optimal organization of government, it nevertheless appears that some conclusions are quite robust. We consider these below.

Division of tasks: well-defined and limited objectives

The first, seemingly robust conclusion is that whenever decisions are delegated to an agency its objectives and responsibilities should be made clear and unambiguous. One reason for this is that it is, in practice, very difficult to communicate those, often diffuse, political priorities that should form the basis for practical decision-making. At lower levels of government decision-makers always run the risk of making decisions that are not consistent with overall political objectives. Furthermore, and perhaps even more important than the risk of outright mistakes, is the fact that there will be a systematic tendency for subordinates – given the opportunity – to prioritize differently from their political superiors.

Quite naturally, bureaucrats will always tend to choose the least controversial decision. For example, an industry regulator, with the double responsibility of promoting competition and ensuring product quality (or safety or supply security) will almost surely give priority to quality over competition. The regulator will do so, not because quality is always more important, but because deficient quality has costs which are immediately obvious to everyone while the loss from imperfect competition may be difficult to ascertain. The point is, of course, not that competition policy concerns should always be given priority; in many circumstances it may be optimal to accept barriers to competition in the interest of pursuing other objectives. But this is not always so. The point is that since the gains from competition may be difficult to ascertain it will be relatively easy to give low priority to competition if other, more obvious concerns are conflicting. Because the decision-maker usually knows more about market conditions than do his superiors, it will be very difficult to detect even systematic tendencies to distort decisions.

The tendency to give low priority to competition will be even stronger if the regulator shares the responsibility for competition policy with a designated competition authority. In this case the regulator will bear the full responsibility for insufficient product quality (or other objectives that are his responsibility alone), but can only be partly blamed for insufficient competition. Clearly, the competition authority can attempt to argue its case by pointing to the competitive implications of a given decision, but in a world of uncertainty and imperfect information it is often one side's word against the other's. And if a particular decision requires mutual consent, or the sector-specific regulator is given the right to make the final decision, competition policy concerns will rarely win.

A different, although somewhat related argument for establishing clear and unambiguous objectives for subordinate authorities, and consequently for centralizing the responsibility for competition policy to a single agency, is the prevalence of government ownership of business enterprises. (This argument may well be particularly important in Norway, where state ownership is more widespread than in many other countries.) To ensure the credibility of the government there should never be any doubt that market participants will be treated equally, irrespective of ownership. If the goals of the regulator are broad and diffuse, or responsibility for competition policy is shared between different authorities, it is more likely that government decisions will be questioned on the grounds of unfair treatment. Or, to put it differently, it is important that possible conflicts between the various interests of the government – as legislator, regulator and owner – should be made explicit and not camouflaged. By providing regulation and competition authorities with clear and unambiguous objectives it will be easier to make explicit possible conflicts of interest and to ensure that such conflicts are lifted to the political level – where they belong.

Jurisdiction: centralization of authority

The arguments for narrowing the objectives of any given agency do not extend to its jurisdiction. On the contrary, there are good reasons for extending jurisdiction as widely as possible. This allows for the best use of available expertise and ensures a credible and consistent policy across different sectors of the economy.

Consistency across sectors has become increasingly more important as our economies are transformed at an ever faster pace. A prime example is seen in the case of telecommunications and broadcasting, where technological innovations have blurred the traditional borders between the two industries. A consistent competition policy – executed by a single, integrated competition authority – eliminates the need for the difficult task of delimiting the responsibilities of different authorities.

An additional reason for avoiding sector-specific agencies is the risk of regulatory capture. It would be naïve to believe that bureaucrats are immune to what is going on in their professional environment, and over time most regulators will find it difficult to distinguish between the interests of those they are dealing with on a regular basis and those of the public at large. Consciously or unconsciously, a regulator may gradually become an advocate for the regulated, rather than the government's tool. The risk of regulatory capture is greater the more frequent and intensive is the contact between the regulator and the regulated. The danger is therefore greater for an industry regulator than for an agency with a jurisdiction covering a larger and more diversified section of the economy.

Clearly, the centralized model of the competition authorities does not solve all problems, and there are at least two potential difficulties that need to be considered. The first concerns the opportunity for making efficient use of the industry expertise of regulators. The other difficulty concerns possible conflicts between competition policy and other policy areas.

In the above discussion, the efficient use of expertise was given as an important reason for advocating the model of a centralized competition authority. For the same reason, it would make little sense to let the competition authority duplicate the industry-specific expertise that is already available at the various industry regulators. A division of labour therefore warrants close co-operation between the competition authority and the various industry regulators to ensure the efficient utilization of their expertise. (This is necessary also to allow the industry regulators to draw on the expertise of the competition authority when analysing the effects of technical regulation on market performance, in cases when such effects are deemed likely.)

Delegation: right of appeal

Regarding the potential conflict between competition policy and other policy concerns, it should be clear that the centralized model of organization does not allow for complete delegation of decision power to the competition authority. As explained above, there are very good reasons for providing agencies with limited responsibilities. However, a fragmented organizational structure requires that conflicts between the objectives of different agencies are solved at a higher (political) level. Consequently, an institutionalized right of appeal to superior authorities for decisions made by the competition authority is unavoidable. This right of appeal must be extended to other government agencies that may want to oppose decisions made by the competition authority (and vice versa).

In practice, a right of appeal would mean that, sometimes, final decisions have to be made at the highest level of government. For example, in Norway the telecommunications regulator is attached to the Ministry of Transport, and the electricity regulator to the Ministry of Oil and Energy, while the NCA is subordinate to the Ministry of Labour and Government Administration. What then happens in cases of a conflict between different ministries? Presumably such conflicts can be solved at the cabinet level only. Consequently, to avoid unnecessarily burdening the political level, the right of appeal could be restricted to decisions involving fundamental conflicts between different policy areas.

An additional, but very different argument for limiting the right of appeal is that the competition authority will in most cases make the *de facto* final decisions. Often private individuals and firms affected by government decisions do not find it worthwhile to exercise their right of appeal. Rather than wasting time and money on the uncertain outcome of an appeal case, it may be better to accept the first decision as final. Consequently, instead of introducing a right of appeal which may not be used, it is better to explicitly delegate the final decision to the competition authority. Clearly, this would necessitate allowing decisions to be appealed to a higher level within the competition authority itself.

It seems natural, therefore, to suggest that a distinction be made between cases involving conflicts between different policy concerns and cases for which the right of appeal concerns failures to comply with rules of procedure. For the first type, appeals should be made to the ministry (or some other authority at the political level); for the second type, an independent body (possibly within the competition authority itself) could be established to deal with complaints raised on procedural grounds.

It may not be easy to draw a clear line between the two types of cases. One possibility would be to follow the principle that appeals should be brought for the competition authority unless

- the case involves individuals or firms that are subject to regulations by other government authorities directly relevant to the case; or
- the case involves publicly-owned firms that have been provided with obligations beyond mere business objectives, and their possibility of fulfilling such duties will be affected by the decision reached; or
- the case has direct relevance for the possibility of pursuing other policy goals.

Whenever there is doubt about whether a case meets these criteria, the appeal should go to a superior, political authority. For the same reason the superior authority must have the final say about the right level of appeal.

Another important issue in the same vein concerns the right of a superior authority to instruct the competition authority. There appear to be good reasons for providing the superior authority with the right to instruct the competition authority to consider a particular case. It is not equally clear, however, that such a right should be extended to include the possibility of restricting what cases the competition authority can deal with. This sort of interference in the dealings of the competition authority is likely to undermine both the consistency and the credibility of competition policy. For the same reason the superior authority should not be given the opportunity to influence the outcome of cases before the competition authority (although, it may of course overturn the competition authority's decision at a later stage).

Conclusion

A discussion along the above lines recently lead the NCA Expert Committee on Competition Policy to advocate the model of a centralized, semi-independent competition authority responsible for economic regulation.[20] Centralization would allow for a division of labour between the competition authority and the industry-specific regulators such that each agency could be provided with a clear and unambiguous goal and a limited set of responsibilities. This is necessary to avoid giving agencies tasks that are not well aligned with their main objectives. If, for example, an industry regulator is given the sole responsibility for product safety (or supply security or the financial viability of firms), and also shares the responsibility (with the competition authority) for competition policy, it should come as no surprise if the regulator decides to put safety first. In such cases only the regulator will be held responsible for insufficient safety, while any blame for imperfect competition will be shared with others. To avoid a systematic tendency to distort decisions to the detriment of market competition, regulators should be relieved of the responsibility of competition policy.

Centralization would also help to ensure the efficient use of competition policy expertise and the consistency of competition policy across different sectors of the economy. Furthermore, there is always a real danger of regulatory capture, meaning that an agency becomes an advocate for special interests instead of the instrument for the regulation of that interest group. Centralization means that, rather than being in the hands of an industry regulator with a narrow jurisdiction, competition policy would be the responsibility of an agency facing an economy-wide clientele with sometimes competing interests.

Making the competition authority responsible for economic regulation would imply that the authority be given more instruments than it presently commands (anyway, this would be the case in Norway). It should be an integral part of competition policy to be able to use direct regulation (of prices in particular) in cases in which it is difficult to establish effective competition. With the current organizational set-up it is in fact not possible to fully exploit the expertise of the NCA. This is unfortunate with regard to both the problem of drawing a line between where competition can work and where other measures are needed to ensure economic efficiency, as well as the problem of choosing the right policy instruments. It follows that the task of economic regulation of natural monopolies should be transferred from industry regulators to the competition authority and that the responsibilities of other agencies should be correspondingly limited (namely, to what has been termed 'technical' regulation).[21]

Extending both the jurisdiction and the set of instruments available to the competition authority has clear advantages, but it does not solve all problems. An obvious drawback with the centralized model is that the competition authority will often find itself in need of industry-specific expertise already available at the industry regulators. Close cooperation between the competition authority and other government authorities is therefore warranted in order to avoid costly duplication of efforts.

It may also be argued that the centralized competition authority model does not provide a solution to the problem of how to weigh competition policy objectives against other policy concerns. However, the solution to such problems should rightly be found at the political level of government. This may partly be done through the design of statutes and procedural rules provided to the various authorities, and partly by allowing decisions to be brought to the political level of government; in particular, it must be possible to appeal against decisions made by the competition authority (and other agencies).

The right of appeal to the political level of government could well be limited to cases for which the consideration for competition comes in direct conflict with other policy concerns. In the majority of cases such conflicts do not arise. In fact, it would be perfectly possible to increase the independence of the NCA quite considerably without violating the principle that political deliberations should be made at the political level of government. This would, however, necessitate the establishment of an independent body (possibly as part of the competition authority) before which appeals, in cases that do not involve policy conflicts, could be made. The right to decide which cases do, and which do not, involve policy conflicts, must necessarily reside with the political superiors of the competition authority.

Notes

1 This chapter is to a large extent based on a report from the NCA Expert Committee on Competition Policy, of which the author was a member (see Chapter 6 in von der Fehr *et al.*, 1998). Although the views expressed here are broadly in accordance with those presented in that report, they may not be fully shared by the other members of the Expert Committee, nor, indeed, by the NCA. I am grateful to Tore Nilssen and participants at the Second Oslo Competition Conference for insightful comments on an earlier version of the chapter.

2 For a discussion of competition policy in regulated industries, with particular reference to the UK experience, see Nuttal and Vickers (1996).

3 The discussion is also entirely non-technical. There is a growing literature dealing which the question of the optimal organization of government, applying techniques from modern micro-economic theory. Where relevant, references to this literature will be provided in notes.

4 A formal discussion of competition and regulation in vertically related markets is provided in Vickers (1995).

5 For an analysis of how the use of administrative procedures work as a means of exerting political control, see McCubbins *et al.* (1987).

6 This argument builds on the so-called 'Revelation Principle' in economic theory, see e.g. Binmore (1992, ch. 11, section 7.3). We consider a 'principal' (the political superior) who may commit to a certain incentive mechanism (a specific institutional set-up, forms of procedure and incentive systems) with the purpose of motivating the 'agents' (the administration) to make decisions in accordance with the priorities of the principal. The mechanism defines a 'game' between the agents, in which their 'strategies' (choices of behaviour) lead to a particular 'outcome' (decisions and rewards). If the agents are 'rational' (in the sense of Game Theory), only those outcomes that constitute an equilibrium in the game may be implemented. The Revelation Principle states that an outcome that is achievable by some mechanism may be implemented as an equilibrium in a game based on a so-called 'direct mechanism', in which agents are plainly asked to reveal all relevant information. Since the outcome can be achieved, there exists a mechanism by which it may be implemented. The principal can therefore announce that this mechanism will be used, and that – instead of the agents themselves playing according to this mechanism – they will be asked to reveal their private information on the basis of which the principal himself will play the agents' equilibrium strategies for them (i.e. players will be instructed to play and will receive their rewards according to the equilibrium of the game). It will then be optimal for an agent to be truthful given that everyone else truthfully reveals his or her information (otherwise the strategy in the corresponding game would not have been optimal in the first place). If the assumptions underlying the Revelation Principle are satisfied, any outcome which may be achieved by delegating decisions may also be implemented by an organization structure in which all decisions are completely centralized.

7 Throughout this chapter it will be assumed that these policies are in fact well defined. For a discussion of the implications of potential conflicts between different political bodies (including that between current and future political bodies) for organizational design, see Macey (1992) and Spulber and Besanko (1992).

8 For a more general discussion of the analysis of policy-making – based on the same

transaction-cost view of organizational imperfections and applying some of the techniques of modern contracts (or principal-agent) theory – see Dixit (1996).

9   K-Kontakt, no. 3, vol. 4, Norwegian Competition Authority, July 1997.

10 Laffont and Martimort (1995) demonstrate this result in a principal–agent model in which two agents each observe the realization of a stochastic parameter. Information may be communicated between the two agents at no cost. Communication between agents and the principal is, however, costly in the sense that only information about the sum, and not about the individual components, may be transmitted.

11 See Holmström and Milgrom (1991) for a formal analysis.

12 *'Using enfranchised advocates generates precious information on the pros and cons of alternative policies, and creates a system of checks and balances. The idea may be applied to justify the existence and behaviour of specialised ministries, biased representatives, multipartism or our democratic legal system'* (Tirole, 1994). Tirole analyses a model in which it is impossible to provide direct incentives for collecting information (i.e. a form of procedure), so that incentives are indirect, depending on the decision which is eventually made. It is demonstrated how competition between agents with differing incentives makes it possible to produce more information. In particular, in the example considered it is impossible to induce a single agent to collect all relevant information, but this becomes possible when more than one agent is present.

13 Holmström and Milgrom (1990) identify another factor that may affect the choice between an integrated organization and the delegation of tasks between different authorities. If the tasks are closely correlated, there are advantages of incentive mechanisms based on comparisons between agents. Such conditions favour competition.

14 Cf. Spulber and Besanko (1992) and Dewatripont and Maskin (1995). McCubbins *et al.* (1987) provide a fairly general discussion of how administrative procedures may be used to exert political control over agencies with delegated decision power.

15 Martimort (1996), in his analysis of the multi-principal nature of government, compares the cases in which a certain project is funded by one and two authorities, respectively. It is demonstrated that it is less likely that sufficient funding for the project to be undertaken will be provided in the case of two independent authorities. This result follows from the complementarity between the authorities' activities. The opposite result would emerge if activities were instead substitutes, since then the two authorities would compete to gain influence over the project, and hence total funding would be excessive.

16 Tirole (1994) provides an example to demonstrate how the government may achieve greater credibility by establishing independent authorities with different objectives. In the example, a regulated firm is undertaking a two-stage investment project. If costs are kept within budget in the first stage, the 'regulator' (who is maximizing total welfare) makes the decision about whether the project should be continued. If costs are excessive, however, the decision about continuing the project is left to the 'finance department' (whose only objective is to minimize government deficits). Compared to the case of an integrated government agency (with the aim of maximizing total welfare), the regulated firm faces a 'harder budget constraint' and hence has stronger incentives to control costs.

17 Cf. Laffont and Tirole (1993) and Spiller (1990). Neven *et al.* (1993, Chapter 6) provide a discussion of regulatory capture and its remedies, with particular reference to European merger policy.

18 The model of Martimort (1996) may be extended by assuming that government decision-makers puts an extra weight α on the welfare of agents affected by their decision. Under certain conditions it can then be shown that separation of responsibilities leads to smaller deviations from the optimal solution.

19 Martimort (1996) shows how the reduced-form model may be given additional content by assuming that regulatory capture is made more difficult if the task of

collecting relevant information is split between authorities (see also Laffont and Martimort, 1994). One integrated authority may gain the entire information rent in the case of maximum efficiency. In the case of separated authorities, each observing only part of the relevant information, any particular agency may at most gain the information rent associated with partial efficiency (i.e. maximum efficiency within the domain of its authority).

20 See von der Fehr *et al.* (1998), pp. 5–6. A broadly similar conclusion, based on some of the same arguments, was reached by the Australian Independent Committee of Inquiry on National Competition Policy, see Hilmer *et al.* (1993), Chapter 14.

21 Cynics – having realized that the Expert Group was sponsored by the NCA – would not be surprised to find that the group recommended extending the powers of the NCA. Naturally, one would hope that the argument given does stand up to scrutiny. Nevertheless, a development in the recommended direction has already been going on for some time, through formal agreements negotiated between the NCA and individual regulators.

References

Baron, D. P. (1995) 'The economics and politics of regulation: perspectives, agenda and approaches', in J. S. Bank and E. A. Hanushek (eds) *Modern Political Economy: Old Topics, New Directions*, Cambridge: Cambridge University Press.

Binmore, K. (1992) *Fun and Games: A Text on Game Theory*, Lexington, MA: D. C. Heath & Co.

Dewatripont, M. and Maskin, E. (1995) 'Credit and efficiency in centralized and de-centralized economies', *Review of Economic Studies* 62, 4: 541–555.

Dewatripont, M. and Jean Tirole, J. (1996) 'Advocates', Nota di Lavoro 43.96, Fondazione Eni Enrico Mattei.

Dixit, A. K. (1996) *The Making of Economic Policy: A Transaction-Cost Politics Perspective*, Cambridge, MA: The MIT Press.

von der Fehr, N.-H. M., Norman, V. D., Reve, T. and Ryssdal. A. C. S. (1998) *Ikke for å vinne? – Analyse av konkurranseforhold og konkurransepolitikk*, SNF-report no 8/98, SNF Foundation for Research in Economics and Business Administration (in Norwegian).

Hilmer, F. G., Rayner, M. R. and Taperell, G. Q. (1993) *National Competition Policy: Report by the Independent Committee of Inquiry*, Canberra: Australian Government Publishing Service.

Holmström, B. and Milgrom, P. (1990) 'Regulating trade among agents', *Journal of Institutional and Theoretical Economics* 146, 85–105.

Holström, B. and Milgrom, P. (1991) 'Multitask principal-agent analysis: incentive contracts, asset ownership and job design', *Journal of Law, Economics and Organization* 7, 1: 24–52.

Laffont, J.-J. and Martimort, D. (1994) *Separation of Regulators against Collusive Behaviour*, working paper, Toulouse: IDEI, University of Toulouse.

Laffont, J.-J. and Martimort, D. (1995) 'Collusion and delegation', *Rand Journal of Economics* 29, 2: 280–305.

Laffont, J.-J. and Tirole, J. (1993) *A Theory of Incentives in Regulation and Procurement*, Cambridge, MA: MIT Press.

McCubbins, M. D., Noll, R. G. and Weingast, B. R. (1987) 'Administrative procedures as instruments of political control', *Journal of Law, Economics, and Organization* 3, 243–77.

Macey, J. R. (1992) 'Organizational design and the political control of administrative agencies', *The Journal of Law, Economics, and Organization* 8, 1: 93–125 (includes comments by K. A Shepsle and M. E. Levine).

Martimort, D. (1996) 'The multiprincipal nature of government', *European Economic Review* 40, 3–5: 673–685.

Neven, D., Nuttal, R. and Seabright, P. (1993) *Merger in Daylight: The Economics and Politics of European Merger Control*, London: Centre for Economic Policy Research (CEPR).

Nuttal, R. and Vickers, J. (1996) *Competition Policy for Regulated Utilities in Britain*, working paper, Oxford: Institute of Economics and Statistics, University of Oxford.

Spiller, P. T. (1990) 'Politicians, interest groups and regulators: a multiple-principals agency theory of regulation, or Let Them be Bribed', *Journal of Law and Economics* 33, 65–102.

Spulber, D. F. and Besanko, D. (1992) 'Delegation, commitment and the regulatory mandate', *Journal of Law, Economics, and Organization* 8, 1: 126–164 (includes comments by S. F. Ross and L. Arvan).

Tirole, J. (1994) 'The internal organization of government', *Oxford Economic Papers* 46, 1–29.

Vickers, J. (1995) 'Competition and regulation in vertically related markets', *Review of Economic Studies* 62, 1–17.

5 Implementation of second-best solutions

The judge or the bureaucrat?
A lawyer's perspective

Anders Chr. S. Ryssdal

Introduction

Perfectly competitive markets are like unicorns – perfect beauties and never seen. Businessmen and competitions officials alike have to muddle through in a world of market imperfections, respectively trying to make money and repair market failures. Both groups try to make sense of confusing market forces, and, fortunately, they both need lawyers to apply the rules of the game.

This means that lawyers – who should alternatively be assumed away or denounced as deadweight costs in any honest economic model – in the real world have an important role to play especially on the enforcement level of competition policy, and this fact provides the subject of my topic here today. If there is more than one way to procedurally impose corrective remedies on the conduct of business – what is often referred to as 'second-best solutions' by competition officials – the issue to be discussed is what method provides the better alternative.

To simplify my presentation, I shall distinguish in the main between two forms of enforcement: on the one hand, *administrative enforcement* where decisions are made by an administrative agency and only later subjected to (limited) judicial review, and on the other hand, *judicial enforcement*, where the competition agency shall have to initially present its case to a court to obtain corrective action.

While administrative enforcement has been the typical European model, enforcement by the Department of Justice through the courts is more customary in the US. In the real world, a number of hybrids exist, and to my knowledge no system operates in pure form. We have expert administrative tribunals that look like courts, and we have activist specialist judges who act like competition officials. The US Federal Trade Commission is a typical example. However, the important distinguishing factor is what degree of independence from political authority the final decision maker can exercise. While administrative enforcement is typically subordinated to some political authority as regards policy instructions and review, the actions of a court can only be corrected through the more cumbersome procedure of changing the substance of the law. That the real world consists of decision-makers whose dependence and independence are only partial, does not detract from the usefulness of applying this distinction at the outset.

The chapter is organized as follows. First, I characterize briefly the new generation of competition statutes. I then turn to highlight what enforcement decisions by competition officials we are interested in. Thereafter, I go briefly into the explanatory value of the concept of Rule of Law when evaluating competition enforcement policy. I then turn to examine some of the considerations likely to impede the implementation of competition policy from an overall economic point of view, before I turn to a closer inspection of how the choice of enforcement mechanism is likely to impact on sources of distortion such as capture theory, information problems and rent seeking.

The new generation of competing statutes

The Norwegian Competition Act was enacted by the Norwegian Parliament 11 June 1993, and entered into force on 1 January 1994. The statutory purpose of the Competition Act is stipulated in Section 1–1 as '[to] ensure efficient use of society's resources by promoting workable competition'. Over the last ten years, Sweden, Finland and Denmark have enacted similar competition laws, with similar statutory purposes or intentions. This focus on efficiency means that the intention as well as the effect of this new generation of Nordic competition Laws can be measured through economic analysis. The Norwegian, Swedish and Finnish competition laws are all based on the prohibition principle, under which price cartels, market-sharing cartels, retail price maintenance, and bid rigging are flatly outlawed in the statutes themselves. In addition, various provisions exist to deter other forms of anti-competitive conduct and, in Sweden and Norway, also anti-competitive mergers.

Other European countries have adopted similar national competition laws. Broadly speaking, two trends are quite noticeable: first, the emergence of *efficiency* as the statutory purpose or at least an important policy consideration, and, second, the introduction of the *prohibition principle* as the preferred design. Important milestones have thus been reached – clear focus and clear ground rules. At least this is what one should think.

The need for enforcement decisions

However, in the real world, neither markets nor legal systems are perfect. Nor are they self-enforcing. And for the purpose of this chapter, it is important to stress that all laws – regardless of their basic design – require *decisions* by the Competition Authorities to be consistently applied. These agencies, sometimes in cooperation with Ministries and courts, possess important enforcement powers, and the *discretionary use* of this power determines the fate of the regulated firms. Under the Norwegian law, several important discretionary decisions are, for example, left with the Competition Authority:

- the detection of illegal cartels requires a *decision to investigate and report* the alleged illegal activity to the criminal prosecution authorities;
- it is possible to apply for a *dispensation* from the general cartel bans, provided that certain statutory requirements are met;
- anti-competitive conduct not outlawed in the law itself, as well as anti-competitive mergers, can still be deemed illegal if the Competition Authority makes a *decision to intervene* against them.

While the first decision is principally an enforcement decision that could theoretically be left to the police, the second and third forms of decisions are policy decisions that require professional analysis to determine whether a possible policy action promotes the statutory purpose of economic efficiency. In turn, this means that decisions by the Competition Authorities can be analysed and criticized by economists on purely professional grounds. Such professional critique operates in addition to formal judicial review of decisions by administrative agencies.

The rule of law

An important part of the basic concept of rule of law in all Western democracies is that public agencies cannot intervene in the private sphere without legal authority. In Scandinavian law, this tenet is known as the legality principle. The description of this basic principle in the legal literature varies from one country to another. But whatever its manifestation, the common denominator is that the executive branch of government is not free to intrude in the private sphere at will. The legal authority to intervene must be vested in *pre-existing* legal rules. This requires legislatures to pass on the need for public regulatory intervention in the first place. The legality principle can therefore be seen as a logical upshot of the separation of powers doctrine that lies at the heart of the constitutional make-up of most political democracies. The content of the law is supposed to be predetermined in scope and purpose and it is for the Parliament to enact legislation. The legality principle is an important legal safeguard. Legislatures do not consist of specialists, but of a large number of elected members. Even if more cumbersome to operate, they are more democratic than administrative agencies.

However, to reconcile the concerns for democratic control with operational needs, the executive branch will normally be empowered not only to apply public law rules in individual cases, but also to exercise rule-making power on a subordinated level; the rule-making power is delegated in part from the legislature. Still, requiring the legislature to pass – at the minimum – on the issue of what rule-making authority to delegate, means retaining some overall parliamentary control. Moreover, the requirement that the legislature gets involved at some point reinforces the protection of individual rights, political control and public interest, and ensures public overview over the regulation process. These are considerations traditionally highlighted in the legal literature.

Whatever the economic implications – and on this basic constitutional level traditional legal research dominates – the legality principle is a synthesis of the separation of powers and rule of law requirements where an important aim is to *constrain* executive action. However, these constraints are weakened as soon as the legislature establishes direct or indirect (by authorizing enabling rules) legal authority for an executive agency to intrude. This observation is well suited as a baseline for the analysis below – for two distinct reasons. On the one hand, to make sense of enforcement policy issues, it is necessary to make the enabling legal instruments i.e. the enforcement decisions, the object of scrutiny. On the other hand, the underlying rationale for the Legality Principle does not extend very far to guide the details of the enforcement effort. Operational policy issues and the need for action in individual cases are assumed to be handled (uncontroversially) by an enforcement agency.

The important point for the present discussion is that enforcement issues should not be dealt with as having been determined at the law-making stage. Details of enforcement policy are often regarded as minor issues politically (while they will in reality often determine the force and direction of competition policy). On the other hand, it is likely that enforcement needs are anticipated by the potential enforcers at the pre-enactment stage. Bureaucrats are often effective lobbyists.

So far, the message has been that the statutes themselves cannot be designed in such a way that full compliance by competition agencies can be guaranteed. Before turning to the enforcement issues in particular it is, however, desirable to take issue with the status of economics as the guiding light for competition policy.

The status of economic analysis

Assuming that economic analysis is fundamental to competition policy, the state of the economics science becomes critical. Economists are the priests of competition policy. Today, there is general agreement that economics qualifies as the most theoretically developed among the social sciences, but it is still not an exact discipline in the scientific sense.

One important source of errors is that the development of economics is characterized by changing opinions and views among scholars. A second, related source of errors may be that new knowledge always threatens established knowledge. Established bureaucrats and economists may treat new insight as dangerous inroads into their territory, threatening to deplete the value of their own human capital.

A third source of errors may be particular to the present state of competition analysis, and lies at the other extreme of the spectrum: the efforts and advances in New Industrial Economics rely heavily on game theory where each model is so specific that it is currently difficult to see how this insight can be generalized in such a way that competition authorities or business firms can anticipate the direction of enforcement efforts. Game theory does not provide a general theory of competition, but represents a highly advanced tool with great explanatory power as long as the individual specifications are correct – a pre-condition rarely met in the real world. Economist John Burton has therefore drawn the following resigned conclusion about New Industrial Economics and competition policy:

> It is unfortunately necessary to move towards adapting the 'negative' stance taken earlier towards standard neo-classical models of perfect competition and monopoly. This reviewer advises that the legal profession should be extremely pessimistic as to the positive role that the New Industrial Economics can as yet adopt in informing competition policy matters. . . .
>
> My main conclusion is unfortunately a rather negative one. Contemporary economic thinking about competition cannot supply either competition policy or competition lawyers with consensus view or a map for a way forward in these difficult matters.
>
> It was US President Hoover who was once led to request wearily – and no doubt lawyers would second this sentiment – 'please find me a one-armed economist so we will not always hear: on the other hand . . .'. A resurrected Hoover would perhaps be even more wary of economists, finding a caco-phony of competing views from conflicting schools of thought with which to contend.
>
> We should also remember, however, that progress in the world of ideas, no less than in the world of business, depends upon competitive rivalry. This process at least allows us over time gradually to weed out erroneous theories, and to move towards more adequate perspectives. Taking the long view, economists over this century have positively clarified their understanding of the competitive process in the market arena; and the resulting agenda for competition is certainly different than it was a half-century ago.
>
> (Burton, 1994)

Even if economics does not provide the final answer to competition policy puzzles, an alternative basis for enforcement would certainly be more precarious: this alternative would have to consist of more or less well-reasoned guesswork based on *ad hoc* and intuitive observations by the decision-maker, his or her view of the evidence, and his or her guesses as to the effects of a particular enforcement effort. The real challenge is not to ignore economic analysis, but to make it as complete as possible. While the value of the general theoretical insight into markets provided by micro-economics has been stressed repeatedly in professional and political circles over the last ten years, the institutional economic element has so far not been adequately incorporated.

In the real world served by lawyers, these general observations can be translated into the following concerns. First, for competition policy to have the desired effect, *inter alia* to prevent violation of statutory bans and to ensure that decisions to intervene can in fact repair marketing perfections, there is a need for vigorous enforcement by competent officials. Competition laws are never self-enforcing, and no private incentives can be established to ensure socially optimal compliance. This means that competition officials must command skills and other resources sufficient to establish a credible threat.

Second, and as a somewhat opposite consideration, the limits on knowledge as to what might be an adequate response to a market imperfection, calls for a somewhat cautious approach to enforcement – especially when it comes to discretionary decisions to intervene. It is clear that neither businessmen, economists nor officials can at all times identify what market developments will in fact (and with hindsight) produce efficiency gains. This again means that it will often be difficult to determine whether new forms of business conduct should be stimulated or restrained.

Third, when policing violations of clear statutory bans, however, such restraint is uncalled for. Cartels engaged in price-fixing, market sharing and bid rigging should be aggressively pursued regardless of demonstrated effects. The only procedural considerations at issue in these cases, are how to secure protection for the defendants according to general legal principles regarding the rights of the accused and due process of law.

Fourth, competition enforcement agencies are like all other administrative agencies influenced by the incentives of their agents, and an important general consideration must be to ensure that the incentives of competition officials are aligned with the fundamentals of competition policy, i.e. policing illegal cartels, intervening against anti-competitive conduct, but not pro-competitive conduct – so that the level of enforcement be optimal and not excessive. Agency imperialism and other wasteful practices should be discouraged.

Departing from these general observations, I now turn first to a closer look at the two methods of enforcement – administrative enforcement, and enforcement by courts, to see how they meet the challenges presented so far.

Administrative vs. judicial enforcement

Administrative enforcement means that the important enforcement decision-making – especially in cases involving administrative intervention against mergers and anti-competitive conduct – is taken with legal effect by an administrative agency. In the Nordic legal tradition, there have been few objections to entrusting this kind of legal decision-making to administrative agencies. It has been argued that administrative agencies command professional competence superior to that of the courts. While it is certainly true that it is difficult to see how the traditional European judge could command sufficient experience to make *initial enforcement decisions*, whether they be of a civil or criminal nature, the respect for professional competence inherent in the Scandinavian tradition, has also inhibited subsequent *judicial review* of administrative decisions, especially in civil cases. Moreover, it has been argued that administrative agencies can act with greater speed than courts, and that they are accountable to political authorities. There is an assumption that their accountability to political authorities, and through the limited power of judicial review also to the courts, will keep the competition authorities in line. However, since in the real world competition agencies can operate unobserved by either courts or political superiors, administrative enforcement is often less than transparent and efforts to oversee them are often less than vigorous.

Judicial enforcement requires the competition authorities to present their case to the courts. When competition cases are litigated according to standard procedural principles, the facts and effects of each case and their analysis can more easily be observed by the general public, media and scholars. Moreover, courts are unaccountable to politicians, which means that political pressure is eliminated. Non-expert judges without professional skills, can supplement their knowledge through the use of expert judges and expert witnesses. But they cannot act on their own volition. Ready enforcement assumes the existence of special enforcement agents to take the first initiative, and this requires a redoubling of investments in the enforcement apparatus if initiative and decision-making responsibilities are split between agencies and courts.

In sum, arguments can be marshalled in favour of both systems. However, to make more sense of the discussion, it is necessary to turn to the enforcement incentives illuminated by institutional economics.

Capture theories

Antitrust enforcement has been subjected to economic analyses of three ultimately related but still different strands. These are analyses of the demand and supply of specialized labour resources, information and public privilege.

The first kind of analyses is often referred to as *capture theories*. The term is used to denote the special ties between an agency's employees and its outside constituents. The essence of capture theory is to identify rational motives for public regulators to conform to, or at least be influenced by, the outside interests of the regulated industry. In its crudest, tabloid and 'bribery-like' form, the hypothesis about capture is fundamentally flawed. Even if individual cases of corruption will always occur, the rational public servant knows that giving in to outside pressure means that his or her own career prospects will be impaired by a tarnished reputation. Why should a private boss trust him or her, when the agency employer obviously cannot?

However, more refined capture theories with better explanatory potential exist – as e.g. that public servants' 'on the job training' and inside knowledge represent a scarce resource that will capture a premium in the labour market for professional expertise. Upon observing that a regulating agency commands such a specialized resource – knowledge – Posner makes the following point:

> Under this view, the hiring of the agency's employees by the regulated industry carries no implication of a reward for past favors, and the relatively low wages paid by the agency carry no implication that its employees are substandard.

> (Posner, 1986)

However, the fact remains that enforcement agencies stand the risk of being impoverished if regulated industries constantly steal away key personnel. In addition, some form of 'capture' is possible also when no change of career takes place, as when industry representatives and agency officials get together socially, and the officials let themselves be pampered (lavish entertainment, lucrative speech assignments, etc.), or have their egos catered to and reinforced in other ways.

This means that capture theories – through the stress placed on individual rationality and the regulation context – often point in the right direction, but are insufficient to serve as an exclusive way to understand enforcement efforts, and to design sound enforcement policy normatively.

On the other hand, if a decision in an instant case should be influenced by capture, judicial enforcement procedure grants litigating parties better opportunities to reveal any undue influence than a purely administrative procedure.

Information asymmetries

Economists and competition authorities cannot conduct case analyses without external input. They need a basis of factual information to work from, and such information has to be collected. However, a number of problems arise when evaluating external information.

Problems associated with the evaluation of evidence

Administrative agencies are normally equipped with powers to produce evidence from regulated firms. However, the evaluation of this evidence – once produced – takes place under greater uncertainty inside the offices of a bureaucrat who acts as both prosecutor and judge, than in a courtroom.

First, evidence often thought to be especially damaging in competition suits such as business plans calling for the 'domination of a market', 'forcing competitors out', 'tying in distributors and suppliers', etc. are often motivated by firms' need to compete, and does not reflect abuse of market power in a social sense. The same goes for examination of all other kinds of business information – statistics about market shares, strategic considerations, etc. When an administrative agency is charged with both evaluating the evidence and making the final decision, there is serious risk that evidence can be misinterpreted. Of course, this does not always happen, but if we are looking for systemic distortions, specialist agencies tend to develop their own professional culture. An important part of this culture is a profound scepticism towards evidence presented by regulated firms.

In a court enforcement system, such errors and misinterpretations are more likely to be eliminated. The adversary system of civil procedure contains safeguards intended to illuminate ambiguous evidence. By questioning witnesses under oath, examining written evidence under the supervision of a judge in open court and observing other rules, civil procedure systems normally provide a better access to the facts of a case. While this technique can certainly be applied at a later stage of judicial review also under an administrative enforcement system, it is well known that only a fraction of administrative decisions are later tried in courts, because of the time and effort required to have administrative mistakes reversed.

In sum, an administrative system is less well positioned to eliminate errors due to misinterpretation of evidence than a judicial system.

Information problems effecting economic analysis

However, the balance between judicial and administrative enforcement may tip in the other direction when it comes to the need for purely professional economic analysis.

An external observer can only observe what is objectively manifested evidence. However, such evidence normally has to be collected from the regulated business firms themselves. This means that business firms risking adverse regulation have important incentives to present information to the Competition Authorities in such a way that the harmful effects are minimized. The theory of rent-seeking has often been applied to the interaction between regulated firms and regulating authorities, and is discussed further in the next section. However, asymmetries may also be discussed in a principal–agent model.

Jan Erik Askildsen (1990) has used this approach. He emphasizes two kinds of problems. First, since welfare theory is normally used to analyse the effects of monopolies, the theory itself provides monopolies with incentives to inflate its costs and hide its profits. Second, since the statutory purpose of economic efficiency also embraces the purpose of dynamic efficiency, a monopolist will often be able to explain high costs through the need for investments in expensive technology while the real reason for inefficient production may be x-inefficiency. Public enforcers often lack information to contradict firms' claims. There is no infallible solution to this problem, because all government efforts to reduce monopoly profits create incentives for the monopoly to reduce its efficiency.

First, information could be presented in a biased way. The monopoly surplus could be transferred in the form of contracts, arrangements, expense-coverage from the firm to the owners rather than as accounted profits. Second, the monopoly surplus can be wasted through transfers to management and other employees, in the form of high salaries and similar work benefits, when owners are less than vigorous (as in the case of publicly held monopolies). Finally, the incentives to improve production efficiency are always less compelling for firms unchallenged by competition.

The policy problem is whether competition policy enforcers will be able to access the information required to determine if monopoly profits are generated in the first place and to devise an adequate remedy. Askildsen suggests that alternative governance techniques requiring a monopolist to reveal its preferences, i.e. by having to choose from a menu of contract terms and price alternatives, can be preferable to an attempt to regulate prices directly. However, if the monopolist acts rationally, only a short-term improvement should be expected. As soon as the new governance technique is understood, monopolists will engage in strategic behaviour to try to avoid revealing its preferences by choosing 'second-best' options precluding government insight.

The root of the problem is that regulated firms rationally seek to bias their presentation of information in order to obtain whatever dispensations, clearances and administrative decisions that suit their commercial interests. For enforcers it will often be difficult to ignore claims that costs are high. A number of industries are dependent on highly qualified labour requiring high wages, costly technology and expensive investments simply to meet the business challenges of tomorrow. Misguided competition policy efforts to regulate prices or limit contractual freedom could actually damage these firms' ability to compete, and as such run counter to the efficiency purpose of the Competition Act.

To assess such information from regulated firms and place this information in the right context, standard methods of evidence evaluation will be insufficient. Professional economic analysis is required, and courts are ill suited to conduct such analysis. It is therefore obvious that some kind of participation from an expert agency is necessary. And the real issue is whether such an expert analysis should be subjected in full to censure by a judge as under a strict court enforcement system, or only subjected to limited judicial review as under an administrative system.

It can be argued that leaving such professional analysis to a judge, even if assisted by expert witnesses or expert judges, causes a greater potential for erroneous decisions than if entrusted to an expert administrative agency. In the US, judges are familiar with economic analyses to a greater extent than in Europe. I seriously doubt whether European judges can adopt the same style as their US brethren in the foreseeable future. This means that those parts of a decision consisting purely of economic analysis are better left to an administrative agency and that judicial review should be limited – but with the important qualification that courts should always have full authority to review underlying facts of any decision.

Rent-seeking

The theory of rent-seeking is by now firmly accepted by economists. The fundamental economic problem is that rent-seeking leads to inefficiency, because private actors will expend real resources in their attempts to influence government agencies to obtain pure transfers. Rent-seeking is fundamentally different from business firms' efforts to achieve temporary monopoly profits through innovation, cost-efficiency and better satisfaction of consumer demands. The latter efforts create temporary monopoly rents, but the resources consumed benefit the economy as a whole, i.e. unlike the resources consumed by rent-seeking. Rent-seeking is a general phenomenon, covering *inter alia* interest groups' incentives to achieve transfers and monopoly protection of their businesses, as well as individual actors' interests in obtaining favourable administrative decisions. The baseline for rent-seeking is that governments exercise a monopoly on the use of legislation and legal force in their territories. By influencing a government agency to obtain a favourable administrative decision, the business firm therefore *ipso facto* benefits from this legally protected monopoly.

The theory of rent-seeking provides entrepreneurs with incentives to obtain special protection under the Competition Act. William J. Baumol and Janusz A. Ordover summarize the issue in the following terms:

> Entrepreneurship, in our view, is an input, whose supply and allocation, like those of other inputs, is determined in part by economic circumstances. If we define entrepreneurs as the individuals who are prepared to depart from the conventional modes of economic operation in the pursuit of wealth, power and prestige, then one can expect them to follow the line of least resistance in pursuit of these goals. Entrepreneurs presumably being no more or less dedicated to morality than are lawyers, landlords, doctors or professors, there will be at least a number among them who are prepared to be flexible to their choice of economic activity, preferring a line of endeavour that contributes to productivity only if it happens to be the most promising way toward the acquisition of wealth and the entrepreneur's other personal objectives.
>
> Along these lines, Schumpeter himself listed the formation of monopoly as among the sorts of (organizational) innovation an entrepreneur will sometimes seek to undertake. . . .
>
> It should now be clear how antitrust fits into this story. To be extent that it prevents or impedes monopolization or reduces its profitability, it can discourage entrepreneurs from embarking on such ventures and cause them to reallocate their talents and efforts into production-enhancing innovation. On the other hand, to the extent that antitrust activity is carried out in ways that facilitate rent seeking [by awarding rents justified for 'dynamic' reasons], it can redirect entrepreneurship the other way, at the expense of productivity growth. Thus, facilitation of rent seeking would appear to have a double cost on society, one static and one dynamic.
>
> (Baumol and Ordover, 1992)

Rent-seeking is the economic term for what in popular political vernacular is often referred to as lobbyism, and lobbying efforts are normally more successful when conducted clandestinely. This means that rent-seekers are more likely to succeed under an administrative system than in the courts. In fact, representative organizations are normally not even heard as parties in a court case. They may of course try to lobby the competition agency in advance, i.e. to refrain from going after their members. Since courts do not commence enforcement actions on their own volition, the potential for such distortion affects both systems. But under a court system, clandestine rent-seeking is at least eliminated at the last stage of enforcement. And all else being equal, it should clearly be considered an advantage that all arguments are presented openly as in a courtroom, rather than clandestinely as is often the case during an purely administrative procedure.

Conclusion

As has become obvious from this chapter, I think that the enforcement of competition policy would generally benefit from a stronger reliance on the courts than is currently the European fashion. We can learn from our US colleagues, not only when defining the economic focus of competition policy, but also when designing the enforcement system. And in my view, competition agencies themselves should welcome a switch to greater reliance on courts. Courts not only safeguard the interests of private parties, but also confer a stamp of approval on the analytical techniques employed by the competition authorities. Greater judicial scrutiny would – in my view – enhance the status of competition policy, assure its impartiality, and eliminate undue influence. By subjecting their decisions to the courts to the greatest extent as possible, competition agencies receive valuable corrections and bolster the reputation of such enforcement policy that is well founded.

References

Areeda, P. and Kaplow, L. (1988) *Antitrust Analysis*, 4th edn, Boston.

Askildsen, J. E. (1990) 'Konkurransepolitikk, regulering og informasjonsskjevheter', *Sosialøkonomen* 6, 26–31.

Bakke, E, and Lehmkuhl, K. (1987) 'Norsk konkurransepolitikk – i dag og i fremtiden', *Norges Handelshøyskole*, Bergen, 23 September.

Baumol, W. J. and Ordover, J. A. in T. M. Jorde and D. J. Teece, *Antitrust: Source of Static and Dynamic Inefficiencies? Antitrust, Innovation and Competitiveness*, New York pp. 82–97.

Burton, J. (1994) 'Competition over competition analysis: a guide to some contemporary economics disputes', in J. Lonbay, *Frontiers of Competition Law*, London, pp. 1–23.

Eide, E. (1992) *Rettsøkonomi – en introduksjon*, Jussens Venner, pp. 193–224.

Hannesson, R. (1986) Brunstad, R. J. and Hope, E. *Markedsstruktur og konkurranse*, Oslo pp. 137–158.

Langenfeld, J. and Sheffman, D. T. (1986) 'Evolution or revolution', *The Antitrust Bulletin* 287–300.

Möschel, W. (1991) 'The goals of antitrust revisited', *Journal of Institutional and Theoretical Economics* 147, 7–23.

Norman, V. D. et al. (1998) *Ikke for å vinne? Analyse av konkurranseforhold og konkurransepolitikk*, Rapport fra en ekspertgruppe nedsatt av Konkurransetilsynet, SNF-report 8/98.

NOU (1991): 27, Konkurranse for effektiv ressursbruk, Innstilling fra et utvalg oppnevnt 2 februar 1990 til å utrede ny pris- og konkurranselovgivning. Presented 1 October 1991.

Posner, R. A. (1986) *Economic Analysis of Law*, 3rd edn, Boston.

Ryssdal, A. C. S. (1994) 'Ny norsk konkurranselov', *Lov og Rett* 7, 387–406.

Ryssdal, A. C. S. (1996) 'Towards a Nordic Competition Law', *Tidsskrift for Rettsvitenskap*, pp. 332–357.

Sandmo, A. (1990) 'Noen refleksjoner på public choice-skolens syn på økonomi og politikk', *Norsk Økonomisk Tidsskrift*, 104, 89–112 on p. 94.

Stiegler, G. J. (1983) 'The process and progress of economics', Nobel Memorial Lecture 8 December 1982, Lex Prix Nobel, Stockholm 1983, pp. 253–272.

Tirole, J. C. (1988) *The Theory of Industrial Organization*, Cambridge.

Tollison, R. D. (1987) 'Is the theory of rent-seeking here to stay?' in C. K. Rowley, *Democracy and Public Choice: Essays in Honor of Gordon Tullock*, Oxford, pp. 143–157.

6 Competition policy with a Coasian prior?

Svend Hylleberg and Per Baltzer Overgaard

Introduction

In a recent report commissioned by the Norwegian government, a group of experts appointed by the Norwegian Competition Authority (NCA) have presented a new framework for Norwegian competition analysis and policy, see von der Fehr, Norman, Reve and Ryssdal (1998). In the following we shall briefly present and discuss some of the main elements of this framework. Being external (and foreign) observers of the Norwegian economy and competition policy, our comments will be of a fairly general nature and mainly relate to (roughly) the first half of the report. In this part of the report, a general and abstract framework for competition analysis is developed taking as its point of departure modern theory of industrial organization and theory of contracting and the firm.[1] In our view, the integration of the latter into competition policy thinking is the most interesting and distinctive feature of the report, and we shall emphasize this below.

A brief outline of the report is as follows. Chapter 1 discusses competition and efficiency (as understood by economists). Starting from the Coase Theorem, the basic point is forcefully made that competition in itself should not be the aim of competition policy; the promotion of competition is warranted only to the extent that competition improves the *incentives* of agents to use scarce resources efficiently. If monopoly power is exploited in a way that economizes on resources in both the short term and the long term, then supernormal profits or rents should go unchallenged.[2] However, the chapter also presents a series of reasons to suggest that an unrestricted exploitation of monopoly power may not work solely to economize on resources. Hence, active, though imperfect, competition may under a fairly broad set of circumstances provide 'better' incentives for economic agents (particularly, firms) to innovate, introduce new products, cut slack, and minimize costs. Thus, it is the incentives to economize attributed to a competitive environment that are important, rather than competition itself. But, in a market environment where those incentives are sufficient despite the existence of (what has traditionally been labelled) market power, then competition authorities should take a benign view of such market power (and *economize* by employing its scarce resources elsewhere).

Chapter 2 gives a thorough overview of factors that might facilitate or limit competition. These include notions of economies of scale related to particular functions performed by an industry or distribution channel; market conditions; entry threats and barriers; and ownership and control. Many of the issues raised are fairly well understood, but three points are worth emphasizing at this point.

First, the report stresses that, as an empirical matter, substantial entry barriers are mostly created by government regulation rather than endogenously and strategically by incumbent firms.[3] This obviously has immediate and general consequences for the approach of the NCA to entry barriers; later in the report it is suggested that more effort might usefully be exerted by the NCA in an attempt to persuade other regulatory agencies to dismantle entry barriers that have little economic or other (social) rationale.

Second, and returning to the key issue of *incentives* to compete, the report points out that the structure of ownership and control within and between industries has an important bearing on these incentives. Since incentives are attributable to individuals or a group of individuals rather than to firms as legal entities, it is important for purposes of competition analysis to determine who owns and/or controls a given firm. Consider an industry with four firms: A, B, C, and D, where a merger between A and C is under scrutiny. Then it seems likely that the assessment of post-merger incentives for competition between A/C, B, and D will depend crucially on the initial ownership structure in the industry. If B is a subsidiary of A, and D is a subsidiary of C, then the merger essentially monopolizes the industry, in the sense that the owners of the merged company A/C control all three firms. In contrast, had the four firms been entirely independent in terms of control, then the number of oligopolist players is reduced from four to three, and fierce competition might conceivably continue. The argument made in the report is that the composition of ownership and control in industries under scrutiny has often been unduly neglected by competition authorities.

Third, in the discussion of market conditions conducive to competition, the report introduces the notion of *market turbulence*. A turbulent market is one which is highly unpredictable from the point of view of individual firms or agents. Unpredictability may relate to future technologies, product varieties, customer behaviour, extent and size of market, number and identity of competitors, behaviour of rivals, etc. The report makes the (casual) observation that markets characterized by weak competition tend to be non-turbulent: markets are stable and predictable; technologies develop slowly and predictably; customer bases are in the main stable; rivals (existing and potential) are well known and few in number. Such an environment tends to foster a tacit understanding, whereby the intensity of competition is kept in check. Based on this, the report argues that (under a broad set of circumstances[4]) a certain amount of market turbulence is a *sine qua non* of active competition. This has the interesting policy implication that the NCA might sometimes take active steps to generate market turbulence, in order to shake-up established behavioural patterns in an industry. As an example, rather than collecting and disseminating information about transactions, customers, prices, quantities and market shares, the authorities might take steps to garble information and prevent it from flowing too freely within an industry. After all, secret price-cutting, discounts, price-discrimination and business-stealing are often essential for active oligopoly competition. Similarly, cutting entry barriers would generally tend to increase turbulence, suggesting that a more concerted effort by the NCA aimed at dismantling entry barriers is called for (preferably at the expense of more traditional 'trust-busting').

In Chapter 3 the objectives and ambition of competition policy are discussed. It is argued that efficiency is and should be the objective, whereas distributional objectives are best pursued by the use of other means. It is also argued that the most effective competition policy is based on creating the right incentives and not on a direct regulation of behaviour. In addition, competition policy should be based on few and simple means with the aim of creating a framework within which competition can take place; a complicated and detailed regulation of markets should not generally be attempted.

Chapter 4 presents what the report calls the incentive-based approach to competition analysis. This approach based on agent incentives should be contrasted with the traditional approach inspired by the SCP-paradigm.[5] Very briefly, the report proposes a three-step approach to the analysis of the competitive environment surrounding a set of products or a collection of firms. Let the firm be the basic unit of analysis. Then, the first step asks whether a firm has any market power to exploit, the second step asks whether the firm has any incentive to exploit its market power, and the third step asks whether the exploitation of market power is accomplished in a socially acceptable way, that is, in efficient and economizing fashion. We should note that the report is less than entirely clear on how case analysis should generally go through these steps, but we hazard an interpretation below.

In Chapter 5 three specific examples from Norwegian industry are presented (in summary form) to suggest how the new approach might be pursued in practice, and Chapter 6 contains a discussion of institutional issues (including the possible tension between competition policy and sector-specific regulation) and some suggestions for institutional reform.

The companion report by Bjorvatn (1998) gives a more detailed discussion of methods of analysis, while that of Sørgard (1998) presents results of recent research on vertical relations and restraints.

The Coasian prior

To explain the title of this chapter, let us return to the starting point. To put the reader in the right frame of mind, the report sets out by presenting the Goose Theorem, which we can briefly state as follows for present purposes: absent any limitations on bargaining and contracting, rational agents will always find a way to realize all potential gains from trade. Hence, the unregulated market outcome will always be efficient, since agents could always gain by renegotiating, if the outcome was inefficient. In its pure form competition policy with a Coasian prior is simple: if allowed to, economic agents will contract and bargain to an efficient allocation, and interference by antitrust authorities whereby certain contracts and bargains are necessarily prevented can only have negative, if any, consequences for the efficiency of final allocations. As a standard, albeit rather hypothetical, example, an immediate implication is that a monopolist should be allowed to perfectly segment customers through whatever set of complex contracts it takes (e.g., first degree price discrimination). Similarly, observed vertical restraints and integration of any form serve only to improve the efficiency of the distribution channel and, hence, should be considered perfectly benign.

Clearly, the assumptions of perfectly smooth and costless contracting and bargaining are heroic, to say the least, and as a practical matter the report certainly does not subscribe to the pure version of the Coase Theorem.[6] However, the report stresses that the Coasian perspective should be taken seriously and integrated firmly into competition analysis. This has important implications for what might be a sensible (in the sense of economic efficiency) predisposition of the NCA towards various observed market arrangements. For example, (on *a priori* grounds (?)) the imposition of vertical restraints, such as exclusive dealing and/or territories, full-line forcing, and RPM on dealers in a distribution network, have traditionally been looked at with a large measure of hostility by competition authorities. But a combination of these may be essential for an entrant to effectively challenge established firms with a new product variety. A ban on such contractual provisions might thus constitute a barrier to desirable entry, and be contrary to the general aim of competition policy.

Thus, from the general Coasian perspective, there is little room for *per se* bans on particular contractual and legal arrangements. Furthermore, efficiency should not be relegated to a defence which is only reluctantly accepted (as is typically the case in current antitrust cases). After all, efficiency is the main objective of policy. Competition policy with a Coasian prior is one that views market arrangements that go beyond the anonymous, linear spot-contracting of the economics text book as something that typically promotes the efficient use of resources, rather than as an attempt to abuse market power.[7]

The incentive approach

The report proposes a three-step approach to the analysis of a given market environment. However, at the general and abstract level, the report does not provide a detailed account of how the practitioner should proceed.[8] At the risk of misinterpreting the suggested three-step approach, let us add some algorithmic structure.

Suppose a collection of firms is considered. The first step asks whether a particular firm has any market power to exploit. Market power must stem from 'exclusive' access to some valuable asset. Exclusivity is, of course, at matter of degree, and assets come in many different shapes and forms. To illustrate, think of taxis in the Greater Oslo area. Suppose, initially, that by Royal decree firm A has the sole right to organize and reap the returns from the taxi industry. The asset relates to the demand for taxi rides, which in turn depends on the price of substitutes. Hence, if there are only poor and high priced substitutes, then this asset is valuable, and A may choose to exploit its market power to allow the owner(s) to become very rich, indeed. If low-priced substitutes are plenty, then A's asset is clearly worth less. Similarly, if B, C, D, E, etc., are allowed to enter the taxi industry, then A no longer has exclusive access to the asset, and the exploitable market power of A is eroded. Generally, if a firm has no market power to exploit, then there is little need to scrutinize incentives or actual behavior any further. In contrast, if significant, exploitable market power exist, then we should go to step two. The second step asks whether the firm has any incentive to exploit its market power, and the analysis should relate to the issues discussed in Chapter 2. If not, the investigation should stop. If a firm under scrutiny has incentives to exploit its market power, then we should go to the final step. The third step asks whether the exploitation of market power is accomplished in socially acceptable ways, that is, in efficient and economizing fashion. If so, then whatever behaviour and contractual arrangements are associated with this exploitation should be considered benign. If market power is exploited in unacceptable ways, then the practitioner should turn his attention to possible remedies.

Having concluded in the final step that market power is exploited in unacceptable ways, the practitioner should first ask whether any effective remedies are available. Such remedies might relate to the analysis conducted in either step three, step two, or step one. In some cases the unacceptable exploitation of market power uncovered in the step three analysis may be remedied directly, e.g., a certain set of vertical restraints might be declared null and void, a firm might be ordered to charge uniform prices across customers, etc. These are means traditionally associated with antitrust action. Alternatively, the practitioner might go back to the analysis of the incentives to compete conducted in step two and attempt to quell the incentives to exploit market power (e.g., by creating market turbulence if possible), or go back to step one and attempt to limit market power as such (e.g., by initiatives to promote entry). These means of intervention could be labelled structural remedies.

Given their focus on incentives, there is little doubt that the authors of the report would welcome an increased use of structural remedies at the expense of more traditional means of intervention. A fundamental weakness of much intervention of a traditional nature is that a ban on certain practices and contractual restrictions might only lead to a substitution towards even less efficient market arrangements. This issue has a long tradition in the literature, particularly in relation to vertical restraints and organization of distribution channels.

Although (some version of) the suggested procedure might foster more simple and straightforward analytical and administrative procedures for the NCA in the long run and thereby economize on scarce NCA resources (mainly by aborting investigations following step one or step two), several problems remain. Immediately below we shall discuss a couple of problems related to methodology in competition analysis,[9] while the next section touches upon some institutional problems for the suggested approach.

The first methodological issue is illustrated by the discussion in Bjorvatn (1998). For instance, in order to obtain a proper basis for answering the questions posed in the three steps, it may often be necessary to estimate the demand structure in a market and the cost structure of firms operating in that market. However, due to lack of data and time, it may be very difficult to perform a proper econometric investigation. Bjorvatn (1998) seems to suggest that a thorough analysis of an economic theory model and calibration or simulation exercises would suffice in cases where an econometric analysis is not feasible. But such a belief, although shared by many theorists, is highly problematic, since a particular theory model and a calibration exercise produce results which have no more bearing on reality than the (unchecked) assumptions put into the model in the first place. Calibration exercises are much more fruitfully used in analysing properties of a model than in analysing properties of the real world.

The difficulties involved in doing proper econometric analysis (useful for competition authorities) are illustrated by the example presented in Sørgard (1998) of the effects of the UK Monopolies and Mergers Commission's suggestion to break up the close vertical relations between UK breweries and pubs; a suggestion which was partly implemented from 1989 to 1992. The example is based on an econometric investigation by Slade (1998) using data from 1973 to 1993. Sørgard and Slade argue that the break-up led to higher prices and higher profits for the breweries contrary to the expectations of the Monopolies and Mergers Commission. However, despite the careful econometric investigation conducted by Slade, there are several specific points of critique which could be raised. Perhaps most importantly, the econometric results, which are based on only 2–4 years of data after the break-up, do not in our view warrant the strong conclusions drawn by Slade and Sørgaard on the effects of the break-up of the ties between breweries and pubs.

In fact, an econometric test for a break point at the end of a sample and with an unclear break cannot be trusted. In addition, the break-up was a major change in the industry, and it is unlikely that all the effects have materialised after 2–4 years. There is even no argument in favour of the short-run and long-run effects being in the same direction. Hence, the econometric evidence supporting the (prior (?)) views of Slade and Sørgard is fragile at best.[10]

The difficulties in obtaining reliable empirical evidence is, and has been, for a long time, a problem for several areas of industrial organization, but there is no substitute for a systematic and thorough collection of data and a proper statistical analysis of these, if we want to avoid the curse of folklore based on hearsay and storytelling.

Practice and institutional problems

Before closing we should ask: is the procedure proposed in the report different from procedures actually followed by the NCA and competition authorities in other countries? Yes, we believe there are major differences. Obviously, several of the more detailed suggestions in the report are in already in use at the NCA and similar organizations elsewhere, but a *systematic* adherence to the principles underlying the suggested procedure does not exist. Nowhere has the Coasian perspective been fully integrated into the heart of competition policy and regulation.

This, we believe, is partly due to disagreements on the premises of competition policy, but also to difficulties in implementing the three-step procedure without an increase in resources or, at least, a major reshuffling of resources already allocated to the competition authority. The current distribution of resources is partly historically determined, but the main determinant is that most cases are the result of complaints which must be handled in accordance with the general rules governing the public administration.[11]

Most economists might agree that distributional problems are best addressed through other means than competition policy, and that competition policy should concentrate on promoting economic efficiency. However, this view is not shared by many politicians, although they may have agreed to the wording and voted for laws embodying a pure efficiency perspective. Probably even more importantly: as a practical matter, such a view may not find much favour with the legal community. The courts may agree as far as the view is a just statement on the efficiency of policy instruments, but the courts do not in general accept a view which may lead to different treatment of what (to most non-economists) appears to be identical cases. Practice shows that (at least) European courts have been very hesitant to accept arguments based on probability statements, notions of frequency, and on hypotheticals such as potential entry.

These problems (from the point of view of the suggested approach) are exarcebated by the fact that cases handled by the NCA are most often the result of a complaint. Rulings by the NCA which are seen by e.g. the plaintiff to be based on convoluted economic arguments he does not really understand and which imply different treatment of what is considered identical cases by the plaintiff (and by the community at large), will undoubtedly be appealed and enter the court system.

Finally, the suggested procedure may be difficult to implement in full. This is partly due to the first set of arguments, since the administration of a law cannot disregard the views (however flawed) of the courts and of the community in which it operates. It is also due to a lack of resources, in so far as the three-step procedure requires a somewhat different and more analytically oriented investigation. This is not to say that the staff at the NCA and other similar organizations are unable to perform the analyses needed, but rather to argue that more resources should be directed towards collecting and analysing information on the structure of different markets, relevant players and incentives. In the long run this may lead to the use of fewer resources, but in the short run it will most likely require more resources devoted to data collection and analyses.[12]

Conclusion

In conclusion, we believe the report represents a major contribution to the discussion of competition analysis and policy of the NCA, and we strongly recommend it to all those interested in these topics. The proposed three-step incentive-based approach to analysis is particularly appealing in terms of its general perspective on competition policy.

However, we would conjecture that the main challenge for the proponents of the procedure is not to convince economists and the economics profession about the advantage of an incentive-based approach, but rather to generate a similar consensus among all the different groups and agencies that shape antitrust (and regulation). The three-step incentive-based approach may be successfully implemented only if the whole system subscribes to its philosophical premises, and it may be hazardous to implement it without creating an understanding among the participants beforehand.

Notes

1　The group of experts was asked to suggest ways and means for the NCA to supervise and analyse markets with a view to implement a policy which leads to an efficient use of economic resources. In addition, the group was asked to provide specific examples to illustrate the suggested approach and methodology. Finally, it was asked to discuss the relationship between competition policy and more (sector) specific regulation and the division of labour between the NCA and other regulatory agencies.

2　In this note we shall subscribe (along with the expert panel) to the view that distributional issues are best addressed through other means than competition policy. Consequently, the sole aim of competition policy is the promotion of economic efficiency. The report acknowledges that this presumption may be contested, and that, although it is in line with competition laws in many countries and certainly with the entrustment given to the panel, it might not necessarily reflect the views of the politicians writing the laws.

3　It should, of course, be noted (as the report does) that entry barriers erected through regulation are often the result of regulatory capture and rent seeking by incumbents.

4　It should be noted that the report recognizes that turbulence may sometimes work in the opposite direction. Uncertainty and unpredictability of future market conditions may lead to short-term 'profit-taking', in the sense that monopoly power is exploited fully whenever it arises.

5　For the sake of argument, we implicitly assume (along with the authors of the report) that current antitrust practice is 'traditional'. We fully appreciate that this is not an accurate description in many cases.

6　Neither does Coase, of course. The world of the pure version of the theorem would be one in which *per se* legality of all forms of exploitation of monopoly power is warranted. Any agreement, contract, restraint on trade, etc., would be motivated by efficiency considerations and be perfectly benign.

7　Of course, for reasons outlined in the report, this prior should not be held too naïvely.

8　In fact, the report stresses that no blueprint for case analysis will be provided. In contrast, eclecticism is called for; presumably, to avoid dressing the practitioner in a strait-jacket similar to the one often attributed to the SCP approach to case analysis.

9　We should emphasize that these methodological issues are not peculiar to the procedure suggested in the report. These are problems that should be addressed by any approach to competition analysis based on modern theory of industrial organization and contracting.

10　These, rather critical, comments are not meant to suggest that Slade and Sørgaard necessarily draw the wrong conclusions. We merely want to warn the practitioner that counsel for the opposing side might have a field day.

11 So, key to the effectiveness of the three-step procedure is whether the vast majority of cases can be aborted quickly through a step one investigation.
12 For a very interesting (lawyer's) perspective on the implementation of the second-best solutions, see Ryssdal (1998).

References

Bjorvatn, K. (1998) *Metoder for analyse av konkurranseforhold*, SNF-rapport 9/9S, Bergen.

von der Fehr, N.-H. M., Norman, V. D., Reve, T. and Ryssdal, A. C. S. (1998) *Ikke for å vinne? Analyse av konkurranseforhold og konkurransepolitikk*, SNF-rapport 8/98, Bergen.

Ryssdal, A. C. S. (1998) Implementation of Second Best Solutions – The Judge or the Bureaucrat? A Lawyer's Perspective, paper presented to The Second Oslo Competition Conference, Oslo, Chapter 5 in this volume.

Slade, M. E. (1998) 'Beer and the tie: did divestiture of brewer-owned public houses lead to higher beer prices?', *Economic Journal* 108: 565–602.

Sørgard, L. (1998) *Vertikale relasjoner: Finnes det enkle, konkurransepolitiske regler?*, SNF-rapport 10/98, Bergen.

7   The Australian competition policy reforms

Allan Fels

Introduction

This chapter reviews the reforms to Australian competition policy introduced in November 1995, paying particular attention to the reforms relating to the regulation of public utilities.

The general reforms have a number of distinctive features including:

- the establishment of a comprehensive competition policy;
- the establishment of a national policy based on an agreement between the Australian government and state and territory governments;
- the establishment of a generic access law embodied in a new part of the Trade Practices Act. This regime applies in principle to all sectors although its main practical application is to public utilities in such areas as communications, energy and transport;
- the transfer of substantial economic regulatory functions to the national competition agency;
- a strong commitment by national state, and territory governments to an effective policy.

This chapter begins by reviewing the concept of a comprehensive national competition policy. It then turns to Australian reforms as they relate to public monopolies; outlines the main features of the generic access law; and discusses the transfer of economic regulatory functions to the national competition agency. The chapter concludes with a case study of telecommunications regulation.

A comprehensive national competition policy

Competition policy is sometimes equated with the traditional antitrust, competition or trade practices laws of a country. However, many other policies affect competition. A *comprehensive* competition policy includes all government policies that affect the state of competition in any sector of the economy including policies that restrict as well as those that promote competition and extends well beyond traditional competition law.

A national competition policy in a federation includes laws and regulations at all levels of government, federal, state and local, that affect the state of competition. A comprehensive competition policy includes:

- prohibition of anti-competitive conduct (traditional antitrust laws);
- liberal international trade policies;
- free movement of all factors of production (labour, capital, etc.) across internal borders;
- removing government regulation that unjustifiably limits competition, e.g. legislated entry barriers of all kinds, professional licences, minimum price laws, restrictions on advertising;
- the reform of inappropriate monopoly structures, especially those created by governments;
- appropriate access to essential facilities;
- a level playing field for all participants, including competitive neutrality for government businesses and an absence of state subsidies that distort competition;
- separation of industry regulation from industry operations, e.g. dominant firms should not set technical standards for new entrants.

A comprehensive competition policy therefore includes policy concerning, among other subjects: international and interstate trade; intellectual property; foreign ownership and investment; tax; small business; the legal system; public and private ownership; licensing; contracting out; bidding for monopoly franchises; and a range of other policies. It is worth noting that some of the above policies have a very direct effect on competition, while others affect the general economic environment and the general climate of competition of the country, e.g. foreign ownership and investment restrictions.

Where does traditional antitrust law fit into this picture? Traditional antitrust law mainly affects conduct in markets. It prohibits anti-competitive agreements, abuse of market power, anti-competitive vertical trade restraints, resale price maintenance, certain kinds of boycotts, etc.

Antitrust law only has a limited direct effect on market *structure*. Merger policy has a substantial effect on the structure of a market. In some countries divestiture powers are included in antitrust laws, but in many they do not exist or are not used. Sometimes the application of antitrust law to anti-competitive conduct may have structural effects. Nevertheless, the impact of antitrust law on key structural variables, e.g. entry and the number of players in a market is often relatively small. In particular, traditional antitrust policy does not override anti-competitive laws and regulations, e.g. laws that restrict entry into a particular industry. This is not to say that antitrust law is not a vital element in a comprehensive competition policy. Traditional antitrust policy does not involve direct regulation of prices or other performance variables, e.g. quality of service.

Where does regulation fit in? Traditional economic regulation of prices and quality of service can be seen as complementing competition policy. Where market power exists and cannot be curbed by competition policy, regulation may prevent or limit or alter the way in which market power is exercised, e.g. price control may seek to prevent the use of market power to charge excessive prices. Regulation of the kind above thus directly impacts on performance variables through the control of conduct rather than through seeking to affect structure.

Regulation may, of course, serve a number of legitimate objectives such as environmental, safety or income redistribution goals which may be seen as lying outside the field of competition policy. However, the way in which these objectives are pursued may have effects on competition and to that extent these elements of regulation cannot be excluded from consideration as part of a comprehensive competition policy.

Regulated sectors are becoming an increasingly important part of competition policy. It is often in these sectors that market power is strongest. The processes of deregulation and privatization (or corporatization or commercialization) often create industry structures in which there are powerful dominant incumbent firms at the outset of the process. So powerful may their position be that reliance on traditional antitrust law may be insufficient and may need to be complemented by various forms of regulation designed to protect or bring about greater competition and to curb the abuse of market power. Whether or not regulation is considered to be a part of competition policy is a semantic issue but because of its close connection with competition policy, it is viewed in this chapter as part of a comprehensive competition policy.

In the real world there has been a long history of regulation conflicting with, rather than complementing, competition policy. A great deal of regulation involves restricting entry into industries, setting minimum prices and imposing obligations in an anti-competitive manner. Thus, at the most general level, regulation may be seen as sometimes being an integral part of competition policy, sometimes as complementing it, and sometimes as conflicting with it.

Structural reform of public monopolies

As part of Australia's recent competition policy reforms each state government has agreed to abide by various principles in the reform of public monopolies. Before introducing competition into a sector traditionally supplied by a public monopoly, governments have agreed to remove from the public monopoly any responsibility for industry regulation, and to re-locate industry regulation functions so as to prevent the former monopolist enjoying a regulatory advantage over its rivals.

Also, before introducing competition into a market traditionally supplied by a public monopoly, and before privatizing a public monopoly, governments will undertake a review into a range of matters, including: the appropriate commercial objectives of the business; the merits of separating any natural monopoly elements from potentially competitive elements of the public monopoly; the merits of separating potentially competitive elements of the public monopoly, and the community service obligations undertaken by the public monopoly; regulation to be applied to the industry; and ongoing financial relationships between the owner and the public monopoly.

Access to facilities

The importance of access to certain key facilities, such as telephone networks, electricity grids or gas pipelines, in order to encourage competition in related markets in telecommunications, electricity or gas production or distribution is recognized in the National Competition Policy. Vertical separation is generally preferable to regulation of access terms and conditions, but for a variety of reasons vertical separation might not occur, and in these cases regulated provision of third party access might be appropriate.

To a large extent, the Australian public policy debate preceding the introduction of the access regime focused on the question of whether s.46 of the Trade Practices Act provides a sufficient basis for regulation access to essential facilities or whether more direct regulation of natural monopoly markets is warranted.

The National Competition Policy Report by the Independent Committee of Inquiry into Competition Policy in Australia (known as The Hilmer Report) in August 1993 addressed this issue and concluded that s.46 alone is unable to deal effectively with access to essential facilities. S.46 of the Trade Practices Act prohibits the misuse of substantial market power and provides that:

> a corporation with a substantial degree of market power cannot take advantage of that power for the purpose of:
>
> * eliminating or damaging a competitor in that or another market;
> * preventing entry to that or another market; or
> * inhibiting competition in that or another market.

The reasons for the conclusion that s.46 could not adequately address the access problem included:

* the inability of s.46 to deal directly with monopoly pricing that is not for a 'prescribed purpose'; (the term 'purpose' has been important in the Australian law);
* the evidentiary difficulties in proving in court that refusal of access on reasonable terms is conduct for a prescribed purpose;
* the general shortcomings of a process that depended upon a court finding of a breach of the law;
* the cost, time and risks involved in obtaining a court resolution of commercial access disputes;
* doubts about the capacity of the courts to determine optimal prices, terms and conditions of access to essential facilities.

The Competition Policy Reform Act 1995 inserts a new Part IIIA into the Trade Practices Act which establishes a legal regime providing for third party access to a range of facilities of national importance.

A single facility might provide a number of services, to which access may be essential for enhanced competition in some cases but not in others. For this reason, the legislation focuses on a service provided by means of a facility. What exactly is covered by this part of the Act? Part IIIA defines 'service' as a service provided by means of a facility, including:

- the use of an infrastructure facility such as a road or railway line;
- handling or transporting things such as goods or people;
- a communication service or similar service.

The definition specifically excludes any production processes (e.g. factories), intellectual property (e.g. copyright and patents), or the supply of goods, except to the extent any of these is an integral but a subsidiary part of the service in question. Examples of the kinds of facilities which may be covered by Part IIIA clearly include gas transmission and distribution, electricity transmission and distribution, railway tracks, airport systems, water pipelines, telecommunications networks and certain sea ports.

There are three mechanisms for the provision of third party access:

1   a potentially compulsory process, whereby the service is 'declared' and then is the subject of arbitration if the parties cannot agree on any aspect of access;
2   a voluntary process, whereby a service provider can offer the Australian Competition and Consumer Commission (ACCC) an undertaking which sets out the terms and conditions on which it will offer third party access, and which the ACCC may accept;
3   state and territory government laws that regulate access and that are deemed 'effective' in terms of their compliance with national policy criteria for access laws. State access laws are not considered further in this chapter, although their operation is similar to the national ones described.

Compulsory declaration process

Any person may apply to the Council to consider whether the service should be declared. There are a number of matters, all of which the Council must be satisfied on before it can recommend the declaration of a service. These are:

1   that access to the service would promote competition in a market (other than a market for the service);
2   that it would be uneconomical for anyone to develop another facility to provide the service;
3   that the facility is of national significance having regard to its size, the importance of the facility to interstate or overseas trade and commerce, or its importance to the national economy;

4   that access to the service can be provided without undue risk to health or safety;
5   that access to the service is not already subject to an effective access regime;
6   that access to the service would not be contrary to the public interest

The compulsory process is shown in Figure 7.1.

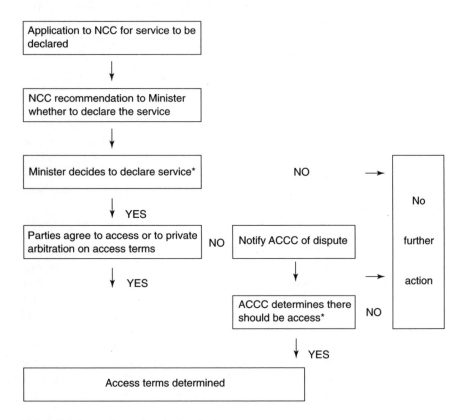

Figure 7.1 Compulsory (i.e. declaration) access process
Note: *Subject to review by the Tribunal.

These are threshold criteria which must be met before the Council can recommend that the service can be declared. Mere satisfaction of these criteria does not, however, automatically lead to a recommendation to declare. The Council can consider any other relevant matter. It must then recommend to the 'designated Minister' whether or not the service be declared. (The designated Minister is a state or territory Minister in the case of a facility owned or operated by a state or territory government body, and the Commonwealth Minister otherwise). Following receipt of the recommendation, the Minister must then decide whether or not to declare the service, and must give reasons for the decision.

The Minister cannot declare the service if the service is the subject of an operative access undertaking. Furthermore, the Minister cannot declare a service unless satisfied of all of the matters set out above. There is a right of review by the Australian Competition Tribunal of Ministers' decisions, exercisable within 21 days of publication of the decision of the Minister.

Declaration of a service does not mean that there is an automatic right of access to the service for third parties. Rather, it represents a right for third parties to negotiate terms of access backed up by compulsory ACCC arbitration if the parties cannot agree on any aspect of access. Where the parties cannot agree on access (or the terms of access), they may decide to refer the dispute to private arbitration. If they do not agree to refer the dispute to private arbitration, an access dispute may be notified to the ACCC. The ACCC can then determine whether access should be provided and, if so, the appropriate terms for access. There are rights of review by the Tribunal of determinations by the ACCC, exercisable within 21 days of the determination.

There are a number of matters which the ACCC must take into account when making a determination, including the interests of the service provider, users and the public. Also, there are a number of constraints on the terms of determinations.

The ACCC must not make a determination that would have any of the following effects:

1   preventing an existing user from being able to obtain their reasonably anticipated requirements for the declared service as at the time the dispute was notified;
2   preventing a person from using the service by the exercise of a right under a contract or determination that was in force at the time the dispute was notified ('a pre-notification right') in so far as the person will actually use the service;
3   depriving a person of a protected contractual right under a contract that was in force at the beginning of 30 March 1995;
4   resulting in a third party becoming the owner, or part owner, of the facility or extensions to it without the consent of the provider;
5   requiring the provider to bear some or all of the costs of extending the facility to meet the access requirements of the third party.

There is a provision which prohibits anyone from engaging in conduct for the purpose of preventing or hindering another person's access to a declared service under a determination.

Voluntary (access undertakings)

This voluntary approach, which is shown in Figure 7.2, allows service providers to offer to the ACCC an access undertaking which sets out the terms

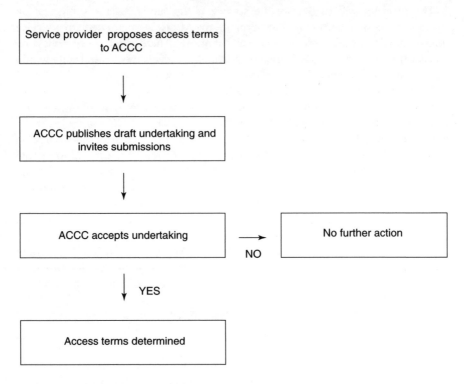

Figure 7.2 Voluntary (access undertaking) process

and conditions on which it will offer access to third parties. If accepted by the ACCC, this will foreclose the possibility that the service will be declared, thus removing uncertainty as to what the access arrangements for the service might be under the declaration route. The reform processes in the telecommunications, electricity and gas industries in Australia are developing access regimes which will most probably be established through this undertakings route.

The ACCC need not accept an undertaking. It might decline to accept an undertaking if, for example, it was uncertain about future conditions and preferred to preserve the possibility of future declaration. Before accepting an undertaking, the ACCC must publish a draft of the undertaking for public comment.

At the end of the period for public comment, the ACCC can decide whether to accept the undertaking. In making this decision it must consider submissions received during the public comment period and have regard to a number of matters including the interests of the service provider, users and the public, and whether there is an existing access regime.

The ACCC can accept an undertaking in respect of services which are already covered by an access regime. This may be desirable where (say) the existing regime is not fully effective. The ACCC cannot, however, accept an undertaking in respect of declared services.

Enforcement

Part IIIA also includes provisions for the enforcement of access determinations, the prohibition on hindering access to a service and access undertakings. Enforcement action is taken in the Federal Court. In the case of a breach of an undertaking, only the ACCC has standing to sue whereas, for contraventions of determinations, any party may sue.

Recognizing that in some instances, once a service has been declared, the third party and the provider may negotiate an access agreement or refer the matter to private arbitration, the legislation contains a provision for registration by the ACCC of access contracts for declared services. The ACCC has the discretion whether to register the contract: in exercising this discretion it must take into account the interests of the public and users. Once registered, the contract can be enforced as if it were an access determination of the ACCC.

It will be seen that Part IIIA of the Trade Practices Act has established a generic access regime applicable in principle to a range of sectors. Clearly, Part IIIA is a somewhat complex piece of law. It balances a number of policy variables. These include the benefits to competition of granting competition; the probable detriments to investments if new entrants can use the facilities of an established player, possibly with ultimate detrimental effects on 'facilities-based competition'; property rights issues (requiring the appeal processes and the involvement of the Courts and Tribunals); federalism issues; and issues about the role of governments (as reflected in the role of designated Minister).

Two somewhat distinctive Australian factors have influenced the form of the legislation. First, there is the Federal character of Australia's governmental structures. Second, Australia's constitution requires a rigid separation of judicial from executive and legislative functions. This latter factor has inevitably involved the courts in playing a role in the access regime. In addition, in any event, the Australian people appear willing to accept relatively strong competition laws which affect property rights substantially providing that the courts have a role in making many of the final judgements. Thus, while the role of the regulator is very important, there is a right of appeal in most of its decisions to a tribunal or to a court.

Since the enactment of Part IIIA of the Trade Practices Act, a significant trend has been the development of tailor-made arrangements for telecommunications, electricity, gas and rail which, while reflecting the broad access regulation framework embodied in Part IIIA of the Act, vary the models to be developed in their approach, detail and descriptiveness in the light of different technology, market arrangements and ownership structure of the sectors. It is not considered that these developments reflect a departure from the generic regime provisions of Part IIIA. In some cases it has been taken for granted that certain facilities would be declared and so the declaration process has been bypassed and the emphasis placed upon the terms and provisions of access. In other cases special requirements, e.g. any to any connectivity in telecommunications, have been written into that regime (which in any case has been built on some of the elements of a pre-existing telecommunications industry access regime that applied from 1991 until recently).

There has been some debate as to whether the access regime should only apply where there is both a natural monopoly service which is required in a related market and the facility operator also compete directly in the related markets. While there are some theoretical reasons for confining any access obligation to natural monopoly facilities required for competition in a related market, it is arguable that confining the obligation to facilities that are also vertically integrated is too limiting. Under this approach, an upstream monopolist which also competes in a downstream market would be subject to the access regime but it would not apply to an upstream monopolist that supplies essential inputs to the downstream market without competing in it directly.

The economic policy rationale for excluding the 'unintegrated' upstream monopolist is not apparent when such a facility operator can replicate the access pricing arrangements of the 'integrated' monopolist by entering into contracts with downstream firms to charge the monopoly price for the essential input. In this situation, the same monopoly rent and associated distortion would be reflected in the downstream market price in the absence of a vertically integrated ownership structure. Thus, if the access obligations to supply the essential input at an 'efficient' price are to be incurred only by an 'integrated' monopolist, and not by the 'unintegrated' monopolist, the resulting disparity of regulatory treatment simply discourages the monopolist from participating in the downstream market at all. As a result, the access regime would fail to achieve its policy objective. There would also be a regulatory disincentive to engage in efficient vertical integration, where this may be warranted by economies of scale and scope and transaction costs savings, with adverse consequences for productive efficiency and final consumers.

In Australia, the regulation of access to essential facilities is not confined to vertically integrated natural monopolies. Rather, it applies to all nationally significant essential facilities whose services are necessary for effective competition in another market. The preceding is by no means a full discussion of the national access regime. Some ACCC publications provide a fuller guide.[1]

It is too early at this stage to provide a useful overview of the actual operation of the access regime. A number of declarations have been sought from the National Competition Council and these are at various stages of completion in terms of appeal processes and the like. The Telecommunications Access Regime is currently in a crucial stage. Electricity, gas, airport matters are currently being resolved. By the end of 1998 a picture will start to emerge of how the regime is working.

How should access conditions be determined?

The COAG access arrangements embodied in Part IIIA of the TPA require that access terms and conditions, including price, for declared essential facilities be determined in the first instance by commercial negotiations between the facility operator and those seeking access. But there is provision for a right of compulsory arbitration by the ACCC to resolve access disputes that cannot be resolved by negotiation between the parties.

The rationale for this approach is that the availability of compulsory arbitration gives third parties seeking access considerable leverage in negotiations with the monopoly facility operator which is expected to contribute to negotiated pricing outcomes closer to 'efficient' access prices. The availability of arbitration (which must consider the implications for competition, efficiency and the wider public interest) combined with the cost, delay and publicity of dispute arbitration, is intended to give the facility operator a strong incentive to negotiate more reasonable terms and conditions of access.

The fallback of compulsory arbitration in those cases where the terms offered are considered to be excessive gives third parties an independent forum in which to have the disputed access terms determined by an objective arbitrator against broadly based public interest criteria.

This declaration/arbitration model has the advantage of limiting the extent of direct intervention to determine access prices and conditions to the (exceptional) cases that cannot be resolved directly by the parties, while at the same time providing strong incentives for the parties to reach agreement on access terms through commercial negotiations rather than resort to final arbitration.

This model is not without its critics, however, and I will mention briefly some of the criticisms that have been made of it. Some commentators have questioned whether an access regime involving direct intervention by exception (i.e. only in those cases where disputes remain unresolved) will be capable of overcoming the monopoly pricing/allocative efficiency problem inherent in the supply of essential facility services. There may be (smaller) access seekers who are unwilling or unable to take a dispute to arbitration and will have no choice other than to accept a monopoly access price. For example, they may be constrained by their informational disadvantages, concerns about retaliation by the facility operator which would impair their ability to compete, or simply be unable to undertake the cost and delay of conducting an access dispute. Under this view, access disputes would be rare but that would not necessarily be an indication that the regime had successfully eliminated monopoly pricing and the resulting allocative efficiency distortions.

A variation on this view maintains that access disputes would be unlikely because the threat of arbitration would give the incumbent essential facility operator an incentive to bribe downstream users of the facility to accept the monopoly price without seeking arbitration in return for a share of the resulting monopoly rent. While the contractual arrangements to achieve this outcome would be subtle, these commentators argue that the absence of disputes would simply indicate that the monopoly solution was being maintained by such side deals between the facility operator and its downstream users.

The solution suggested to address these perceived shortcomings is direct access price regulation to cover all of the services supplied by the facility, not just those that give rise to disputes. For example, price or revenue caps could be

applied to squeeze out monopoly rents, while providing incentives to pursue efficiency improvements, or alternative approaches to public utility price regulation
could be used.

My current position on this debate is that we have no practical experience yet
of the effectiveness of the arbitration model or the significance of these potential
shortcomings. However, the arbitration model will be implemented with these
criticisms clearly in mind. To the extent that they prove to be of substance and
cannot be addressed by administrative means, consideration can be given to the
need for some form of direct price regulation in the light of that experience.

Prices oversight

In Australia, at the Commonwealth level, there are three levels of price oversight (not control) surveillance, monitoring and inquiries. Price surveillance is a
system whereby firms are declared. Currently around 10 organizations are subject to declaration. The ACCC considers notifications from declared firms and
indicates to notifying firms whether it supports the proposed price increase.
Firms are not required to comply with the PSA's recommendations, the system
relying on moral persuasion. Since the inception of the system in 1984, declared
firms have on all occasions followed the regulator's recommendations. The
outcome of notifications is placed on the public register.

The Prices Surveillance Act has been amended to provide a time limit for
declaration and to extend the surveillance provisions to potentially apply to state
and territory government businesses. The PSA is now required to place the
reasons for its notification decisions on the public register.

Price monitoring is a less intrusive form of oversight. Previously, the
PSA undertook monitoring on an informal basis. The reforms formalize this
monitoring role.

The Competition Principles Agreement indicates that price oversight of state
and territory government businesses is generally the responsibility of the particular government concerned. Some states have their own price oversight legislation.
For example, the New South Wales Independent and Pricing Regulatory Tribunal
(IPART) investigates and reports on the determination of maximum prices
for government monopoly suppliers and the pricing policies of such suppliers,
including electricity, rail and water authorities in New South Wales. The
Victorian Office of Regulator-General is responsible for the economic regulation
of a range of government business enterprises, including electricity, gas and
water, with the power to regulate prices of prescribed goods and services supplied
by or within a regulated industry. These arrangements will continue as part of the
national competition policy. Price surveillance under the Prices Surveillance Act
will, however, apply to state and territory government businesses, where:

1   the state or territory concerned has agreed; or
2   the Council has, on the request of an Australian government (Common-
    wealth, state or territory) recommended declaration of the business on the

basis that the business is not subject to effective oversight and the Commonwealth Minister has consulted the appropriate Minister of the state or territory concerned. The details of, and information on this process are set out in the Competition Principles Agreement.

The interaction between competition policy and regulation

There has been significant debate in Australia as to the most appropriate framework for administering economic, technical and competition regulation. Among the issues debated have been the merits of general vs industry specific competition regulators and of integrated vs separate administration of economic, technical and competition regulation. There has also been debate about the role of national and state regulation. This section of the chapter outlines Australia's approach to this debate and its attempts to improve the interaction between its competition and regulatory authorities.

Before discussing the actual policy outcomes in Australia, it is worth briefly reviewing some of the general debate which has occurred in recent years. The debate originated because of the privatization, commercialization and varying degrees of deregulation that occurred in relation especially to public utilities in the communications, energy and transport sectors. The need for some kind of economic regulation that extended beyond the usual bounds of the Trade Practices Act emerged. A number of options presented themselves. At one extreme, it would have been possible for each state and territory of Australia as well as the Commonwealth to establish a separate regulator for each industry. Thus in the state of Western Australia there would have been a gas regulator, an electricity regulator, a rail regulator, and so on, and this would have been mirrored in other states. Another approach might have been to combine the regulators in each state so that there was a general regulator in each state as well as at Commonwealth level. Another option would have been to have established regulatory processes for each industry in Australia. There could also have been a general regulatory regime administered by one national regulator. The final option would have been to include all these regulatory functions as part of the role of the national competition regulator.

A further set of issues concerned the relationship between technical and economic regulation – should they be combined or kept separate? For example, should all telecommunications regulation, both economic and technical, have been located in a communications regulatory agency? Or should all of it including technical regulation have been located in the national competition regulator or should the economic and technical regulation of communications have been separated (although hopefully coordinated)? In such a model, conventional competition law and general economic regulation would have been operated by the Australian Competition and Consumer Commission, while technical regulation would have been done by a communication agency with a close working relationship between the two agencies, in particular to ensure that the technical regulation did not have anti-competitive effects.

With respect to the debate about whether there should be industry-specific or general regulation, the arguments in favour of general regulation have included that general regulation is more suitable in an era or convergence. The process of convergence is occurring in areas such as energy (between gas and electricity), communications (between telecommunications, information technology and the media), financial services (between different providers of financial services, e.g. banks and insurance). There has even been convergence between the energy and communications sectors as energy transmission facilities are seen as providing possible facilities for telecommunications transmission. Likewise, financial services and telecommunications are becoming closely linked. An associated benefit of general regulation is that it permits 'one-stop shopping'. In Australia, for example, a new telephone entrant, Optus, wishing to provide paid television services found itself dealing with the telecommunications regulator, the competition regulator, the broadcasting regulator, the spectrum management allocator as well as the Departments of Communication and of Treasury (the latter is responsible for competition policy). General regulation is also likely to involve some resource saving as there are economies of scale and scope in regulation. There is also a greater likelihood of consistency across sectors or across different industries.

Another point for general regulation is that it is argued that such regulators are less likely to be captured than an industry specific regulator. While on the face of things there are many instances of specific regulators who have proved themselves not to be captured, a further possible concern is that over the course of time industry-specific regulatory bodies may distort decisions in ways that are more favourable to the preservation of their own activities than to pro-competition deregulation.

The arguments in favour of industry-specific regulation are that the industry-specific regulators may have better technical economic knowledge and expertise; that it is generally easier to combine industry specific economic regulation with detailed technical regulation in one organization which is likely to lead to more enlightened economic decision-making. There are also some dangers in relying upon a general regulator. There is something to be said for ensuring a degree of diversity in regulation and in not putting 'all the eggs in one basket'. There may also be a better prospect for adequate funding of an industry-specific than a general regulator.

It is difficult to carry this debate too far. Whichever solution is chosen, there are ways of overcoming its limitations. Australia has tended, however, on balance, to favour general rather than industry-specific regulation. At national level there is the Australian Competition and Consumer Commission which does the major national economic regulation. At state level the Regulator General in Victoria and the New South Wales Independent Pricing and Regulatory Tribunal (IPART) perform general rather than industry-specific regulation.

The next element in the debate has concerned national versus local regulation. The general arguments for national regulation have included that most markets are national these days; indeed, the process of deregulation itself tends to break down barriers between states and create national markets; there are economies of scale and scope in having national rather than local regulation, and national regulation avoids inconsistencies which can occur between many local regulators in different states. There is also a shortage of regulators at local level. The argument for local regulation is that it is often more politically acceptable than national regulation. Moreover, some markets may be local. Local regulators may have a better local knowledge and feel. Again, it is difficult to generalize in the abstract. In Australia the pattern has been to give regulatory matters with national elements to the national regulator. Where, however, there are purely state issues, these are left to the local regulator. Some states say that in the long term they expect local regulation to gravitate to a national level.

On the basis of the above debate, it is concluded that there is a case for national regulation. The question then arises as to whether there should be a separate national regulator or whether it should be integrated with the competition regulator. The arguments for integrating national regulation with competition regulation are that regulation has significant effects on competition and is therefore best linked with the regulation competition; that regulation on its own is often anti-competitive and tends to downplay competition and replace it with other values. If, however, regulation is performed by the competition regulator, then a healthy competition culture will pervade regulatory decision-making; there are also substantial benefits from close coordination of regulatory and competition policy decision-making. The arguments for separate regulation include that this avoids confusing the competition regulator's role; that the competition regulator does not become distracted and overwhelmed with messy regulatory details; and that a regulatory mentality may actually swamp the competition mentality rather than the opposite because of the sheer numbers who are required to conduct regulation. Again in Australia, the argument has tended to go in favour of integrating regulation and competition policy in one agency.

Against this background the chapter now reviews the position that has been achieved at this stage in Australia. Australia has a general competition law that applies across all industries and is administered by a single competition authority, the Australian Competition and Consumer Commission (ACCC).

The ACCC and the newly established National Competition Council (NCC) also perform several important economic regulatory functions. For example, the ACCC has various responsibilities in relation to the terms and conditions (including setting prices) of access to certain essential infrastructure facilities such as telecommunications, gas and electricity and in monitoring prices in industries where competition is weak. It also has a quality of service monitoring role in respect of airports. These responsibilities reflect a government view that there are advantages in placing these economic regulatory functions with the general competition agency. In the case of the NCC, the main regulatory function is in relation to establishing rights of access to the services of certain essential infrastructure facilities. Other significant aspects of economic regulation such as the granting of licences are typically administered by industry-specific regulators or by more general government regulators. Technical regulatory issues that do not have a significant competition element are typically administered by industry-specific regulators or may be subject to goods and services standards set by Australia's principal standards organization, Standards Australia.

General vs. specific competition regulation

Australia has a national competition law that is consistently applied across all industries and is administered by a single independent agency. This general approach promotes consistency, certainty and fairness in the universal application of the competition law. It also enhances the regulator's ability to take an economy-wide perspective; reduces the risk of regulatory 'capture' by industry; and minimizes duplication. There may also be administrative savings.

There may be advantages in having industry-specific competition regulation in industries characterized by complex technology or having natural monopoly or other special elements. In the case of telecommunications, specific competition laws are contained in Part XIB of the Trade Practices Act 1974 (TPA), which is administered by the ACCC and which complements rather than replaces general competition law.

Industry-specific competition provisions are also contained in Part X of the TPA, which provides a regime for regulating the conduct of those international liner cargo shipping companies which collaborate as conferences under agreements registered with the Department of Workplace Relations and Small Business (which has responsibility for maritime policy). Part X provides special (but conditional) exemption for exporters from the competitive conduct provisions of the TPA without the need for authorization by the ACCC. Failure on the part of conferences to meet Part X conditions and provide efficient and economical services can result in an investigation by the ACCC and a recommendation to the Minister for Workplace Relations and Small Business. The government will be reviewing Part X as part of its legislative review programme during 1998–99.

Integrated vs. separate administration of economic, technical and competition regulation

Technical regulation and some significant aspects of economic regulation are administered in Australia by industry-specific bodies or more general government regulators. This recognizes that the national competition authority should focus on anti-competitive conduct and not become embroiled in overly detailed or complex regulatory matters unless they have a clear connection with competition issues in, for example, network industries.

Separation of regulatory duties between competition, technical and economic regulators does entail the risk that competition regulators will not always have the same level of technical knowledge that can be achieved by an integrated regulator. This has not been a serious problem to date in Australia and the risks are less in industries where the ACCC has both an economic regulatory role as well as its normal competition role. In addition, various mechanisms are in place to improve coordination between regulators (see below).

Role of the ACCC

In addition to its core 'competition' function, the ACCC has a number of key 'economic regulatory' functions. Under the general or 'economy-wide' access regime for essential infrastructure facilities established in Part IIIA of the TPA, the NCC advises the government as to rights of access and, where these are established, the ACCC acts as an 'arbitrator of last resort'. That is, the ACCC has the power to arbitrate on access disputes and determine the final terms of access (including price) if access seekers and owners of essential facilities fail to reach a commercially negotiated settlement.

More specific 'economic regulatory' functions are performed by the ACCC under the access regimes for telecommunications (discussed below) and for gas transmission pipelines (with the exception of those in Western Australia). The gas role includes monitoring compliance with ring fencing obligations and approving access arrangements (covering services, reference tariffs, trading and expansions) in accordance with an industry code. In addition, from 1999 the ACCC will assume the role of transmission regulator for the electricity industry. This will involve setting a revenue cap for electricity transmission networks.

There is a strong emphasis in all these areas on the desirability of commercially negotiated outcomes. Generally speaking, the regimes establish frameworks within which industry participants operate commercially and the role of the regulator is as light-handed as possible.

State regulators

Economic regulation of state-based markets mainly occurs at the state government level. This state-based regulation is moving toward more general regulators such as the New South Wales Independent Pricing and Regulatory Tribunal (IPART) and the Victorian Office of the Regulator General (ORG). These bodies have responsibilities, including technical ones, across a range of industries and, as discussed below, have a close association with the ACCC.

Addressing regulatory uncertainty

With the 'division of labour' between various regulators, there is potential for some degree of overlap of functions between the ACCC, which administers competition regulation across all sectors of the economy, and those technical and economic regulators that operate within specific industries or within certain states across a number of industries. For this reason, a number of steps have been taken to minimize uncertainty regarding the jurisdiction of particular regulators and avoid confusion for consumers and the business community.

For example, the ACCC has frequent information exchanges with a variety of economic and technical regulators through regular liaison meetings and the exchange of publications and other information. The ACCC also has a significant public and business education role. In addition, chairpersons of various Commonwealth and state economic regulators (such as the Australian Broadcasting Authority, the New South Wales IPART and the Victorian ORG) are associate members of the ACCC; and certain members of the ACCC are appointed as associate members of the Australian Communications Authority and the Australian Broadcasting Authority. This helps to bridge the 'knowledge gap' that can arise when competition, economic and technical regulators are separate bodies.

Further, in conjunction with a number of Commonwealth and state regulatory agencies and policy advisers, the ACCC publishes a quarterly newsletter entitled the *Public Utility Regulators Forum*. The *Forum* was established in recognition of the need for cooperation among the various state-based regulators. It aims to focus understanding of similar issues and concepts faced by different regulators; minimize regulatory overlap for large users operating across jurisdictions; provide a means of exchanging information; and enhance the prospects for consistency in the application of regulatory functions.

Telecommunications case study

On 1 July 1997, the Commonwealth government introduced a new legislative reform package designed to introduce full and open competition in the telecommunications industry in Australia. These reforms substantially increased the ACCC's regulatory role in the telecommunications sector.

Background

Prior to 1992 Telstra (formerly Telecom) was the wholly government-owned monopoly provider of telecommunications services. Telecom also performed the role of regulator prior to this function being transferred in 1989 to an independent industry regulator, AUSTEL. In 1991 the government decided to issue a second carrier licence (to create a 'managed duopoly') and to expand AUSTEL's role to include telecommunications industry competition matters. During this time the ACCC's role was for the most part limited to consumer protection issues.

Optus acquired the second carrier licence and began providing services in competition with Telstra in November 1992. Soon afterwards a legislated triopoly in mobile telephony was formed with Vodafone commencing services in October 1993. Limited opportunities for resale of Telstra's services were also allowed from 1991.

With the introduction of full and open competition in Australia on 1 July 1997, telecommunications was brought within the reach of the general anti-competitive provisions of the TPA. Because of uncertainty, however, as to whether these general provisions would deal effectively with the complexity and limited level of competition in some telecommunications markets, it was also decided that additional industry-specific provisions should be introduced into the TPA to regulate anti-competitive conduct in the industry. The industry-specific provisions in Part XIB of the TPA give the ACCC powers to issue competition notices to carriers and service providers engaging in anti-competitive conduct. These notices are enforced through the courts and, if carriers are found to have contravened the provisions, they face significant pecuniary penalties and restitution orders.

The ACCC is also responsible for administering an industry-specific access regime for telecommunications under Part XIC of the TPA. The aim of this regime is to provide for the long-term interests of end users of telecommunication services through ensuring 'any-to-any connectivity' (maximizing positive network externalities); promoting diversity and competition in the supply of carriage, content and other services; and promoting the efficient use of, and investment in, network infrastructure. The new telecommunications access regime provides a framework for regulated access rights to be established for specific carriage services and related services, and establishes mechanisms within which the terms and conditions of access to the network service can be determined. There will always, however, be a primary reliance on commercially negotiated outcomes. Arbitration by the ACCC is a fall-back option.

The TPA provides extensive information-gathering powers and the ACCC is able to make record-keeping rules for specified industry participants to assist it in the administration of the telecommunications specific provisions. It is intended that these industry-specific anti-competitive provisions will eventually be aligned, to the fullest extent practicable, with the general trade practices law. Finally, it should be noted that the ACCC is responsible for administering price cap arrangements applying to Telstra.

Technical regulation for telecommunications, such as spectrum management, has been transferred from AUSTEL to a new independent regulator known as the Australian Communications Authority (ACA). The ACA also administers economic regulation in respect of licensing, carrier and service provider rules, numbering and universal service arrangements.

Reasons for regulatory changes in telecommunications

As noted above, it was considered that the special nature of the telecommunications industry warranted adoption of non-generic competition regulation for a transitional period. As competition in the telecommunications sector increases over time, there is an expectation that the need for special provisions will decline and reliance on the general competition law will be more likely to suffice. To assist this movement towards reliance on general competition law, it was decided to have the industry-specific competition provisions administered by the ACCC under the TPA and to leave technical and licensing issues to the ACA. It should be emphasized that the industry-specific competition provisions are broadly consistent with the general provisions of the TPA and complement rather than replace the general law.

The ACCC's role in telecommunications brings an 'economy-wide' perspective to competition regulation in a sector experiencing rapid integration or 'convergence' with other industries such as information technology, financial services, broadcasting and, more recently, participants in the energy reticulation markets. This convergence has seen new service forms develop, while existing forms are merging to create new hybrid services. Hence, it is increasingly difficult to categorize services in traditional terms which may involve a simple linkage between a particular service and a particular technology used to deliver that service. Clearly, the convergence phenomenon has implications for the roles of different regulators and increases the arguments for general rather than industry specific regulation.

Interaction between the ACA and ACCC

Some telecommunications issues involve areas of overlap between the ACA and the ACCC. In general, where one agency has responsibility for a particular issue that may overlap with the other agency, there are legislative requirements for consultation and notification. For instance, while the ACA is generally responsible for specifying technical standards, where such standards are integral to competition within the market, the ACCC may assume primary responsibility for their issue. Moreover, given that the telecommunications access regime is inextricably linked to technical matters within the industry, the ACCC must consult the ACA on various matters, such as the model terms and conditions to apply to telecommunications services subject to an access regime.

The chairperson of the ACA is currently an associate member of the ACCC, which enables the ACCC to call on relevant technical expertise when dealing with complex competition issues in the telecommunications industry. Furthermore, as already mentioned, a member of the ACCC is an associate member of the ACA, which further reduces the possibility that conflicts or overlaps will exist or develop to any significant degree.

Personnel changes in the ACCC

When the new telecommunications regime commenced in July 1997, a number of AUSTEL's experienced personnel were moved to the ACCC, along with its competition functions, so that the ACCC would have sufficient technical expertise to deal with the 'specifics' of the telecommunications industry. In addition, the ACCC has appointed a full-time Commissioner responsible for telecommunications issues.

Experience to date

Reform of the telecommunications market since July 1997 has seen a number of new carriers commence operations and offer competing services. Two aspects of the regulatory regime have contributed to their success. First, the ACCC has additional powers to intervene if necessary in the marketplace and respond to anti-competitive conduct. Second, the legislated access regime provides the ACCC with discretion, after public consultation, to declare network services that it considers should be made available to all market participants. A number of basic network services essential for competition were declared from 1 July 1997, including originating and terminating access for fixed and wireless services, certain trunk transmission services, digital data access, and a conditioned local loop service. Further, the mere threat of regulatory intervention through mandated arbitration by the ACCC provides an incentive for access providers and seekers to come to a negotiated settlement. Recently, the ACCC has (among other things) raised the issue of declaring ISDN access services and sought public input into whether it should also declare local call resale as a service to which the access regime applies.

As noted above, the new regulatory regime has seen the entry of a number of new carriers. There have also been price reductions and service enhancements for consumers and Telstra's market shares in international, domestic long-distance and mobile telephony have declined. Notwithstanding these successes, Telstra retains a near monopoly position in local telephony and controls a large proportion of the telecommunications infrastructure. Reflecting this situation, there have been calls in the industry from new entrants for some additional regulatory initiatives to further assist in the development of competition. The issues most commonly raised are the need for improved cost information disclosure requirements by the incumbent (to assist access seekers in the access negotiation process) and the need for an improved form of regulatory scrutiny of the incumbent's internal cost allocation. The question of whether these proposals should be accepted will require the government to balance the claims of new entrants for additional regulatory assistance with the need to ensure that Telstra is not unreasonably constrained in responding to its competitors. The benefits to consumers from the new regime come as much from the actions of Telstra in responding to competition as from the initiatives of the new entrants themselves.

Conclusion

Australia has generally adopted a 'mandated' division of labour approach to regulation on the basis that having a general competition law administered by a single independent statutory body, the ACCC, promotes consistent application of competition regulation across all sectors of the Australian economy. However, governments have recognized the desirability of the ACCC having 'economic regulatory' roles in some industry sectors, in particular, essential infrastructure and network industries. Industry-specific competition regulation has been employed sparingly (currently telecommunications and conference shipping).

In the longer term, as competition increases in industries previously exempt from the TPA or otherwise benefiting from legislative barriers to competition, and convergence between industries such as information technology and telecommunications continues, greater reliance will be placed on general competition laws rather than industry-specific regulation. This will mean that the ACCC will need to continue to develop its in-house expertise in relation to a number of industries and continue to consult frequently with industry-specific regulators to assist in the smooth operation of competition, economic and technical regulation.

Note

1 *National Access Regime*, November (1995); *Access Undertakings: An Overview*, July (1997); *Access Pricing Principles, Telecommunications: A Guide*, July (1997). These papers can be purchased from the ACCC, 360 Elizabeth Street, Melbourne, Victoria 3000.

8 Competition policy in the information economy

Carl Shapiro

Introduction

The recent monopolization action brought by the United States against Microsoft has galvanized public interest in competition policy as applied to the high-technology sector. Yet the *Microsoft* case is but one in a series of public enforcement actions, and private antitrust suits, that are determining how antitrust laws will be applied to the information economy. This chapter describes the economic characteristics of information industries, draws out the implications of these characteristics for competition policy, and illustrates how antitrust policy has evolved recently in the United States in the high-tech sector.

Some commentators have suggested that enforcement officials should leave the high-tech sector alone, since it is fluid, experiencing rapid technological change, and by and large displaying vigorous competition. Yet few can deny that pockets of monopoly power remain, usually associated with the control of some information bottleneck: local telephone companies, cable television operators, and Microsoft present themselves as examples, but many more companies enjoy powerful positions, often based on their control over interfaces or standards, if not genuine bottlenecks of network hubs. The leading goal of competition policy in the information economy should be to hasten the erosion of such monopoly power, and to prevent the use of monopoly power to destroy competition in adjacent markets.

This chapter is organized into four parts. The first part offers a strategic guide to the network economy. Competitive strategies in the information economy are distinct from strategies in other sectors of the economy, and competition policy must be attuned to the new strategies that firms are employing. While durable monopoly power has always been rooted in underlying scale economies, the sources of those scale economies, and the resulting barriers to entry, are distinctive in the information economy. Demand-side economies of scale associated with network externalities are especially important in many high-tech markets.

The remaining parts of the chapter explore the three broad areas of antitrust law in the United States: merger enforcement, limits on the ways in which rivals firms can cooperate, and limits on the behavior of dominant firms.

In the merger area, I do not detect any need for a special 'high-tech' enforcement policy. Certainly, we are in the midst of an enormous merger wave, but this consolidation has taken place under the watchful eye of the antitrust authorities. Both the US Department of Justice and the Federal Trade Commission have been actively involved in reviewing high-tech mergers, and have sought to block or modify certain mergers. A review of selected mergers shows that established guidelines for merger review are working in the information and communications sector.

The information economy *does* call for greater inter-firm cooperation to set standards, to supply complementary components that form a system, to build interconnecting networks, and to cross-license or pool patents to enable new products. Happily, the needed cooperation looks to be proceeding without undue antitrust barriers. Literally thousands of standards are being hammered out among horizontal rivals every year, all this generating little or no antitrust liability. The one dark cloud in this picture is the residual fear in the antitrust bar that clients cooperating with rivals to establish new standards or launch new technologies will be judged by *per se* rules intended to outlaw price fixing. And the limits on cross-licensing and patent pools are still being set.

Concerning dominant firms, there is certainly no reason to believe that the information economy spells the end of monopoly power, but neither is there justification to expand the reach of competition policy, such as by imposing mandatory licensing of intellectual property. The traditional limits on unilateral conduct by dominant firms, such as prohibitions on exclusive dealing and tying, can be fruitfully applied in the information economy. These points are illustrated below with a brief analysis of the recent Justice Department action against Microsoft.

A brief strategic guide to the information economy[1]

One hears a lot these days about the 'new economy'. The implication is that time-tested economic principles must be discarded, and new principles sought. Were this true, it would presumably imply a need for a top-to-bottom re-thinking of competition. Fortunately, history can still be our guide, both to business strategy and to competition policy. While we cannot rely much on the classical model of perfect competition and price-setting firms, we do not need a fundamentally new economics. There has merely been a shift in emphasis, as networks, interconnection, compatibility, interfaces, and intellectual property rights have become increasingly important sources of competitive advantages.

The telephone industry illustrates my point nicely. Just 100 years ago, the Bell System (later to become AT&T) was successfully consolidating its position as the dominant telephone company in the United States. At the time, the Bell System controlled less than half of the telephones in the United States, and faced direct competition in many locales. The key was that the Bell System was the technical leader in offering long-distance service, and adopted a strategy of refusing to interconnect its local rivals with its long-distance network. Before long, the Bell

System began to benefit from positive feedback: by controlling the largest national network, the Bell System could offer a superior product, and this superiority fed on itself until the Bell System emerged victorious over its local rivals, and securely in control of the long lines. The point: networks, interconnection, and leveraging are not a new phenomenon, just increasingly important.

At the risk of over-simplifying, I offer here six basic principles for firms competing in the information economy. Understanding these principles is key for fashioning competition policy.

1. Innovation is king

Perhaps the defining characteristic of the information economy is rapid innovation. No company can afford to stand still, whether it designs microprocessors for computers, writes software, offers communications services, or creates information content. Failure to seize opportunities for innovation is likely to be fatal. Of course, a dominant firm will not lose its grip overnight, and a technical pioneer will keep its reputation even if it falls being the cutting edge of technology, but the classical notion of the sleepy monopolist just does not fit this sector. Ultimately, performance is driven by innovation, not pricing. Competition is typically Schumpeterian in character, with a fierce struggle to be the next temporary monopolist.

2. Intellectual property as sword and shield

Precisely because innovation is king, intellectual property rights play a greater role than ever before in competitive strategy. Copyrights have always been crucial in publishing; now content providers must carefully guard against rampant piracy on the Internet. Patents have always been a sword, usable against infringing firms that would rob the innovator of its just rewards; now patents often serve as a shield as well, used to mount counterclaims against others who bring infringement claims. Mutually blocking patents are all too common, creating a need for cross-licenses and patent pools. Trade secrets have always been a way to preserve a competitive advantage; as patents become cross-licensed and products rapidly reverse-engineered, trade secrets and carefully protected software source code loom larger than ever.

3. Versions, versions everywhere

Information products exhibit very strong economies of scale: most of the costs are 'first-copy costs', with the incremental cost of additional copies being far smaller than the average cost. This pattern is accentuated by the Internet, since physical replication is no longer necessary and distribution costs are minuscule. With large fixed costs, the imperative to engage in price discrimination grows. We see very large gross margins, typically 80 per cent or more in software, and we see multiple versions designed to appeal to different customer groups: a low-end version for new users, a fully featured version for power users, a business version with site licensing for local area networks, etc. Neither price discrimination, versioning, or high gross margins is necessarily indicative of any lasting monopoly power. Both competitive strategy and antitrust analysis must reflect the ubiquity of *information product lines*.

4. Nurture your complements

Products have always worked together to form systems: automobiles, spare parts, service, fuel, driver training, and roads combine to form a 'transportation system'. But never before have so many products been so tightly bound up through interfaces. The personal computer is a complex system, incorporating a microprocessor, various other chips, busses than connect these parts, a monitor, an operating system, interfaces with local and global communications networks, and on and on. As a result, companies spend a great deal of time forming alliances, setting standards, and working with partners to make sure their products work together effectively to comprise an overall 'system'. In the network economy, every company must pay close attention to the provision of *complements*; Microsoft and Intel form one of the most prominent examples of such a partnership.

Antitrust thinking about substitutes (competitors) is far more advanced than antitrust thinking about complements (partners). That must change. Cooperation among *complementors* is generally pro-competitive. See the discussion below on cooperation. The Technical Appendix sketches out of the most basic economic theory of the pricing of complements.

5. Networks rule

To the extent there is a 'new economy', it is the economy of networks rather than an older economy based on sheer scale. Many networks are self-evident: the telephone network, the network of fax machines, a credit-card acceptance network, a network of automatic teller machines and ATM cards, or the Internet itself. As a general rule, large networks offer more value to users than small networks, creating a virulent form of scale economies often denoted by network externalities (or network effects) which generates positive feedback: the strong get stronger and the weak get weaker. Put differently, there are now strong *demand-side* economies of scale: customers value a popular product (network) more than an unpopular one. For just this reason, the terms on which outsiders can gain access to a dominant network can be critical for the very nature of competition in these industries.

The role of networks and network economics in the information economy is even larger than it might appear at first, because of the presence of many *virtual* networks: the network of users of Apple Macintosh computers, the network of owners of compact disk machines, the network of users of Zip drives, or the network of users of Microsoft Word. As these networks have grown in importance, compatibility standards and the control over interfaces have become central to rivalry. Some of the most pressing issues in competition policy revolve around the control over bottlenecks and interfaces: a company controlling one component of a system may be able to wrest control over adjacent components by redesigning the interface between its core component and these other components. In part, this is what Microsoft is alleged to have done, i.e., gain control of the browser component based on its control over the operating system. Since the browser is itself an interface to the Internet, many observers are asking where Microsoft's dominance will stop.

6. Monopoly power lives

Clearly, there are strong forces in the information economy that favor scale. On the supply side, the creation of information involves strong economies of scale, and the design of many new products involves substantial fixed (and sunk) costs of R&D. On the demand side, network effects favor popular products and established networks. Together, we have fertile ground for market power. But not so fast. The winds of innovation blow strong, and are a powerful counterweight to these forces. My rule of thumb: be wary of branding a company as dominant for antitrust purposes if it recently gained a leading position, but look seriously at barriers to entry if you observe a company that has held a dominant position for several years or more. I reject the simple position that monopoly power cannot persist in the network economy, even while recognizing that many of today's leading companies must continue to improve quality and reduce price to protect their current positions.

Horizontal mergers[2]

Keeping these strategic principles in mind, we are now prepared to examine several substantive areas of antitrust law, in this order: horizontal mergers, vertical mergers, standard-setting and cooperation, and the conduct of dominant firms. The remainder of this chapter focuses on the US experience for the simple reason that most of my specific knowledge and experience relates to the United States. Horizontal mergers are analyzed by the US Department of Justice and the Federal Trade Commission under their 1992 *Horizontal Merger Guidelines* (the *Guidelines*). Here I discuss how those *Guidelines* have been applied in the high-tech area.

Unilateral competitive effects

In most high-tech mergers, the focus of merger enforcement is on unilateral competitive effects: the danger that the merged firm, acting independently of any remaining rivals, will find it profitable to raise its prices after the merger. This concern is founded on economic theory which demonstrates that there is quite generally an incentive to raise prices following the consolidation of rival brands.[3] Theories based on coordinated competitive effects, including the danger that a cartel will successfully form in the industry, while historically the focus of merger enforcement policy, have taken a back seat to unilateral effects in the high-tech area.

Two key factors influence the magnitude of these unilateral competitive effects (this is not to say that entry, product repositioning, or efficiencies can be ignored): the gross margins for the merging brands, and the *diversion ratio* between those two brands.[4] The diversion ratio from brand *1* to brand *2* measures the fraction of sales lost by brand *1* when its price is raised that are captured by brand *2*. Unilateral competitive effects are greatest when gross margins are high and when the diversion ratio is high.

This line of reasoning indicates that mergers involving information products can indeed lead to significant unilateral competitive effects, unless entry is relatively easy. Gross margins throughout the high-tech sector tend to be larger than in other areas of the economy. Indeed, they *must* be large to cover the fixed costs of R&D, the first-copy costs of creating information, and the fixed costs of building and maintaining networks for the transmission of information. There is nothing sinister about high gross margins, nor does their presence suggest any monopoly power. But high gross margins can accentuate concerns in the merger context.

Merger synergies

The strong production and demand-side economies of scale present in many high-tech markets open up the possibility of significant efficiencies associated with horizontal mergers. For example, efficiencies would result if development costs can be saved by having one rather than two teams develop new products. Whether efficiencies of this type would make up for any loss in variety and loss in direct competition requires a fact-specific inquiry in any given case.

Some efficiencies flowing from high-tech mergers may be achievable without the necessity of a merger. For example, while the degree of compatibility between two sets of products can be increased through a merger, such changes may well be possible through cooperation on development efforts and the licensing of copyrights without the necessity of a full merger. Under the *Guidelines*, efficiencies of this sort, which are not 'merger-specific', cannot be used to defend or justify an otherwise anti-competitive deal.[5]

Selected cases[6]

Although most mergers, high-tech or otherwise, gain government approval, the FTC and the DOJ have had a significant impact on the information sector in blocking or seeking modifications of several prominent mergers. I have selected a few cases to illustrate how antitrust principles have been applied to high-tech mergers. The cases reported here are heavily skewed towards deals that were either abandoned or modified in response to antitrust challenge, in part because there is far less public information concerning transactions that were cleared without modification. I should note, however, that many enormous high-tech deals have been cleared without modification, including the acquisitions of Lotus by IBM, of Nynex by Bell Atlantic, and of Pacific Bell Telephone by SBC. Furthermore, Microsoft has engaged in a long series of acquisitions that have not been challenged, including HotMail, WebTV, and Vermeer.

Borland and Ashton-Tate (1991)

In 1991 Borland International announced its intention to acquire Ashton-Tate. The key product overlap was in the area of database management programs. The two leading programs at the time were Ashton-Tate's dBase program and Borland's Paradox program. This case was an important early test of how mergers in the personal computer software industry would be treated by the antitrust agencies. Would the deal be blocked as the merger of the two leading suppliers of personal computer based 'relational database' programs, or would the deal be permitted in the light of the highly dynamic nature of software markets?

To satisfy DOJ concerns, Borland agreed to issue FoxPro a license to the dBase code; FoxPro was a rival to dBase then in litigation with Ashton-Tate over infringement of dBase copyrights. The license was intended to insure that the installed base of dBase users had a viable alternative outside of Borland's control. Since then, the Paradox program has lost most of its following, dBase has faded out, Microsoft purchased FoxPro to serve the high end of the market and promoted Access at the low end, and Microsoft now dominates the personal computer database market. Some would point to this case as evidence that software markets are so fluid that mergers are of little concern. I draw a more limited conclusion: that licensing fixes to mergers can indeed enable new competitors.

Adobe and Aldus (1994)

In 1994 Adobe announced its intention to acquire Aldus. The two companies sold the leading brands of professional illustration software: Adobe Illustrator and Aldus Freehand. The parties argued with some effect that each was driven to upgrade its product in order to earn revenues from its own installed base. This was not the only dimension along which competition took place, however. There was evidence, for example, of substantial direct pricing competition between the two programs, both for new customers and for sales to their own installed bases. In the end, the FTC required the merged firm to divest the FreeHand professional illustration software owned by Aldus to a third firm, Altsys Corporation, which had originally developed the software. Again licensing was seen as a fix to a direct horizontal overlap in software products.

Microsoft and Intuit (1995)

In 1994, Microsoft proposed a $2 billion acquisition of Intuit, Inc. Intuit was the owner of Quicken, the leading personal financial software package. Microsoft's Money product performed many of the same functions. The government viewed Quicken and Money as competing in a market for 'Personal Finance/Checkbook' software. In that market, Quicken was the leading product, with a 69 per cent unit share, followed by Microsoft's Money with a 22 per cent unit share. The DOJ described Microsoft as Intuit's most significant competitor, and stated that the proposed acquisition would eliminate competition between Microsoft and Intuit, which had benefited consumers by leading to high quality, innovative products at low prices

The Antitrust Division rejected Microsoft's proposed 'fix' in which some of its Money assets would have been transferred to Novell Inc. The Division believed that Novell would not be as effective a competitor with Money as was Microsoft. The Division also did not accept Microsoft's arguments that entry was easy,[7] and that competition from banks (e.g., on-line banking) would discipline the pricing of Quicken. Moreover, in this situation a licensing fix was regarded as inadequate. In response to DOJ's challenge, the parties abandoned the transaction in July 1995.

Computer Associates and Legent (1996)

In 1996 Computer Associates proposed to acquire Legent for $1.7 billion. The focus of the antitrust inquiry was on certain mainframe computer software markets. In particular, Computer Associates and Legent were the largest and second-largest vendors of systems management software products for IBM mainframe computers.

Mainframe software markets are different from personal computer software markets in a number of respects: mainframe software is a much more stable market, which is experiencing little if any growth; technological change is not so rapid; there is very substantial lock-in by individual customers, although network effects are less pronounced; the software itself is extremely sophisticated; and vendor reputation is critical, due to the 'mission critical' nature of much of this software.

Computer Associates agreed to grant licenses for Legent's products in each of five software markets of concern to the Antitrust Division. The five areas all involved computer systems management software products used with mainframe computers running the VSE operating system: security software; tape and disk management software; job scheduling software; and automated operations software. The goal of the settlement was to establish a new viable competitor in each of these areas. Two aspects of this case are noteworthy. First, notice that the relevant product markets are quite 'narrow', reflecting the fact that users need solutions in each of these categories, and the specialized nature of the software that meets these needs. Second, the government found that entry was quite difficult, a reminder that ease-of-entry is not a silver bullet for merging software companies.

Autodesk and Softdesk (1997)

Autodesk, Inc. negotiated a consent decree in 1997 with the FTC to settle Commission concerns about its proposed $90 million acquisition of Softdesk, Inc. Autodesk develops and markets computer-aided design (CAD) software for use in the architecture, engineering, and construction industries, including 'Auto-CAD', a design engine for use on Windows-based personal computers. Autodesk products account for some 70 per cent of the installed base of Windows-based CAD engines, with approximately 1.4 million users. Softdesk, which primarily sells CAD application software, was developing and testing its own CAD engine, IntelliCADD, and was within months of introducing IntelliCADD into the market, when the Autodesk acquisition of Softdesk was announced.

Compatibility issues were central in this enforcement action. The FTC asserted that 'IntelliCADD, if brought to market, would have provided substantial direct competition to AutoCAD because it offered compatibility and transferability with AutoCAD generated files and application software – features other CAD engines do not offer.' The FTC further alleged that 'the large installed base of AutoCAD users necessitates that any new CAD engine developed and offered in the market offer file compatibility and transferability with AutoCAD in order to be an effective competitor.'[8]

The FTC asserted that Autodesk's acquisition of Softdesk, as originally proposed, would have substantially lessened competition in the development and sale of CAD software engines. Under the terms of the settlement, IntelliCADD was divested to Boomerang Technology, Inc., which in turn assigned and sold its rights and title to IntelliCADD to Visio Corporation. The settlement did not include the IntelliCADD development team, although it did prohibit Autodesk and Softdesk from interfering with the ability of Boomerang to recruit or hire employees of Softdesk who worked on development of IntelliCADD.

Primestar (1998)

In April 1998 the Justice Department sued to block the sale of direct-broadcast satellite (DBS) assets from MCI and News Corp. to Primestar, which is largely owned by cable companies, including Tele-Communications Inc., Time Warner, Comcast, and Cox Enterprises. The key asset involved was an orbital slot capable of beaming programming directly into homes throughout the entire continental United States. Since there are only three such slots, the Justice Department was concerned that letting this slot fall into the hands of cable operators would mute the threat from DBS to local cable franchise monopolies in the delivery of video programming to the home. Facing the DOJ objections, Primestar abandoned its plans to purchase this orbital slot.

This case illustrates concern over the distribution of information, the Internet notwithstanding. Presumably, the concerns in the Primestar case would be far less if telephone companies (or others) had already put into place widespread fiber optic lines to homes and thus offered strong broadband competition for cable companies; but such a distribution network appears to be very expensive to build out, leaving DBS as the current best alternative to cable for multichannel video distribution.

Vertical and complementary mergers

Although the focus of merger enforcement, in high-tech and generally, is on horizontal mergers, it is worth taking a quick look at *vertical* or *complementary* mergers that have been reviewed or challenged by the antitrust agencies in the United States. These mergers involve products that work together rather than serve as substitutes for one another.

Impeding two-level entry

The primary concern in vertical or complementary mergers should be based on the two-level entry theory. Under this theory, a complementary merger can make entry more difficult by requiring an entrant to develop products in two markets at once: two distinct types of software, or hardware and software, or content and distribution. A variant of this theory arises when the integrated firm degrades the compatibility of products sold by rivals that compete with its own products in one of the markets.

For the two-level entry theory to be applicable, market power and entry barriers must be significant at each of the two levels. The market power must be such that an entrant into a single level is significantly disadvantaged by not being able have its component work with the otherwise complementary component produced by the merging firms. These theories, and their application, are subtle, in part because the alternative to a merger may be a complex long-term contract.

Synergies

There can be genuine synergies involved in vertical and complementary mergers. As discussed above (see the Technical Appendix), integration can overcome inefficiencies associated with the pricing of goods or services that stand in a vertical relationship to each other. Less well known, perhaps, is the fact that these same efficiencies can arise for complementary mergers.

Selected cases

Silicon Graphics and Alias and Wavefront (1995)

In 1994 Silicon Graphics, Inc. (SGI), a maker of high-end graphics workstations, announced its plans to acquire two relatively small software houses specializing in 'entertainment graphics software', Alias Research Inc. and Wavefront Technologies. This software is used in producing high-resolution two- and three-dimensional images, e.g., the dinosaurs in *Jurassic Park* and the characters in electronic games. SGI was responding in part to Microsoft's acquisition of the third leading firm in this segment, SoftImage, Inc.

This double deal had significant horizontal as well as vertical aspects. The parties argued in part that SGI had no incentive to raise the price of the software, since this would cut into the sales of the SGI hardware running that software. Ultimately, expressing more concern over the vertical aspects of the deal than its horizontal element, the FTC, in a 3–2 vote, required SGI to enter into a porting agreement with one of DEC, HP, IBM, Sun or another company as approved by the Commission, to make sure that Alias's software was available on these other platforms.

The FTC also required that SGI:

> establish and maintain an open architecture, and publish the Application Program Interfaces (APIs), for [SGI's] computers and operating systems in such manner that software developers and producers may develop and sell Entertainment Software for use on [SGI's] computers in competition with Entertainment software offered by [SGI].[9]

For those watching the Microsoft case, and for those contemplating mergers in the software or hardware industry, the SGI precedent of opening up APIs is worthy of note. Although the FTC action can be criticized on a number of grounds, including the fact that SGI's market position has deteriorated markedly over the past three years (calling into question whether SGI ever had any meaningful power), it stands as an example of mandated 'open interfaces'. Critics assert that such provisions are burdensome or unenforceable, but I am unaware of any disputes that have arisen under this consent decree regarding the definition of 'open'.

Time Warner/Turner (1996)

The FTC conducted an extensive review of Time Warner's acquisition of Turner Broadcasting. The FTC was concerned in part that Time Warner would use its extensive cable properties to protect the position of CNN from competition by the Fox News Channel and MSNBC. This would supposedly be accomplished by denying Fox News and MSNBC carriage on the Time Warner cable systems.

As in the Primestar case, concerns here were rooted in the distribution bottleneck that cable operators enjoy for multichannel video programming. Ultimately, the FTC forced Time Warner to agree to carry one of these rival channels on its systems. Interestingly, after Time Warner cut a deal to carry MSNBC, Fox sued Time Warner on antitrust grounds seeking to gain carriage for Fox News as well. That lawsuit was later settled, with Fox News indeed gaining access to the Time Warner cable customers.

Cadence Design Systems and Cooper & Chyan Technology (1997)

Cadence Design Systems, Inc., of San Jose, California, agreed in 1997 to settle FTC charges that its $400 million acquisition of Cooper & Chyan Technology, Inc. (CCT) would substantially reduce competition for key software used to automate the design of integrated circuits. The FTC was primarily concerned with the vertical aspects of this transaction. In particular, Cadence's 'Virtuoso' layout environment was seen as a 'platform' on which a variety of software could run. The FTC acted to ensure that other brands of software – competitive with that offered by CCT – would not be blocked from running on the Cadence platform. This case illustrates that many software companies, not just Microsoft, can be characterized as controlling a key 'platform' with which other programs must work.

Standard-setting and cooperation[10]

High-technology firms are constantly forming alliances, jointly developing standards, meeting to make sure their products work smoothly together in a system, signing licenses and cross-licenses, and generally cooperating in a fluid environment. In a very real sense, organizational form in the network economy has itself tilted towards loose networks of alliances rather than clear boundaries between hierarchical organizations. Even the most bitter of rivals, Microsoft and Netscape, have agreed to support various software standards, including Virtual Reality Modeling Language for viewing three-dimensional images on the Internet, and the Open Profiling Standard for privacy on the Internet.

Open compatibility standards fundamentally change the nature of competition. Standards lead to expanded network externalities. Standards reduce the technology risk faced by consumers who would otherwise fear picking a losing technology and being left stranded. Truly 'open' standards reduce consumer lock-in to any one vendor. Standards shift the locus of competition: incompatible systems compete *for* the market; compatible products compete *in* the market. Standards shift competition more towards price and away from features, which are at least partially standardized. Standards lead to component competition, which favors specialists, rather than competition between entire systems, which favors generalists. Antitrust authorities need to understand the deep impact of standards on competition, even as they give companies a wide berth to establish standards cooperatively.

I cannot do justice to the whole area of cooperation and compatibility here. Suffice it to say that there are significant efficiencies to be achieved through such cooperation. Competition authorities are well advised to be cautious in treating cooperation that crosses company boundaries any more harshly than cooperation within a single company, so long as the purpose and effect of the cooperation is to establish new products and standards, ensure compatibility, and the like. To do so could stifle the innovative forces expressing themselves in all manner of loose-knit cooperation. In the United States at least, companies seem quite comfortable meeting to establish standards without fear of antitrust sanctions, so long as they confine their activities to genuine standard-setting activity. There are some cases in which companies are wary of cutting licensing deals within a formal the standard-setting process for fear of antitrust sanctions, and there is the occasional attack on standards, but by and large antitrust is not standing in the way of needed cooperation to establish compatibility standards.[11]

Furthermore, there are fundamental economic reasons to encourage, rather than discourage, cooperation among the suppliers of complements. As I show in the Technical Appendix to this chapter, cooperation by two companies selling complements is likely to lead to lower prices than would independent conduct. The precise form taken by this cooperation – pricing commitments, long-term contracts, or full integration – is less important for my current purposes than the simple point that such cooperation generally benefits consumers. This notion cuts against the deep instincts of antitrust lawyers, but is beyond doubt as a matter of economics.

Antitrust lawyers are well versed in the evils that can arise when companies selling substitutes, i.e., direct rivals, collude or merge. They rarely recognize, however, that these evils turn into virtues when the companies are selling complements. To the economist, these situations are perfectly analogous, and indeed a single theory can be applied in both cases with a simple change of sign from positive to negative to study complements rather than substitutes. In practice, analyzing vertical relationships is not so simple, since one must ask whether companies standing in a vertical or complementary relationship to each other can and will devise contractual relationships that lie in between simple uniform pricing and full integration (merger).

Cooperation between two companies owning patents that block each other's products is a good example of the principle. Without some form of cooperation, neither company can bring a product to market. (The same would be true if each company possessed know-how that could only lead to a commercially viable product when combined with the other company's know-how.) This being the case, competition cannot reduced if the companies agree to jointly market and sell a product using both of their patents. Alternatively, they could sign a cross-license, or form a patent pool if they seek to license their patents to third parties as well. Assuming that the patents were valid and blocking, it is hard to see how cooperation between the two companies could do anything other than augment competition. Three recent cases involving patent pools are the FTC's 1998 action against Summit and VisX in the market for laser eye surgery, and the Justice

Department's 1997 approval of the MPEG consortium and 1998 approval of cooperation to promote the DVD standard.

A much harder set of cases arises when products that *today* are complements have the prospect of evolving over time to become substitutes. This pattern arises as part of the Microsoft case: will Netscape's browser evolve from a complement to Windows to a genuine substitute for Windows, in conjunction with the Java programming language?

Unilateral conduct by dominant firms

Finally, I turn to the thorniest area for competition policy in the information economy: the nature of the limits to be placed on conduct by dominant firms.

General principles

I have made it clear that monopoly power is not a casualty of the information age. Monopoly power lives, often based on control over bottlenecks or interfaces. Certainly one should not merely look at a fleeting high market share as indicative of monopoly power, but neither does rapid innovation imply the absence of any such power.

The primary role of competition policy, in my view, is to prevent dominant firms from blockading innovation that would threaten their current position. I see no reason why antitrust law, at least in the United States, needs to transform itself to deal with dominant firms in the information, communications, and entertainment industries in the years ahead.

Nintendo's position in the video game market offers a good example of the uses and limits of antitrust in high-tech: Nintendo held a dominant position from roughly the mid-1980s through the early 1990s, at which time competition from the Sega Genesis, and later the Sony Playstation, grew stronger. Yet I still consider Nintendo's exclusivity policies with game developers to have been anticompetitive: from 1985 until 1992 Nintendo would only allow a game to appear on its system if the game developer agreed not to make that game available on the rival Atari and Sega systems for a two-year period.[12] Policies that prolong monopoly power can be anti-competitive, even if that power will ultimately be eroded by the forces of technological progress.

Looking at the traditional areas of monopolization and abuse of dominance, some categories of conduct in high-tech markets seem quite amenable to antitrust limits, while others present more hazards than opportunities for competition policy. I see no reason why exclusive dealing contracts and their close cousins cannot be attacked on antitrust grounds in the information sector as in other areas. The same is true of tying when used to blockade two-level entry. But I urge caution when invoking the 'essential facilities' doctrine, especially when this involves mandatory licensing, as in the recent *Image Technical Services* v. *Kodak* case from the Ninth Circuit Court of Appeals. And the usual hazards associated with predatory pricing cases are brought into stark relief for information products, with their very low marginal costs.

US v. *Microsoft*

The highly visible case of the *United States* v. *Microsoft* provides an excellent vehicle for seeing high-tech antitrust in action. I will not recount here in detail the primary allegations being made by the Justice Department, but less the extensive factual record that has now been developed at trial. Suffice it to say that the case is ultimately about whether Microsoft has acted to defend its operating system monopoly by blockading an entrant, Netscape with its browser, that could grow to become a threat. The case also involves claims that Microsoft has suppressed competition in the browser market itself, but I consider the core concern to be that of defense of the operating system monopoly. Indeed, one of Microsoft's arguments is that there is no distinct browser market, because the operating system will some encompass the functionality that once was offered only in stand-alone browsers.

The Justice Department complaint described various exclusionary contracts that Microsoft allegedly entered into with various partners and customers, specifically Original Equipment Manufacturers (OEMs), Internet Service Providers (ISPs) and Internet Content Providers (ICPs). Whether or not the facts ultimately show that these contracts damaged competition, Justice's attack of exclusionary contracts entered into by a monopolist is squarely within established antitrust jurisprudence. Some samples from the Complaint:

> Virtually every new PC that comes with Windows, no matter which OEM has built it, presents users with the same screens and software specified by Microsoft. As a result of Microsoft's restrictive boot-up and desktop screen agreements, OEMs are deprived of the freedom to make competitive choices about which browser or other software product should be offered to their customers, the ability to determine for themselves the design and configuration of the initial screens displayed on the computers they sell, and the ability to differentiate their products to serve their perceptions of consumers' needs. These restrictive agreements also maintain, and enhance the importance of, Microsoft's ability to provide preferential placement on the desktop (or in the boot-up sequence) to various Internet Service Providers ('ISPs') and Internet Content Providers ('ICPs'), in return for those firms' commitments to give preferential distribution and promotion to Internet Explorer and to restrict their distribution and promotion of competing browsers.

> Microsoft's agreements with ISPs allow Microsoft to leverage its operating system monopoly by conditioning these ISPs' inclusion in Windows' lists on such ISPs' agreement to offer Microsoft's Internet Explorer browser primarily or exclusively as the browser they distribute; not to promote or even mention to any of their subscribers the existence, availability, or compatibility of a competing Internet browser; and to use on their own Internet sites Microsoft-specific programming extensions and tools that make those

sites look better when viewed through Internet Explorer than when viewed through competing Internet browsers. Microsoft's anticompetitive agreements with ISPs have substantially foreclosed competing browsers from this major channel of browser distribution. Over thirty per cent of Internet browser users have obtained their browsers from ISPs.

Microsoft has also entered into exclusionary agreements with Internet Content Providers ('ICPs') - firms such as Disney, Hollywood Online, and CBS Sportsline, that provide news, entertainment, and other information from sites on the web. One of the new features included in Internet Explorer 4.0 is the provision of 'channels' that appear on the right side of the Windows desktop screen after Internet Explorer 4.0 has been installed on a Windows 95 PC. The same channels will appear automatically on the Windows 98 desktop screen if Microsoft is permitted to tie Internet Explorer 4.0 to Windows 98 in license agreements with OEMs and in sales to consumers. Microsoft provides different levels of channel placement, 'platinum' being the most prominent. Under Microsoft's Internet Explorer 4.0 channel agreements, beginning in mid-1997, ICPs who desired 'platinum' placement (and even some seeking lower-level placement) were required to agree: (a) not to compensate in any manner the manufacturer of an 'Other Browser' (defined as either of the top two non-Microsoft browsers), including by distributing its browser, for the distribution, marketing, or promotion of the ICP's content; (b) not to promote any browser produced by any manufacturer of an 'Other Browser'; (c) not to allow any manufacturer of an 'Other Browser' to promote and highlight the ICP's 'channel' content on or for its browsers; and (d) to design its web sites using Microsoft-specific, proprietary programming extensions so that those sites look better when viewed with Internet Explorer than when viewed through a competing browser.

Given the extensive coverage afforded to this case, and my overall point that the Microsoft case is by far from the only one at the intersection of antitrust and the information economy, I will not offer here any detailed analysis of that case. Suffice it to say that the outcome of this case will have potentially profound implications for how *monopolization* claims are viewed in high-tech industries. However, the case is unlikely to lead to great changes in the law or in enforcement policies regarding mergers and standard-setting, whatever its final outcome.

Conclusion

In a world of networks, where interfaces, compatibility, standards, and bottlenecks take on great significance, competition authorities cannot afford to stand on the sidelines just because innovation is rapid. On the contrary, competition authorities have a duty to prevent today's dominant firms from stifling innovation that threatens their leadership.

I am hopeful that competition authorities are up to the task. Looking at the US experience, merger policy is on a sound footing, and antitrust is not impeding companies from cooperating when necessary to combine their offerings and to establish standards. Regarding unilateral conduct by dominant firms, the Justice Department's recent action against Microsoft will likely have a profound effect on how monopolization cases are viewed in the information economy.

Acknowledgements

I am deeply indebted to my co-authors on related projects. I have learned a great deal about the information economy, the Internet, and on-line commerce from my colleague Hal R. Varian, Dean of the School of Information Management and Systems at the University of California at Berkeley. This chapter draws from our book, *Information Rules: A Strategic Guide to the Network Economy*, Harvard Business School Press, 1999. See http://www.inforules.com for more information. I also am relying heavily on my colleague Michael L. Katz, and our joint paper, 'Antitrust in Software Markets,'which can be obtained at http://haas.berkeley.edu/~shapiro/software.pdf.

Technical appendix: pricing of components and systems

The Model

Consider a situation in which two components, A and B, are used in fixed proportions to constitute a system. Let the unit cost of components A and B be c_A and c_B respectively. Call the unit cost of a system $c_S \equiv c_A + c_B$. By making c_A and c_B invariant with respect to the institutional setting (see below), we are assuming that there are no economies or diseconomies of scope if the system is assembled within one firm vs. two. The focus here is thus entirely on pricing incentives for a given cost structure. The results here are well known in the fields of microeconomics and industrial organization, but their implications for antitrust may not be fully appreciated. The treatment here is intended to illustrate some standard theoretical results, not to break new ground.

There are many examples of (actual or nearly) fixed-proportion components in the information sector, including (a) a computer and a monitor; (b) a computer and an operating system; or (c) a microprocessor and a chipset within the computer. We explore here the pricing of the components, and the system, in three different institutional settings.

The first setting is that of an *integrated firm* that manufacturers and assembles the entire system. Call the unit cost of the system $c_S \equiv c_A + c_B$. Call the price of the system to consumers, to be set by the seller, p_S.

The second setting is a *vertical chain* in which firm A manufactures and sells component A to firm B, which then combines the A component with the B component and sells the resulting system to consumers. Firm B sets the system price p_S. In this case, call p_A the price for component A that firm A charges to firm B.

The third setting involves the *complements*: each of the two firms, A and B, sells its component to the consumer, which then combines the components into a system. In this case, call the prices charged by the two firms p_A and p_B; the system price faced by the consumer is $p_A + p_B$.

Consumers ultimately care about the total price of the system, p_S, which governs the demand for systems. Call this demand relationship $\chi_S = D(p_S)$, where χ_S is unit sales of systems, and the demand function, $D(\cdot)$ is downward sloping, exhibits declining marginal revenue, and satisfies the usual regularity conditions for oligopoly theory. We will illustrate our results using the constant-elasticity demand curve, $D(p_S) = p_S^{-\varepsilon}$. Note for use below that in this special case $- D(p_S/D'(p_S)' = p_S/\varepsilon$. Note also that in general $- D(p_S)/D'(p_S)$ is equal to the difference between price and marginal revenue at the price p_S, or, equivalently, at output level $D(p_S)$.

Integrated firm

With a single, integrated, firm, we have a standard monopoly pricing problem. The firm's problem is to pick p_S to maximize

$$D(p_S)(p_S - c_S).$$

The standard solution can be written as

$$p_S - c_S = -\frac{D(p_S)}{D'(p_S)}.$$

With constant-elasticity demand, this gives the standard mark-up rule

$$p_S = \frac{c_S}{1 - 1/\varepsilon}.$$

Vertical chain

If firm A sets a single, uniform price p_A selling to firm B, which in turn sets a single uniform price selling to consumers, we have the standard "chain of monopolies" problem. A standard result is that prices are higher under this structure than with an integrated monopolist.

The resulting price is obtained in two steps. First, consider how firm B prices the system for a given price p_A set by firm A. Effectively, firm B now has a unit cost of each system of $p_A + c_B$. Naturally, this leads to a higher system price to consumers that would unit costs of $c_A + c_B$, as in the integrated case just above. Firm B thus prices according to the rule

$$p_S - (p_A + c_B) = -\frac{D(p_S)}{D'(p_S)}.$$

With constant-elasticity demand, substituting for $-D/D'$ gives

$$p_S\left(1-\frac{1}{\varepsilon}\right)=p_A+c_B.$$

The next step is to determine A's optimal pricing, given B's demand as reflected in the equation just above. This is analogous to the Stackelberg problem in standard oligopoly theory. Firm A sets p_A to maximize $D(p_S)(p_A - c_A)$, where p_S is determined by the relationship just above. In the case of constant elasticity of demand, using the linear relationship between p_S and p_A noted above, a series of calculations leads the following expression for the resulting systems price:

$$p_S = \frac{c_S}{(1-1/\varepsilon)^2}.$$

Complements

If firms A and B each set prices independently for their components, the problem is analogous to Cournot oligopoly, as opposed to the Stackelberg solution just derived. Firm A sets p_A to maximize

$$D(p_A + p_B)(p_A - c_A),$$

taking p_B as given. Since $dp_S/dp_A = 1$ in this situation, the resulting first-order condition is simply

$$D(p_S)+D'(p_S)(p_A-c_A)=0.$$

Firm B does likewise, giving the analogous condition for p_B of

$$D(p_S)+D'(p_S)(p_B-c_B)=0.$$

Adding up these two first-order conditions gives

$$2D(p_S)+D'(p_S)(p_S-c_S)=0,$$

which can be rewritten as

$$p_S=c_S-2\frac{D(p_S)}{D'(p_S)}.$$

Note that this equation is identical to the equation for the integrated firm, except for the factor of two on the right-hand side.

In the special case of constant-elasticity demand, we have

$$p_S = \frac{c_S}{1-2/\varepsilon}.$$

Notice that this special case becomes internally inconsistent if the elasticity of demand is less than two. (Each firm will want to set arbitrarily high prices.)

Pricing comparisons

We know that in general the system price set by the integrated firm is lower than the price under the vertical chain or complements. The intuition behind this result is as follows. Lower prices for one component generate a positive external effect of the owner of the other component. These externalities are internalized through integration, leading to lower prices. However, this intuition alone does not tell us whether the prices are highest under complements or the vertical chain.

In the case of constant elasticity of demand, the resulting systems prices are

$$p_S^I = \frac{c_S}{1-1/\varepsilon},$$

for the integrated firm,

$$p_S^v = \frac{c_S}{\left(1-1/\varepsilon\right)^2},$$

for the vertical chain, and

$$p_S^c = \frac{c_S}{1-2/\varepsilon},$$

for the independent pricing of complements. Direct comparison of these prices reveals that the system price is lowest for the integrated firm, somewhat higher for the vertical chain, and highest of all under the complements arrangement.

In the case of constant elasticity of demand, prices are lower under the vertical chain than under complements because the upstream firm, which we have denoted by firm A, recognizes that firm B will *raise* its own component price in response to A's higher price. Put differently, the system price will go up by more than one unit, for every unit increase in p_A. Another way to say this is that firm B's reaction curve (optimal p_B as a function of p_A) is upward sloping. (This follows from the fact that a monopolist facing constant elasticity of demand, firm B, more than passes through any increases in unit costs, p_A.) Recognizing this reaction, firm A sets a lower price under the vertical chain than under complements pricing. It follows that the systems price is lower, because firm B is setting its optimal component price given p_A under either the vertical chain or complements structure.

More generally, the comparison of system prices between the vertical chain and complements depends upon whether the reaction curve of firm *B* is upward or downward sloping. Put differently, prices are higher under complements if and only if cost increases are more than passed through to final consumers. Formally, this occurs if and only if $dp_S/dp_A > 1$ in the vertical chain setting. (We always have $dp_S/dp_A = 1$ in the complements setting.) Since in general the vertical chain systems price is given by

$$p_S + \frac{D(ps)}{D'(ps)} = p_A + c_B,$$

the comparison hinges on the derivative of the left-hand side of this equation with respect to p_S. A few steps of calculus tell us that prices are higher in the complements case if and only if the ratio $D(p_S)/D'(p_S)$ is declining in p_S, which is equivalent to

$$D'(p_S)D'(p_S) < D(p_S)D''(p_S).$$

(For simplicity, I am assuming that these various conditions hold or fail uniformly at all points on the demand curve.) This condition is always met for constant elasticity of demand.

Note, however, that the condition just provided always *fails* for linear (or concave) demand. Under those conditions, prices are higher in the *vertical chain* setting.

We can illustrate these points by solving the linear case explicitly. Suppose that demand for systems is given by $D(p_S) = K - p_S$. For simplicity, and without (further) loss of generality, let c_A and c_B equal zero. The integrated firm maximizes $(K - p_S)p_S$, which involves a systems price of $K/2$. Under complements, firm *A* maximizes $(K - p_A - p_B)p_A$, which gives a reaction curve of $p_A = (K - p_B)/2$. Solving for the equilibrium prices gives $p_A = p_B = K/3$, for a systems price under complements of $2K/3$.

Finally, under the vertical chain arrangement, firm *B*'s response to p_A is $p_B = (K - p_A)/2$, so firm *A*, the first mover, maximizes $(K - p_A - (K - p_A)/2)p_A$. The solution to this is given by $p_A = K/2$, causing *B* to set a component price of $K/4$, with a resulting systems price of $3K/4$. In this case, the systems price responds *less* than one-for-one to increases in p_A, so firm *A* is led to set a higher price under the vertical chain than under complements. In the linear case, firm *A* charges $K/2$ for its component, rather than $K/3$, an increase of $K/6$. However, firm *B* lowers its component price in response from $K/3$ to $K/4$, a decrease of only $K/12$ (the slope of *B*'s reaction function is only 1/2). As a result, the final systems price rises from $2K/3$ under complements to $3K/4$ under the vertical chain, an increase of $K/12$.

Notes

1 For a thorough treatment of competitive strategy in the information economy, see Carl Shapiro and Hal R. Varian, *Information Rules: A Strategic Guide to the Network Economy*, Harvard Business School Press, 1999.
2 This section is drawn in part from my paper with Michael Katz, 'Antitrust in Software Markets'.
3 This is true whether the firms engage in pricing competition or quantity competition. See Davidson and Deneckere (1985) and Farrell and Shapiro (1990), respectively.
4 See Shapiro (1996b) for an accessible treatment of gross margins and diversion ratios in merger analysis. See Werden and Froeb (1994) for a more extensive analysis using the 'logit' model of demand.
5 The DOJ and FTC revised the 1992 *Guidelines* in 1997 to articulate more fully how efficiencies would be handled in the merger review process. Although the stated intention of the agencies was to be more receptive to efficiency claims, it remains to be seen how this will work in practice.
6 I have been involved in many of these merger reviews. In particular, I worked for the FTC in the Adobe/Aldus merger, for the DOJ in the Microsoft/Intuit and Computer Associates/Legent deals, for the merging parties in the Borland acquisition of Ashton-Tate, and for DIRECTV in the Primestar matter. In the vertical mergers discussed below, I was retained by the acquiring firm in the Silicon Graphics/Alias/Wavefront, the Time Warner/Turner, and the Cadence/CCT deals. The statements in this chapter are not intended to represent the views of either the government agencies or the companies involved.
7 The experience of Computer Associate's 'Simply Money' program in this market is instructive regarding entry barriers in software. Even though Computer Associates virtually gave its program away, and received some favorable reviews, it still could not gain wide acceptance.
8 FTC press release, 31 March 1997, at www.ftc.gov/opa/9703/autodesk.htm.
9 *Decision and Order in the Matter of Silicon Graphics, Inc.,* Docket No. C-3626, November 1995. The FTC also required that SGI offer independent entertainment graphics software companies participation in its software development programs on terms no less favorable than those offered to other types of software companies.
10 See Chapter 8 of *Information Rules* for a more complete discussion of compatibility and cooperation.
11 See my recent paper with Michael Katz for a more extensive discussion of standard setting and antitrust. The highly successful CD standard has been challenged in a private action, *Disctronics Texas, Inc., et al.* v. *Pioneer Electronic Corp. et al.* Eastern District of Texas, Case No. 4:95 CV 229.
12 I testified for Atari Corporation against Nintendo in their antitrust trial. Nintendo was not found to have violated the antitrust laws.

References

Anton, J. and Yao, D. (1995) 'Standard-setting consortia, antitrust, and high-technology industries', *Antitrust Law Journal* 64, 247–265.
Arthur, W. B. (1989) 'Competing technologies, increasing returns, and lock-in by historical events', *The Economic Journal* 99, 116–131.
Balto, D. (1997) *Networks and Exclusivity: Antitrust Analysis to Promote Network Competition*, Federal Trade Commission, April.

Bulow, J. I. (1982) 'Durable–goods monopolists', *Journal of Political Economy* 90, 314–332.

Coase, R. (1972) 'Durability and monopoly', *Journal of Law and Economics* 15, 143–149.

Davidson, C. and Deneckere, R. (1985) 'Incentives to form coalitions with Bertrand competition', *Rand Journal of Economics* 16, 473–486.

Dybvig, P. H. and Spatt, C. S. (1983) 'Adoption externalities as public goods', *Journal of Public Economics* 20, 231–247.

Economides, N. and White, L. J. (1994) 'Networks and compatibility: implications for antitrust', *European Economic Review* 38, 651–662.

Farrell, J. and Katz, M. (1998) 'The effects of antitrust and intellectual property law on compatibility and innovation', *Antitrust Bulletin*, forthcoming.

Farrell, J. and Saloner, G. (1985) 'Standardization, compatibility, and innovation', *Rand Journal of Economics* 16, 70–83.

Farrell, J. and Saloner, G. (1986) 'Installed base and compatibility: innovation, product preannouncement, and predation', *American Economic Review* 76, 940–955.

Farrell, J. and Shapiro, C. (1990) 'Horizontal mergers: an equilibrium analysis', *American Economic Review* 80, 107–115.

Federal Trade Commission (1996) *Competition Policy in the New High-Tech, Global Marketplace*, Washington, DC: Staff Report, May.

Gilbert, R. (1998) 'Networks, standards, and the use of market dominance: Microsoft (1995)', in J. Kwoka and L. White (eds) *The Antitrust Revolution: The Role of Economics*, Oxford University Press, forthcoming.

Gilbert, R. and Shapiro, C. (1998) 'Antitrust issues in the licensing of intellectual property: the nine no-no's meet the nineties', *Brookings Papers on Economics: Microeconomics*, forthcoming.

Katz, M. and Shapiro, C. (1985) 'Network externalities, competition and compatibility', *American Economic Review* 75 (3), 424–440.

Katz, M. and Shapiro, C. (1986a) 'Technology adoption in the presence of network externalities', *Journal of Political Economy* 94, 822–841.

Katz, M. and Shapiro, C. (1986b) 'Product compatibility choice in a market with technological progress', *Oxford Economic Papers* 38, 146–165.

Katz, M. and Shapiro, C. (1992) 'Product introduction with network externalities', *Journal of Industrial Economics* 40 (1), 55–84.

Katz, M. and Shapiro, C. (1994), 'Systems competition and network effects', *Journal of Economic Perspectives* 8 (2), 93–115.

Klein, J. I. (1998) 'The importance of antitrust enforcement in the new economy', available at www.usdoj.gov/atr/speeches

Lemley, M. and McGowan, D. (1997) 'Legal implications of network economic effects', Austin, TX: School of Law, University of Texas at Austin.

Liebowitz, S. J. and Margolis, S. E. (1990) 'The fable of keys', *Journal of Law and Economics* 33 (1), 1–26.

Rohlfs, J. (1974) 'A theory of interdependent demand for a communications service', *Bell Journal of Economics* 5 (1), 16–37.

Shapiro, C. (1996a) 'Antitrust in network industries', available at www.usdoj.gov/atr/speeches

Shapiro, C. (1996b), 'Mergers with differentiated products', *Antitrust* Spring, 23–30.

Shapiro, C. and Varian, H. R. (1999) *Information Rules: A Strategic Guide to the Network Economy*, Harvard Business School Press 1999.

Varian, H. (1989), 'Price discrimination', in R. Schmalensee and R. D. Willig (eds.) *The Handbook of Industrial Organization*, Amsterdam: North Holland Publishing.

Veblen, T. (1899) *Theory of the Leisure Class*, New York, Dover Publications.

Werden, G. and Froeb, L. (1994) 'The effects of mergers in differentiated products industries: logit demand and merger policy', *Journal of Law, Economics and Organization* 10, 407–426.

9 Regulating manufacturers and their exclusive retailers

Margaret E. Slade

Introduction

In most Western economies, a very large fraction of retail sales are subject to some form of exclusive-dealing clauses.[1] Within this class, new-automobile sales dominate. Other products and services, however, such as gasoline, fast food, and business services, are also important. Most of these exclusive-retailing arrangements can be grouped under the umbrella of franchising.

Within the realm of franchising, there are two commonly used modes. Traditional franchising, which involves an upstream producer and a downstream seller (e.g., gasoline), is more important from a sales-revenue point of view. Business-format franchising, however, is growing faster.[2] With business-format franchising, production takes place at the retail outlet (e.g., fast-food). In this chapter, I consider the traditional manufacturer–retailer relationship.

The products that are sold through exclusive-retailing arrangements are most often branded and are thus not homogeneous from the consumer's point of view. It is well known in the economics literature that differentiation, whether it results from the brand name, the spatial location of the retail outlet, or any other source, endows a seller with some degree of pricing power.[3] Furthermore, manufacturers of consumer products are apt to operate in markets that can be classified as oligopolistic rather than perfectly competitive. At the upstream or manufacturing level, pricing power can be due to economies of scale that limit entry, exclusive trademarks, or unique product features.

When both upstream and downstream firms possess some degree of pricing power, the monopoly market failure is compounded. Indeed, since each firm extracts a profit, there are successive output restrictions that result in retail prices that are higher than those that would be chosen by a single vertically integrated producer/retailer pair. This phenomenon is usually referred to as double marginalization.[4] Furthermore, the manufacturer's profit is lower, and the sum of manufacturer and retailer profits can be lower under double marginalization than under integration.[5] One might therefore expect manufacturers to sell their products themselves or through vertically integrated subsidiaries. However, although such arrangements exist, they do not dominate retail markets. Indeed, retail markets tend to be organized according to one of several standard forms.

Consider the sequence of choices that a manufacturer faces, which are summarized in Figure 9.1. First, the manufacturer must decide whether to operate a retail outlet himself or to contract with an independent retailer. For those outlets that are operated under contract, he must decide whether to employ an exclusive or a common sales agent (i.e. one that sells only his products or one that sells the products of several competing manufacturers). In addition, he must decide whether he or the retailer should own the store or salesroom. Finally, he must

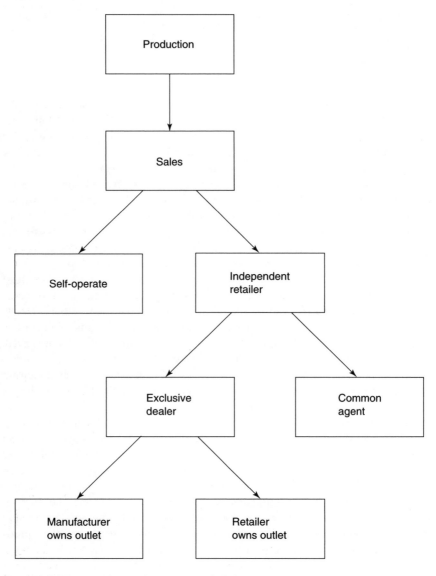

Figure 9.1 The manufacturer's sequence of choices

decide whether to use a linear wholesale-pricing scheme, a two-part tariff, or some more complex form of non-linear-pricing schedule.

The decisions concerning the ownership and operation of retail outlets give rise to three standard forms of retail organization under exclusive trademarks. These forms vary from industry to industry, from firm to firm within an industry, and even from outlet to outlet within a firm. Nevertheless, there is a remarkable regularity in the way that retail markets are organized that transcends industry and national boundaries. I describe each of these standard forms in turn with the caveat that not all arrangements that fall into one of these classes are exactly as described.

Type 1: Company-owned and operated outlets

With this arrangement, the dealer is an employee of the manufacturer. The dealer, who owns neither the outlet nor the inventory of products, normally receives a salary that is, to a large extent, independent of the realization of sales. Such operations are often called direct sales. In addition, many manufacturers employ commissioned agents, who receive a small commission per item sold as well as a salary or *per diem*. Those agents, however, do not take possession of the merchandise. Moreover, the manufacturer sets the retail price. I include commissioned agencies in the same class as direct operations.

With direct operations, the manufacturer is the residual claimant. With commissioned agencies, in contrast, there is some degree of revenue sharing. Nevertheless, the manufacturer is the principal responsible party.

Type 2: Company-owned and dealer-operated outlets

Many retail outlets are owned by the manufacturer but are operated by the retailer. This arrangement can take the form of a lease for the rental of the premises or a licensing agreement.[6] Under either of these forms, the dealer purchases the product at a wholesale price that is set by the manufacturer and sells it at a retail price that she sets herself. The dealer, who owns the inventory of merchandise, is normally responsible for the furnishings and fixtures, whereas the manufacturer, who owns the land and the building, is responsible for major capital improvements.

With this organizational form, the dealer is the residual claimant. Nevertheless, the rental rate or license fee can be used by the manufacturer to extract profit from the retailer.

Type 3: Dealer-owned and operated outlets

Owner operators, like lessee dealers, purchase products at a wholesale price that is set by the manufacturer and sell them at a retail price that they set themselves. In contrast to lessees, however, they own all of the assets, including the land and the premises, and they are responsible for all of the capital improvements.

With this organizational form, transactions are truly arm's length, and the retailer is the residual claimant with respect to all aspects of the business. Furthermore, the methods that are available to the manufacturer to extract profit from the retailer are more limited.

In the next section, I discuss some of the theories that attempt to explain why different types of retail organizational forms are chosen. The third section deals with certain laws that govern those choices, and the fourth section assesses three cases of government regulation of the relationships between manufacturers and their exclusive retailers. These cases, which are drawn from the gasoline, automobile and beer markets, involve the prohibition of certain types of upstream/downstream contracts.

The choice of retail organizational form

A number of theories have been proposed to explain how the choice among exclusive-retailing alternatives is made as well as the decision concerning whether to employ an exclusive dealer or a common agent. In my discussion of these theories, I attempt to characterize the types of establishments that are more apt to fall into each class.

Company employee or independent retailer

The self-operate/contract-out choice has received much attention in the theoretical literature,[7] where it is usually modeled in a principal/agent setting. With the standard paradigm, the manufacturer or principal, who is assumed to be risk neutral, faces a trade-off between providing his risk-averse retailer or agent with incentives to work hard and insurance against market risk.[8] Moreover, since it is generally believed that markets (firms) are better at providing the former (latter), a compromise can involve risk and profit sharing.

There are a number of features that economic theory predicts should characterize company-operated outlets in any industry or country. For example, they should be larger, located in more urban environments, and have fewer repeat customers.

A larger outlet is associated with increased agent risk, not because the market is riskier *per se* but because more capital is subject to the same degree of risk. Vertical integration, by substituting the principal's capital for the agent's, insures the agent from the vagaries of the market.

An urban environment facilitates direct monitoring of an agent's activities. In particular, when outlets are centrally located, it is easier to verify that the premises are clean, the merchandise is properly stored, and that the agent provides the services that the manufacturer desires. When direct monitoring is easier, incentive-based motives for vertical contracting are less important.

A lack of repeat customers provides dealers with greater opportunity to free ride on the manufacturer's good name or recognized trademark, since substandard service will not be detected until it is too late. The principal, in contrast, when operating an outlet himself, can internalize this externality that damages the reputation of all of his units. In addition, when combined with a greater degree of customer choice due to a central location, a lack of repeat business can imply more risk at the outlet level. When outlet-level risk is greater, the need for the principal to insure the agent increases, which in turn makes vertical integration more appealing.[9]

Finally, when the dealer's effort is more important, which can be due to a need to supervise more employees, a higher value added at the outlet level, or a need to have previous experience in the business, independent retail outlets are more likely.

Indeed, when an agent's duties are more entrepreneurial, their compensation tends to be more entrepreneurial as well.

Exclusive dealing or common agency

In many settings (e.g., department stores), a common agent sells the products of several manufacturers. In other settings, in contrast (e.g., automobile salesrooms), manufacturers employ exclusive retailers. Prior to the mid-1980s, there were two main competing theories of exclusive dealing and its consequences. On the one hand, proponents held that this practice enhanced efficiency, since it protected a manufacturer's investment in cost-lowering activities. On the other hand, opponents held that this practice enhanced the market power of the upstream firms by enabling them to exclude rivals from retailing facilities. However, more recent theories of exclusive dealing show that, when a contract attempts to solve more than one market failure, the effects of exclusive-dealing clauses are almost always ambiguous.[10]

It is clear that, when a leased retail establishment must undergo major capital improvements, exclusive dealing can be justified as a way of protecting the manufacturer's investment (as in Marvel, 1982). Specifically, modernization is apt to lower the cost of selling any product, not just one produced by the manufacturer. In addition, retailer training is a form of cost-lowering investment that must be protected under a wider set of contractual arrangements.

Both Martimort (1996) and Bernheim and Whinston (1998) show that a high degree of interbrand substitutability favors exclusive dealing. In the former paper, when goods are close substitutes, exclusive dealing provides an extra informational benefit, whereas in the latter, competition among manufacturers who sell through a common agent drives wholesale prices down and therefore lowers manufacturer profits. When brands of different manufacturers are highly substitutable, therefore, exclusive-dealing contracts emerge as a natural consequence.

It is possible to obtain the Bernheim and Whinston result – that wholesale prices can be driven towards marginal costs when manufacturers sell through a common agent – in a model without moral hazard or risk aversion. Specifically, in a game of complete information, profit-maximizing manufacturers set price-cost margins equal to minus one times the reciprocals of the perceived elasticities of demand for their products.[11] When customers can obtain the brands of competing manufacturers within a single establishment, those elasticities are apt to be larger in magnitude. This is particularly true of low-cost items such as beer purchased in a public house and much less true of high-cost items such as automobiles purchased in a showroom. When substitutability is important, and when search costs are high relative to retail prices, wholesale prices charged to independent retailers are apt to be lower than those charged to exclusive dealers. With this explanation, manufacturers prefer exclusive dealing for the simple reason that it increases their optimal price/cost margins.

On the other hand, manufacturers tend to prefer to sell through a common agency when there are economies of scope (i.e., economies of selling the products of several manufacturers). For example, a customer who wishes to purchase a dress from one manufacturer might want to experiment with accessories made by several designers in an attempt to find the most desirable combination.

Company or dealer ownership of retail facilities

A manufacturer might want to own retail facilities (or not) for a number of reasons. For example, when there are capital-market imperfections, manufacturers might have access to cheaper capital than retailers. On the other hand, if a business is growing rapidly, retailers can provide manufacturers with capital and thus overcome manufacturer capital constraints. These reasons can be important for new and rapidly growing businesses. However, it is unlikely that they explain the prevalence of stable ownership patterns in mature industries.

Another reason why manufacturers might want to own and lease retail facilities has already been suggested – ownership provides them with a means of extracting profit from retailers and thus overcoming the double-marginalization problem. For example, when retailers have price power, it is profit-maximizing for them to set retail prices above the sum of wholesale prices and retail-selling costs. Higher prices cause sales to fall and, for a given wholesale price, cause manufacturer profits to decline. When manufacturers own retail facilities, however, they can recoup their losses by charging higher retail rents. Moreover, this process normally results in lower retail prices than under double marginalization and therefore benefits the consumer as well.

Ownership of retail facilities, in contrast, is less attractive in situations where retailer investment and reputation are very important. Indeed, a retailer has little incentive to invest unless tenure is secure, and security of tenure can be increased through the use of long-term leases or retailer ownership.

Linear wholesale prices or two-part tariffs

A two-part tariff is a selling arrangement in which a buyer pays a fixed fee to enter the relationship and a constant price per unit purchased. For example, a franchise fee plus a per-unit royalty that is paid to the upstream firm by the franchisee is a form of two-part tariff.

The most common argument in favor of two-part tariffs is very similar to the argument in favor of manufacturer ownership of retail facilities. Indeed, any fixed fee (i.e., one that is independent of the amount of the product that is sold), not just a yearly rental rate or license fee, can be used by manufacturers to extract profit from retailers. Indeed, with a two-part tariff, the manufacturer can sell the product to the dealer at marginal cost (and thus avoid double marginalization), the retailer can then set a higher-than-competitive markup and take the profit downstream. Finally, the manufacturer can capture this profit through the proper choice of fixed fee. The consumer also benefits from the two-part tariff, since retail prices are lower.

It is difficult to think of a situation where linear wholesale pricing is strictly preferred by manufacturers, since they can always set the fixed fee at zero. In other words, linear pricing is a special case of a two-part tariff.

Exclusive retailers and the law

In the United States, between the passage of the Sherman Act in 1890 and some time in the 1940s, most restraints on distribution, with the exception of resale price maintenance, were generally upheld as lawful.[12] After that time, however, standards began to grow stricter, and, by the mid-1960s, virtually every restraint on distribution had become suspect, and many had become illegal *per se*. This harsher attitude provoked a response by members of the 'Chicago school', notably Aaron Director and Lester Telser, which in turn led to a swing back towards a rule-of-reason approach. The arrival of the Reagan administration brought further change, which culminated in the publication of the Vertical Restraints Guidelines by the Antitrust Division of the Department of Justice. Those Guidelines embodied the view that the principal role of vertical restraints was to enhance efficiency. Moreover, a prominent feature of the Guidelines was the emergence of market-power 'screens' that exempted restraints that were imposed on brands with small market shares.

With the election of Clinton, however, the tide turned against the Chicago antitrust revolution, and the Guidelines were rescinded. Nevertheless, they have not been replaced, and no clear position on vertical restraints in general and exclusive dealing in particular has emerged in recent years.

In the United Kingdom, vertical relationships are governed by both UK and EU law.[13] Like the US, UK legislation provides no clear guidance as to the legality of vertical restrictions with the exception of resale price maintenance, which is frowned on by most competition authorities. Instead, the Monopolies and Mergers Commission has taken a case-by-case approach. The principal policy framework that governs relationships between manufacturers and their retailers therefore comes from the European Community.

Article 85(1) of the Treaty of Rome prohibits vertical agreements in fairly broad terms. However, it is possible to obtain block exemptions for many types of restrictions for specific industries. In particular, there are block exemptions for exclusive dealing in automobile, gasoline, and beer retailing. Exemptions do not give blanket approval. Instead, restraints are allowed subject to certain provisions. Moreover, agreements that are voluntarily undertaken by both parties are viewed with more favor than unilateral imposition of restrictions by manufacturers.

It seems that public policy towards vertical restraints and agreements is currently undergoing review and revision in the United States, the United Kingdom, and the European Union, and it is not yet clear which way the tide will turn. It is therefore a good time to assess a number of cases where competition authorities have intervened in the market in order to restrict certain industry practices that involve manufacturers and their exclusive retailers.

Three cases of regulation of manufacturers and their exclusive retailers

When one examines the actual regulation of manufacturer/retailer relationships, it becomes clear that its occurrence and stringency vary substantially across jurisdictions. For example, in the United States, manufacturer ownership of retail facilities is prohibited in both the automobile and the beer industries, whereas it is allowed in the gasoline industry. Furthermore, such ownership is common in all three industries in the United Kingdom. Another example is provided by wholesale distribution of beer, which is governed by individual US states. In some states exclusive sales territories are prohibited, in others they are mandated, and in still others, it is up to the wholesaler to choose a system.[14] Regulations and attitudes seem to be determined more by historical accident than by systematic policy based on economic reasoning.

In what follows, I examine three cases that are drawn from the US gasoline, the UK beer, and the US automobile industries. These cases were not chosen to illustrate a particular point. Rather they were selected because each had undergone considerable prior economic and econometric analysis. Nevertheless, the three have something in common. Each illustrates how piecemeal interference with a complex system of vertical arrangements can worsen matters from both the firms' and the consumers' points of view.

Tables 9.1 and 9.2 summarize a few facts about the three industries. Each compares the United States to the United Kingdom. All numbers in the tables pertain to the late 1980s, as consistent data were available only for that period.

Table 9.1 shows four-firm concentration ratios – the percentage of industry output produced by the four largest companies in the market.[15] In the United

Table 9.1 Four-firm concentration ratios, late 1980s (%)

Product	US	UK
Automobiles[a]	N/A	65
Beer[a]	82	59
Gasoline[b]	29	58

Notes: [a] Retail sales of manufacturer's brand.
[b] Wholesale sales of manufacturer's brand to retailers.

Table 9.2 Retail sales by contract type, late 1980s (%)

	Company owned and operated	*Company owned, dealer operated*	*Dealer owned and operated*
Automobiles			
US	0	0	100
UK	N/A	N/A	N/A
Beer			
US	0	0	100
UK	23	53	25
Gasoline			
US	23	43	34
UK	15	37	47

Kingdom, the numbers are close to 60 per cent in all three industries. There is more variability in the US numbers, however. In particular, the US beer industry is much more concentrated. This is perhaps due to the fact that US beer is mass produced and tends to rely on advertising rather than taste differences to create brand loyalty.

Table 9.2 shows the percentage of products that are sold under three types of contracts in each industry and country, where establishments are classified according to the ownership and operation of the outlet, as described above. As with concentration ratios, the United States is the outlier in that it prohibits company ownership in two out of three of the industries considered. In the remaining industry, gasoline, the US and UK numbers are roughly similar.

With this background information in mind, I turn to the three cases.

Gasoline retailing in the United States: the case of divorcement and open supply

Although US oil companies are generally allowed to operate their branded service stations themselves, company operation has met with considerable resistance and has even been outlawed by several states. In addition, although US service stations normally sell only one brand of gasoline, exclusive-dealing restrictions have also met with substantial opposition. These two movements have been labeled divorcement and open supply, respectively.

In the 1970s and 1980s, several US states passed laws prohibiting refiners from owning and operating retail outlets.[16] In other words, these laws prohibit direct and commissioned-agent (type 1) operations but allow companies to own leased (type 2) stations. In addition, in 1987, divorcement was proposed at the federal level, at least for the major refiners. However, it was not enacted. Proponents of divorcement argue that permitting refiners to act as both suppliers and competitors of lessee dealers is unfair and anti-competitive. Opponents argue that there is no evidence that refiners engage in discriminatory practices and that, more importantly, such discrimination would be contrary to the companies' self interest.

Open-supply legislation would prohibit refiners from requiring that their dealers not purchase gasoline from other sources (exclusive dealing).[17] Furthermore, it would allow the gasoline that was obtained from other sources to be sold through the affiliated refiner's branded outlets. Proponents claim that open supply would increase consumer choice, whereas opponents claim that it would limit consumer access to particular brands.

Behind these proposals is the idea that they would enhance competition, which would ultimately lead to lower retail prices. Nevertheless all systematic evidence points in the opposite direction. In particular, since divorcement forces company-operated stations to be converted to leased operations or to be sold to independents, it is important to know whether on average the latter types of stations post lower prices.

A number of researchers have examined this question and none has answered it in the affirmative. For example, Temple, Barker, and Sloane, Inc. (1988) found that the average price of regular unleaded gasoline sold at lessee-dealer stations was 1.5–2.2¢ per gallon higher than that sold at company-operated stations, and Shepard (1993) found a positive but statistically insignificant difference in average prices. Both of these studies assess differences in average prices across operating arrangements in a stable environment.[18]

Perhaps the most comprehensive study of divorcement was performed by Barron and Umbeck (1984), who considered a changing environment. These researchers looked at the effects of the divorcement legislation that was passed by the state of Maryland in 1974 on both retail prices and hours of operation, and found that divorcement led to higher prices and curtailed hours. They attributed higher prices at lessee dealerships to double marginalization and to external demand effects.[19] As discussed earlier, double marginalization results when there are successive stages of excess profit taking,[20] whereas external effects are due to pricing spillovers across stations of the same chain that can only be internalized by the refiner.

Open supply is much less common in gasoline retailing, and it is therefore not possible to assess average price differences across exclusive gasoline dealers and common agents.

It is interesting to note that divorcement of gasoline service stations has been consistently opposed by the US Federal Trade Commission. Furthermore, the Monopolies and Mergers Commission studied the situation in the United Kingdom and concluded that neither company operation of retail facilities nor exclusive-dealing restrictions were detrimental to consumer interest (MMC 1990). However, as we will see, the MMC reached a very different conclusion concerning the beer market.

Beer retailing in the United Kingdom: the case of divestiture

A large fraction of UK public houses are owned by brewers and operated under exclusive-dealing clauses.[21] This situation can be contrasted with the United States, where brewer ownership of retail facilities and exclusive-dealing clauses

are prohibited by federal and state laws. The US restrictions on brewer ownership, however, did not arise as a result of competition-policy considerations.
Instead, the motive behind the laws, which were passed after the repeal of prohibition in the 1930s, was the fear that alcohol retailing would become controlled
by organized crime.

Although UK brewer ownership of public houses and exclusive-dealing
clauses are permitted by a block exemption from Article 85(1) of the Treaty of
Rome, in 1989 the UK Monopolies and Mergers Commission recommended
measures that eventually led brewers to divest themselves of 14,000 licensed
premises. Unlike the situation in the US gasoline industry, where company-
operated outlets (or managed houses in the terminology that is used in the beer
industry) were sold or converted to leases, most of the divested pubs fell into
the tenanted class. In other words, with US gasoline, company operation was
outlawed, whereas with UK beer, company ownership came under attack. The
MMC (1989) claimed that their recommendations would result in lower retail
prices and greater consumer choice. The economic reasoning that lay behind
these claims, however, is not clear in their report .

My guess is that the MMC expected that the leased houses that were sold
would be purchased by independent retailers who would operate them as 'free'
houses (i.e., houses that are not constrained by exclusive-purchasing agreements). Had that happened, consumer choice within a pub would have increased.
Furthermore, the demand for individual brands would probably have become
more elastic as competition from the brands of rival manufacturers strengthened.
More elastic demand would lead in turn to lower profit-maximizing price/cost
margins and thus lower prices.

This counter-factual hypothesis can be assessed by examining systematic differences in the prices of the beers that are sold in tied and free houses.[22] If
demand is more elastic in the latter, prices should be higher in the former. Table
9.3 shows the results of a regression of the retail price of draft beer on a number
of explanatory variables. The data consist of a short panel of over 60 brands of
draft beers sold under two retailing arrangements (tied and free houses) in two
regions of the country (greater London and Anglia).[23] The table shows that, after

Table 9.3 Beer price equation

Variable	Coefficient	t statistic
TIED	12.61	13.1
ALCOHOL	17.88	19.3
COVERAGE	0.149	2.9
LONDON	5.614	6.0
FIRSTPERIOD	−2.102	−2.2
CONSTANT	86.67	20.6
Standard error of the estimate = 9.9	$R^2 = 0.77$	Mean of dependent variable = 165 pence per pint

Note: Product and brewer fixed effects not shown.

accounting for differences in product types (e.g., ale, stout, lager, bitter, or mild) and brewer identity, beer prices are significantly higher in tied houses (TIED = 1). In addition, prices are higher when the alcoholic content is greater (ALCOHOL is larger), when the brand is sold in a larger percentage of pubs (COVERAGE is higher), and when the region is London. Finally, prices were lower in the first period.

The change that actually occurred in the UK beer market after the 'Beer Orders' were passed, however, was very different. Indeed, most of the divested pubs were purchased by newly formed public-house chains, when many non-brewers, often in the food, hotel, or entertainment business, took advantage of the massive sales and purchased large blocks of licensed premises. Furthermore, many of the chain owners entered into long-term exclusive-purchasing agreements with the national brewers – the pubs' former owners. This meant that, in spite of the change in ownership, consumer choice did not improve.[24] Finally, the evidence points to increased, not lower retail prices after divestiture.

Both Keyworth *et al.* (1994) and Slade (1998b) assess the behavior of prices before and after the Beer Orders and conclude that divestiture was associated with higher prices. Furthermore, Slade (1998b), who has data by ownership type, finds that divestiture caused a significant increase in the difference between the prices charged in tied and free houses. Finally, this difference is attributed principally to the increased scope for double marginalization that emerged after the change in ownership.[25]

Recall that I argued earlier that fixed rental fees can be used by manufacturers to extract supercompetitive profits from retailers and thus avoid double marginalization. The move from leased houses to chains, however, removed the rental charges and therefore exacerbated the double marginalization problem. With this scenario, unlike the scenario in which pubs are purchased by independents, prices should rise after divestiture, as they in fact did.

We have seen that prohibition of manufacturer operation and/or ownership of retail facilities has been associated with increased marginalization and higher prices in the US gasoline and UK beer markets. In some markets, however, operation and ownership by upstream firms have been outlawed for decades. Furthermore, manufacturers might have other means to overcome the double marginalization problem. This suggests the possibility that higher prices might be a temporary feature that disappears when the ownership-transition period is complete.[26]

Automobile retailing in the United States: the case of dealer entrenchment

US retail automobile and beer markets have much in common. Indeed, manufacturer ownership of retail outlets is prohibited in both,[27] and distribution is often characterized by exclusive-territorial restrictions.[28] In the automobile industry, manufacturers justify exclusive-sales territories on the grounds that exclusivity encourages dealers to invest in showrooms and repair facilities as well as in more general forms of product promotion. The downside to exclusive territories from the manufacturers' point of view, however, is that they endow dealers with increased pricing power.

We have seen that dealer market power can be overcome when manufacturers own retail facilities. Indeed, rental rates can be used to extract retailer profits. This remedy, however, is not available in the auto industry because manufacturer ownership is prohibited by US law. Nevertheless, there are other restrictions that manufacturers can impose on their dealers in an attempt to alleviate the situation. For example, quantity forcing (i.e. minimum-sales quotas) can be used to increase supply and cause retail prices to fall. Furthermore, dealers who refuse to cooperate with manufacturers on pricing policy can be disciplined by having their franchises terminated or through having new dealerships located in their territories. Unfortunately, although these disciplinary practices can be efficiency enhancing, they can also be abused.

The regulatory environment in the US auto market prior to the 1940s tended to favor manufacturers in that the methods that they could use to discipline their retailers were virtually unrestricted. Public sentiment in favor of dealers began to increase, however, and this sentiment was embodied in the 1956 'Dealers' Day in Court Act'. Since that time many states have passed legislation requiring licensing of both manufacturers and dealers, prohibiting quantity forcing, and making it difficult for manufacturers to terminate dealer franchises or to locate new dealerships in existing territories. If the principal purpose of those practices had been the avoidance of double marginalization, retail prices should have risen when they were prohibited. If, on the other hand, those practices were routinely abused, no price increases should have accompanied the new legislation.

Smith II (1982) used the cross-sectional variation in the stringency of state regulation of automobile dealerships to test the dealer-entrenchment hypothesis (i.e., the hypothesis that prohibiting manufacturer disciplinary measures resulted in increased dealer market power and higher retail prices).[29] He found evidence in favor of entrenchment, but the evidence is not strong.

Conclusion

It is often thought that manufacturer/retailer relationships involve large upstream firms with considerable pricing power and small, competitive downstream outlets. For this reason, economists usually model vertical restraints in a principal/agent framework in which the principal has all of the bargaining power. Furthermore, much regulation was intended, at least originally, to protect the 'little guy'.

When public bodies interfere in the market, however, the result is not always what they intended. For example, instead of witnessing many independent small business people coming forward to purchase the divested UK public houses, pub chains formed. Moreover, those chains have used their bargaining power to obtain volume discounts from their suppliers.[30] In a similar fashion, European hypermarkets have entered retail gasoline markets and have used their strength to bargain with refiners over wholesale prices.[31] Many manufacturer/retailer relationships are thus better characterized by bilateral–monopoly bargaining than by bargaining with all rent going to the upstream party.

In addition, a number of researchers have shown that considerable rent can be left downstream to retailers, and that franchise markets can be characterized by queues and rationing.[32] When this is the case, an efficiency-wage model is more appropriate than one with a competitive retail sector.

Given that economists have at best an imperfect understanding of the complexity of retail markets, it is not surprising that regulators have made many mistakes. Indeed, public intervention has more often resulted in massive wealth transfers than in protection of the consumer. In particular, no clear-cut welfare gains were associated with the three cases that I have just discussed. With such a track record, public policy-makers and legislators should be cautious when they attempt to regulate manufacturers and their exclusive retailers.

A conclusion that emerges from my analysis is that a thorough review of public policy towards manufacturer/retailer relationships is long overdue. One would hope that, at very least, such a review would facilitate coordination of regulations across jurisdictions (e.g., eliminating the contradictory treatment of exclusive territories by different US states). Furthermore, in a world where markets are becoming increasingly more integrated, international boundaries seem less and less relevant to the design of competition policy. For example, it is difficult to justify outlawing manufacturer ownership of retail outlets in some industries in the United States while at the same time allowing ownership in the those same industries in the EU. Finally, given that, worldwide, public policy towards vertical agreements is in a state of flux, the time is ripe for international cooperation on this score. Unfortunately, I cannot offer a panacea. Hopefully, however, I have stimulated some thoughts on the subject.

Notes

1 For example, in the US, this fraction is about one third.
2 With business-format franchising, the franchisor provides a trademark, a marketing strategy, and quality control to the franchisee in exchange for royalty payments and up-front fees.
3 By pricing, monopoly, or oligopoly power I mean the ability to set price above marginal cost or to earn a rate of return that exceeds the competitive level.
4 See Spengler (1950) for a discussion of the double-marginalization phenomenon.
5 In the discussion of double marginalization, I assume that the market is monopolistic or monopolistically competitive and thus exclude more complex forms of strategic behavior.
6 The principal difference between these two forms is that the dealer has greater security of tenure under the former.
7 For example, see Knight (1921), Coase (1937), Williamson (1971), Alchian and Demsetz (1972), Rubin (1978), and Rey and Tirole (1986).
8 This literature also discusses incentives to invest in relationship-specific assets. Such assets, however, are apt to be less important with retailing than with input procurement.
9 Although, in theory, higher risk and a lack of repeat customers should lead to more

vertical integration, empirical assessments of these predictions show that they are not always valid (see Lafontaine and Slade, 1997 and 1998). The prediction that company-operated units should be larger and located in more urban environments, in contrast, is confirmed by the data.

10 Examples of multiple-market failures include double-sided moral hazard (Marvel, 1982, e.g., manufacturers promote the trade name and retailers provide customer service), games where principals control two or more choice variables (Besanko and Perry, 1993, e.g., manufacturers choose advertising levels as well as wholesale prices), moral hazard with risk-averse agents (Bernheim and Whinston, 1996, section 5, e.g., retailers' levels of customer service cannot be observed by manufacturers), and adverse selection with coordination problems (Gal-Or, 1991 and Martimort, 1996, e.g., retailers have superior information about their clientele and local demand conditions).

11 This is a general profit-maximizing condition. The perceived elasticity, however, will depend on the contractual arrangement.

12 For a more detailed discussion of the history of distribution law in the United States, see Steuer (1994).

13 For more details on UK and EU legal treatment of vertical agreements, see Dobson and Waterson (1996).

14 See Sass and Saurman (1993) for an analysis of exclusive territories in the US beer industry.

15 For automobiles and beer, these ratios pertain to retail sales of the manufacturer's product. For gasoline, in contrast, since many refiners sell their own product to smaller companies where it is resold under a different label, these ratios pertain to wholesale sales to retail establishments.

16 These states are Maryland, Delaware, Connecticut, Virginia and the District of Columbia.

17 Proposed legislation at the federal level would have allowed dealers to purchase up to 30 per cent of their gasoline supplies from refineries other than the one with which they were affiliated.

18 The MMC (1990, p. 95) looked at UK prices by contract type and also found that they were higher under tenants or licenses that under company ownership.

19 The strategic effects of divorcement could also lead to higher prices at leased operations, as in Slade (1998a).

20 Barron and Umbeck (1984) assume that a refiner's ability to use rental rates to extract profit from retailers is very limited.

21 For a history of brewer ownership and operation under exclusive-dealing clauses, see Vaizey (1960).

22 A tied house is one that operates under an exclusive-purchasing clause.

23 The data were collected by StatsMR, a subsidiary of A.C. Nielsen Company.

24 The introduction of a 'guest beer' at the same time, however, did result in more choice.

25 It is also argued that strategic considerations exacerbated the price increases.

26 An argument against this possibility is that higher prices have been found to be associated with less manufacturer control even in stable environments (e.g., Temple, Barker, and Sloane, Inc., 1988 and Shepard, 1993).

27 The severity of the strictures on manufacturer ownership of outlets, however, has lessened in recent years.

28 For an earlier account of the automobile distribution system, see Pashigian (1961).

29 Smith's data come from 1979, long after the original legislation was passed.

30 Discounts have not been passed on to the tenants of chains and have therefore not resulted in lower retail prices.

31 In the case of hypermarkets, retailer bargaining has resulted in lower consumer prices.

32 For example, Bresnahan and Reiss (1985), Temple, Barker, and Sloane, Inc. (1988) and Lafontaine (1996).

References

Alchian, A. A. and Demsetz, H. (1972) 'Production, information costs, and economic organization', *American Economic Review* 62, 777–795.

Barron, J. M. and Umbeck, J. R. (1984) 'The effects of different contractual arrangements: the case of retail gasoline', *Journal of Law and Economics* 27, 313–328.

Bernheim, B. D. and Whinston, M. D. (1998) 'Exclusive dealing', *Journal of Political Economy* 106, 64–103.

Besanko, D. and Perry, M. K. (1993) 'Equilibrium incentives for exclusive dealing in a differentiated-products oligopoly', *Rand Journal of Economics* 24, 646–667.

Bresnahan, T. F. and Reiss, P. C. (1985) 'Manufacturer and dealer margins', *Rand Journal of Economics* 16, 253–268.

Coase, R. (1937) 'The nature of the firm', *Economica* 4, 386–405.

Dobson, P. W. and Waterson, M. (1996) *The Public Policy Implications of Increasing Retailer Power*, University of Nottingham discussion paper.

Gal-Or, E. (1991) 'Common agency with incomplete information', *Rand Journal of Economics* 22, 274–286.

Keyworth, T., Lawton Smith, H. and Yarrow, G. (1994) *The Effects of Regulation in the UK Beer Market*, Oxford: Regulatory Policy Research Centre.

Knight, F. (1921) *Risk, Uncertainty, and Profit*, Chicago: Houghton Mifflin.

Lafontaine, F. (1996) *Journal of Law and Economics*.

Lafontaine, F. and Slade, M. E. (1997) 'Retail contracting: theory and practice', *Journal of Industrial Economics* 45, 1–25.

Lafontaine, F. and Slade, M.E. (1998) 'Incentive contracting and the franchise decision', Chapter 2 in K. Chatterjee and W. Samuelson (eds) *Advances in Business Applications of Game Theory*, Kluwer Academic Press, forthcoming.

Martimort, D. (1996) 'Exclusive dealing, common agency, and multiprincipals incentive theory', *Rand Journal of Economics* 27, 1–31.

Marvel. H. (1982) 'Exclusive dealing', *Journal of Law and Economics* 25, 1–25.

Monopolies and Mergers Commission (1989) *The Supply of Beer*, London: Her Majesty's Stationery Office.

Monopolies and Mergers Commission (1990) *The Supply of Petrol*, London: Her Majesty's Stationery Office.

Pashigian, B. P. (1961) *The Distribution of Automobiles: An Economic Analysis of the Franchise System*, Englewood Cliffs, NJ: Prentice-Hall.

Rey, P. and Tirole, J. (1986) 'The logic of vertical restraints', *American Economic Review* 76, 921–939.

Rubin, P. (1978) 'The theory of the firm and the structure of the franchise contract', *Journal of Law and Economics* 21, 223–233.

Sass, T. R. and Saurman, D. S. (1993) 'Mandated exclusive territories and economic efficiency: an empirical analysis of the malt-beverage industry', *Journal of Law and Economics* 36, 153–177.

Shepard, A. (1993) 'Contractual form, retail price, and asset characteristics', *Rand Journal of Economics* 24, 58–77.

Slade, M. E. (1998a) 'Strategic motives for vertical separation: evidence from retail gasoline', *Journal of Law, Economics, and Organization* 14, 84–113.

Slade, M. E. (1998b) 'Beer and the tie: did divestiture of brewer-owned public houses lead to higher beer prices?', *Economic Journal* 108, 1–38.

Smith II, R. L. (1982) 'Franchise regulation: an economic analysis of state restrictions on automobile distribution', *Journal of Law and Economics*, 25, 125–157.

Spengler, J. J. (1950) 'Vertical integration and antitrust policy', *Journal of Political Economy* 58, 347–352.

Steuer, R. M. (1994) 'The turning point in distribution law', in T. P. Kovaleff, (ed.) *The Antitrust Impulse: An Economic, Historical, and Legal Analysis*, Armonk, NY: Sharpe, 1137–1203.

Temple, Barker, & Sloane, Inc. (1988) *Gasoline Marketing in the 1980s: Structure, Practices, and Company Policy*, document prepared for the American Petroleum Institute, Washington, DC.

Vaizey, J. (1960) *The Brewing Industry, 1886–1950: An Economic Study*, London: Pitman.

Williamson, O. E. (1971) 'The vertical integration of production: market failure considerations', *American Economic Review* 61, 112–123.

10 Deregulating Norwegian airlines

Kjell G. Salvanes, Frode Steen and Lars Sørgard

Introduction

According to conventional wisdom, deregulation can result in substantial benefits for society. The key word is, as we all know, competition. It can result in
lower prices, and thereby force the firms to lower their costs. In a survey of the
effects of deregulation of American industry, Winston (1993) concluded that 'the
evidence clearly shows that microeconomists' predictions that deregulation
would produce substantial benefits for Americans have been generally accurate'.
However, the experience from the deregulation of the Norwegian airline industry differs from what we have seen in the United States. Deregulation also
changed the conduct in this industry, but not exactly in the way we expected.
Apart from some secret price cuts in exclusive dealing contracts between each
carrier and some large customers, prices did not fall in the most important market
segment, the business travellers segment. There was no substantial improvement
in service frequency concerning time scheduling of flights, but rather a tendency
of local clustering. The battle for market shares has resulted in intense rivalry
along other dimensions than price, such as advertising, service and number of
flights. On the other hand, the large number of flights has resulted in an increased
number of seats available in the leisure travellers' segment, where we have
experienced lower prices.

In what follows, we will first describe the initial, pre-deregulation situation in
this particular industry. Then we will explain the consequences of deregulation,
focusing on the effect on prices, capacity and time-scheduling of flights. Finally,
we summarize and discuss briefly how entry might affect the market outcome.

The regulation era: legal monopolies and market segmentation

The largest routes in Norway are of almost equal size to the routes between many
specific airports within Europe as well as within the United States.[1] Therefore,
the experience in the Norwegian airline industry can be of interest for what
may happen in airline industries in other countries. As in most countries, the
Norwegian airline industry has been heavily regulated. For each route, one single

firm was given the exclusive right to offer flights. Both prices and time location of flight departures were regulated. In October 1987, a second airline was permitted a limited number of flights for a few particular routes – with a maximum of four flights at on each route. The first carrier could, though, act as a monopolist on the residual demand on those routes. Both prices and time location continued to be regulated by the government. However, there are indications that the regulation was not a binding constraint on each firm's price setting.[2]

The airline industry in Norway, as well as in many other countries, provides us with a textbook example of third degree price discrimination. The business travellers typically have a low price elasticity of demand, while the leisure/holiday travellers' demand typically is more sensitive to price changes. The two kinds of customers were segmented by setting restrictions on the travelling pattern for the low price tickets. In particular, low price tickets had to be bought and often paid for in advance, and the night between Saturday and Sunday had to be spent away from home. Thereby, each carrier succeeded in charging a high price from the business travellers and at the same time a low price from the leisure/holiday travellers.

Figure 10.1 illustrates the effect of third degree price discrimination. The difference in price elasticity in the two segments is illustrated by a flatter demand curve in the leisure segment than in the business segment. When marginal revenue in each segment is set equal to marginal costs, the final price to the consumers differs between the two segments. We will argue that the market segmentation still remains, and that the post-deregulation rivalry has widened the gap between prices in these two segments. Prices in the leisure segment have fallen, while prices in the business segment have remained high.

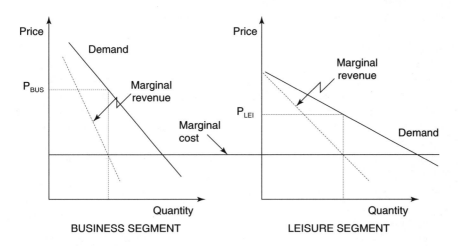

Figure 10.1 Price discrimination

Compete, collude, or both?

In April 1994, all routes, except those between the smallest airports, were further deregulated. Free entry was permitted, and the airlines were free to set prices as well as departure times for their flights. However, there were two restrictions on entry. First, only Norwegian firms were allowed to enter. Second, there was a limited number of slots available at Fornebu, the airport near Oslo, at peak hours. The latter was not a *de jure*, but a *de facto* entry barrier.

It turned out that the two incumbent firms for the routes in question, SAS and Braathens, became the only active firms in the deregulated system. Prior to deregulation, both firms threatened to cut prices following deregulation. However, a study indicates that there was no price reduction on the full fare tickets in the business travellers' segment following deregulation, and only a minor increase in the share of discounted tickets.[3] The study, however, is not an empirical test. The conclusions are drawn from observing descriptive statistics. Therefore, one could ask whether the firms colluded on prices or whether customers shifted from purchasing full fare to discounted tickets. If the latter is true, we have *de facto* competition on prices although the prices of full fare tickets are not affected by the deregulation. Furthermore, the exclusive dealing agreements between each carrier and some of the large customers (large firms) are not taken into account. In these contracts prices are cut secretly. It is thus not clear whether prices in the business segment are quite high as the referred study indicates, or whether the secret price cuts and the shifts to discounted tickets are of large importance.

There are also some casual observations suggesting that there has been a large increase in capacity following deregulation.[4] However, one possible explanation could be that this is due to a general growth in demand. Alternatively, the capacity increase might also be triggered by collusion on prices. A high price-cost margin in the business segment gives each firm strong incentives to increase its capacity to capture market shares. Hence, it is natural to ask whether the firms competed on capacity and colluded on prices in the business segment after the deregulation. This is what we have set out to test.

We made an econometric study where we test for the nature of competition concerning both price and capacity setting (Salvanes *et al.*, 1998a). We have data for twelve routes in the period 1985–96, and half of them remained monopolies also after the deregulation in 1994. Prior to deregulation, we assume that there was a *de facto* collusion on both prices and capacity. Then we proceed in two steps.

First, we test whether there was a structural break in the capacity level following deregulation. We find a significantly larger increase in capacity on those routes where both firms were active than on those routes where only one firm was active after deregulation. This suggests that deregulation triggered competition on the duopoly routes.

Second, we ask what nature of competition prevailed after deregulation on the duopoly routes. There are two possible outcomes: either they compete on capacity and collude on prices, or they compete on both capacity and prices. The former we label semi-collusion, and the latter competition.[5] To distinguish between these two cases, we have derived how a change in demand is expected to affect the choice of capacity. This is illustrated in Figure 10.2.

Note from Figure 10.2 that if market size is large, then we expect capacity to be more sensitive to changes in market demand in the semi-collusive regime than in the competitive regime. To understand this, note that an expansion of own capacity will result in a lower price in the competitive regime. This dampens the incentive to expand capacity. In the semi-collusive regime, on the other hand, such a capacity expansion does not affect the price. The only – and important – effect is that it increases the firm's market share, since its market share is determined by its share of total capacity.[6] The larger the market size, the larger the absolute increase in sale by increasing the market share by a certain amount. Hence, a firm has stronger incentives to expand its capacity, the larger the market size. With a limited market size, however, there is no reason to expand its capacity more than the increase in market size, because the absolute increase in sale from increasing the market share is limited.

We tested the relationship between market size and capacity, and found that a change in market size has a significantly larger relative impact on large routes than on small routes. However, monopoly routes are typically small routes and duopoly routes are primarily large routes. The difference can therefore be due to a comparison of monopoly and duopoly routes rather than to the nature of competition on duopoly routes. Therefore, we have also tested for the duopoly routes only. Again, we find that a change in market demand has a significantly larger impact on large routes than on small routes. This is consistent with semi-collusion, where they collude on prices and compete on capacity, but inconsistent with competition. One interpretation is that a high price–cost margin in the business segment triggers intense rivalry for capacity in order to capture market

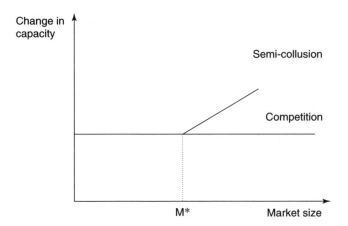

Figure 10.2 Market size and the relationship between market size and change in capacity

shares in that particular segment. Almost 60 per cent of the tickets are full price (non-rebated) tickets (Lian, 1996), while the exclusive dealing agreements with large customers amounts to less than 20 per cent of the total demand (Konkurransetilsynet, 1998). Then approximately 40 per cent of the passengers are using a full price ticket, which suggests that the business segment is very important for the two carriers. It is therefore plausible that collusion on prices in the business segment has triggered a battle for market shares in that segment.

One might think that semi-collusion is a very rare phenomenon, and therefore not of interest for other markets. However, in the literature we find numerous examples of semi-collusion both in theory and in real life.[7] Just to mention a few, semi-collusion was observed in the American cigarette and cement industries in the 1920s and 1930s, the German cement industry in the 1930s, the Norwegian cement industry in the 1950s and 1960s, among Japanese exporting firms in the 1950s and 1960s, and in ocean shipping.[8] This illustrates that such a nature of competition should be taken into consideration as one possible scenario when discussing the possible effects of deregulating a particular industry.

Why collusion on prices?

As reported above, we have found support for collusion on prices and competition on capacities. The former is consistent with a descriptive study, concluding that firms colluded on prices in the business segment, and it suggests that the secret price cuts in the exclusive dealing agreements are of minor importance (see note 4). Let us point out four factors that can explain why the firms have succeeded in avoiding price competition in the business segment.

First, there is a potential for collusive behaviour in this particular industry. There are only two active firms, and until April 1997 foreign firms were not permitted to serve domestic routes in Norway. Price changes will either be announced in the press or made through a travel agency, which in both cases will quickly be observed by the rival. Hence, both firms can quickly respond to the rival's price changes. Furthermore, both firms have expanded their capacity significantly following deregulation. As a result, both firms are able to expand their sale in the business segment and thus cut prices significantly following any possible cartel breakdown.

Second, the two firms had almost equal market shares in the domestic market initially, and it was natural to continue with the initial market sharing in the deregulated system. In fact, there were only minor changes in the market shares on each route as well as in the total market shares after deregulation.[9] On 24 out of the 32 city-pair routes, the initial monopoly carrier continued to be a monopolist. For the remaining eight routes, the pre-deregulation dominant firm continued to have a dominant position. On average, the dominant firm had a 13 per cent points' reduction in market share on these eight routes, and it had no less than 60 per cent market share on any of the routes in the deregulated regime.[10]

Third, for those routes where both firms did have flights, there exists a system for coordinating prices. The firms are permitted to consult each other concerning price setting. To allow for late changes of flight schedules for normal (not discount) tickets, from one airline to another, the airlines have 'transferable' prices. To implement such a policy, the firms are permitted to meet regularly to inform each other concerning future prices on non-rebated tickets – labelled interline tickets. Hence, there exists an institutional pre-play communication system where each firm can inform its rival about its future prices on normal tickets.

Fourth, the firms signalled an aggressive response to any move by its rival. In particular, each firm matches the rival's offer. For example, prior to deregulation Braathens introduced a rebate ticket *Billy* to match SAS' rebate ticket *Jackpot* and set a price NOK 5 below the *Jackpot* price. SAS responded immediately by reducing its *Jackpot* price by NOK 5. A statement by a representative for Braathens suggests that this is a deliberate policy for the firms in question: 'We will match any offer by SAS within an hour, and we cannot accept that SAS has cheaper discount tickets than we have' (C. Fougli to *Dagens Næringsliv*, 20 January 1994, our translation). Such apparently aggressive behaviour is analogous to the introduction of a meet-competition clause. As shown in the literature, a meet-competition clause may have a dampening-of-competition effect (Salop, 1986). An explanation of this principle, which may also serve as an illustration of the companies' strategy, was provided by Audun Tjomsland, the public relation manager for Braathens:

> The two Norwegian firms on the Norwegian routes, Braathens and SAS, are of equal size and can follow each other during a price war. The firm that starts a price war will quickly be followed by the rival firm, so that the firm that starts a war will have an advantage only for a day or two. Accordingly, the firms are reluctant to trigger a price war.
>
> (*Bergens Tidende*, 31 July, 1995, our translation)

Although the study we referred to suggests that there was no fierce price competition in the business segment following deregulation, casual observation suggests that there has been more price competition in the leisure segment, where the firms offer discounted tickets. As mentioned above, the two firms competed on prices with identical kind of offers like *Billy* and *Jackpot*, respectively. These were discounted tickets with restrictions which made them unattractive for business travellers. There are numerous other examples of discounted tickets with restrictions, where the firms matched the rival firm's offer. For example, in the summer of 1996 both SAS and Braathens introduced 50th anniversary tickets, which also were discount tickets with restrictions.

Clustering of departures?

Given no collusion on prices in the business segment, how would we expect firms to locate their flight departures? According to the theory of location, it is ambiguous whether a firm should locate close to its rival or not.[11] On the one hand, it should locate close to its rival to capture market shares. On the other hand, it should locate far away from its rival to dampen price competition. Typically, then, there are incentives for a firm to locate close to its rival – clustering – if there is competition on location, but not on prices.[12] However, the fact that each firm has several products – or more than one flight on each route – makes it troublesome to make clear-cut predictions from theory even when there is no competition on prices. There are examples, though, where theory predicts local clustering, as shown in Figure 10.3.[13]

In the two examples shown in Figure 10.3, the battle for market shares results in local clustering or, put differently, pairwise flights. However, there are many examples where we expect inherent instability. In particular, the firm with a large number of flights will try to squeeze the firm with a low number of flights by locating flights close to theirs on both sides. Theory, then, has no clear-cut predictions. Moreover, if we observe price competition, the theory is even less clear-cut.[14] Then the question is: what do we actually observe?

We have done an econometric study of the location of flight departures (Salvanes *et al.*, 1998b). We investigated twelve routes, six of which remained monopolies after the deregulation. Before we proceeded to actually test for the effect of deregulation, we tested whether regulation did have an impact on location. We found that deregulation did not have any significant impact on the time location of flights on the monopoly routes. This suggests that the change in location pattern we have observed is not due to some binding regulatory constraint that was abolished, but rather due to the nature of competition that emerged when some routes changed from monopoly to duopoly routes.

We then know that the possible changes we observe in time-scheduling on those routes that are becoming duopolies, are changes from monopoly to duopoly and not from regulation to duopoly. There are three main findings we can report from our empirical testing, all of which can be illustrated with the time locations on the two routes Oslo–Bodø and Oslo–Stavanger, shown in Figures 10.4 and 10.5.

First, deregulation seems to have no or only a limited effect on the time-scheduling pattern within each airline. In particular, the first carrier – the one with the largest number of flights – seems to spread its flights throughout the day both before and after deregulation.

Second, the second carrier on each route has a tendency to locate its departures close to those of the incumbent firm. This is particularly clear on the route

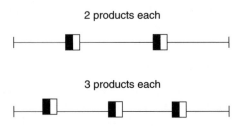

Figure 10.3 Location with no price competition

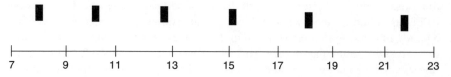

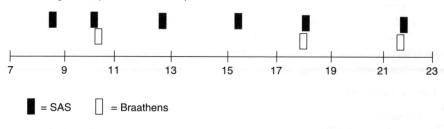

Figure 10.4 Flight departures Oslo–Bodø before and after deregulation

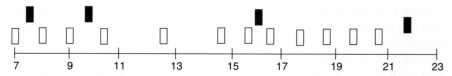

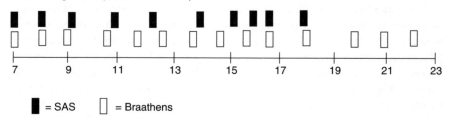

Figure 10.5 Flight departures Oslo–Stavanger before and after deregulation

Oslo–Bodø, the smaller of those two routes. On the larger route, the picture is not so clear-cut. This leads us to our third observation.

Third, the tendency towards pairwise flights seems to be more prevalent in the morning segment as well as in the afternoon segment than in general. This is especially the case if we look at the route Oslo–Stavanger. In these segments, 7:00–10:00 and 15:30–18:00, the typical passenger is a business traveller.

One interpretation of our results is the following. The dominant carrier on each route has a policy of offering a high degree of service frequency. It spreads out its flights on those routes where it faces a rival. The second carrier, however, has a policy of offering flights primarily in the business segment, and to locate close to its rival to capture passengers. This is consistent with what we found when we investigated the nature of competition concerning capacities. We then found support for price collusion, which triggered intense rivalry on capacities. Our results concerning location suggest that the rivalry on capacities indeed was a battle for market shares in the business segment.

Interestingly, we have then found a tendency towards clustering only in the segment with collusion on prices. This illustrates a general conclusion from theory, which says that a relaxation of price competition will give the firms incentives to locate close to each other in order to capture market shares.[15]

Policy implications

The deregulation of the Norwegian airline industry was supposed to promote competition, which it certainly did. But competition was distinctly different from what we traditionally expected it to be. We did not observe a general fall in prices or an increase in service frequency. Instead, we observed collusion on prices in the business segment. Such a high price-cost margin in the most important segment triggered competition on capacities. This is an example of a prisoners' dilemma situation, where both firms increase their capacity in order to increase market shares. The firms seem to be aware this problem. For example, Braathens explained its poor result in the first quarter of 1996 as follows: 'Braathens explains this [poor result] by increased competition. The firm has increased its capacity, but this has not helped much. The growth results in an increase in employment and other costs of production' (*Dagens Næringsliv*, 10 May 1996, our translation).

A few months earlier, SAS had announced several new initiatives: 'Among the initiatives are recruitment on the ground and in the cabin, adjustment of time-scheduling of flights, an increase in capacity amounting to 400,000 seats annually, better food on business class between Norway and other countries' (*Bergens Tidende*, 9 March 1996, our translation. The battle for market shares resulted in pairwise flights in the business segment, and the increase in service frequency was therefore very limited, at best. The large number of seats available implied that the airlines had idle seats available for the leisure segment. Therefore, after deregulation they competed fiercely for the passengers in the leisure segment. No surprise, then, that after deregulation we have observed an even larger difference between the prices in the business segment and the leisure segment.[16] Some of the effects of deregulation are illustrated in Figure 10.6.

The fall in prices in the leisure segment following deregulation is beneficial to society, shown by the trapezium which is marked in Figure 10.6. The installment of extra capacity, shown in Figure 10.6 by the increase in capacity from K_0 to K_1, is costly for both the firms and society. The costs associated with this install-

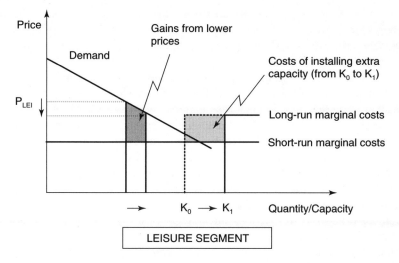

Figure 10.6 The effects of deregulation

ment of extra capacity – which is partly idle capacity – are shown with the rectangle which is marked in Figure 10.6.

We see that the welfare effect of deregulation is ambiguous. On the one hand, lower prices in the leisure segment are beneficial to society. In addition, secret price cuts in the exclusive dealing contracts are beneficial to society as well. Finally, although the increase in the number of flights has no or only a limited effect on frequency, the flexibility for business travellers is probably improved. A late rescheduling can now be easier, because there are more vacant seats available.[17] On the other hand, excess investment in capacity is costly for society. This is typically also true for some other decisions by each firm which is triggered by collusion on prices, such as advertising. One could then argue that society would be better off with one monopoly airline serving the business segment, supplemented by low price airline(s) competing only in the leisure segment. This would be a remedy against the local clustering of flight departures in the business segment, it could dampen the excess investment in capacity, and at the same time ensure price competition in the leisure segment. This illustrates that semi-collusion, which we earlier argued can be present in many industries, can be detrimental to welfare.

However, this does not solve the main problem in this industry: the lack of price competition in the business segment. What, then, should the government have done? There are some antitrust policy lessons to be learnt from the experience in Norway. In particular, the government should have made it difficult for the firms both to find a market-sharing arrangement and to coordinate prices. A second carrier should never have been allowed to enter the market prior to deregulating, as it did in Norway. Both firms were active on the largest routes before deregulation, and this made the transition from regulation to deregulation a very smooth process.[18] Now it is too late to take any action in this respect.

On the other hand, the government still has the option of denying the airlines the opportunity to consult each other concerning prices on full price tickets. Obviously, such an arrangement promotes collusion on prices and should therefore be abolished.

In October 1998, the new main airport for Oslo – Gardermoen – opened. The number of available slots will increase, though only gradually. Several new airlines have announced that they will enter the market, and one firm – Color Air – established flights on some particular routes already in August 1998. Hopefully, this might destabilize the semi-collusion we have observed in this industry before the opening of Gardermoen. However, it is of interest to observe how SAS and Braathens responded to Color Air's entry prior to the opening of Gardermoen. Color Air has low prices, and both SAS and Braathens responded in August 1998 by undercutting their prices on the routes in question. However, the two incumbent firms have restrictions on these discounted tickets so that they are not attractive to business people. Apparently, then, the incumbent airlines hope that the new entrant is a rival only in the leisure segment. If so, we shall not see any changes in the rivalry in the business segment. Given the existence of semi-collusion, this should come as no surprise. The present capacity competition between SAS and Braathens implies that a third carrier also has to install a large capacity to be attractive for the passengers in the business segment. It is doubtful whether it would be profitable for a third carrier to engage in such intense rivalry for capacity, even if collusion on prices in the business segment is maintained. So even if prices are high, the endogenous investment in capacity in this particular industry may deter potential entrants.

Despite the doubts raised here, there is still a chance that the new entrants will destabilize the collusion on prices in the business segment. But if they do not succeed in that respect, then what could the government do? As mentioned above, the ban of price coordination is still a measure that can destabilize collusion on prices in the business segment. If that is not enough, other measures must be implemented. The anti-trust authorities have decided not to publish the rebates each airline has given in exclusive dealing contracts with large customers. This is a good thing, because secrecy concerning price setting gives each firm stronger incentives to cheat on the collusive outcome. The government is a very large customer, and might destabilize the collusive outcome if they, for example, decided to have an exclusive dealing agreement for a quite long time period for the total government purchase in this market, and encouraged other large customers to do the same. No doubt, this will create some turbulence in this industry. Although turbulence is not what we would like to promote in general in the airline industry, that kind of turbulence in this particular industry is a good thing for society.

Notes

1 Not surprisingly, the number of flights between city pairs as, for example, San Francisco–Los Angeles and London–Amsterdam, is much higher than between city pairs in Norway. However, when we take into account the fact that there are several airports in each of these large cities, then the number of flights between specific air-

ports is at the same level as the number of flights on the largest routes in Norway (Strandenes, 1990).

2 The regulation dates back to the 1940s. At that time the Norwegian economy was heavily regulated, with no focus on antitrust issues. Each firm had to apply to the civil aviation authorities concerning price changes. Then each firm could argue that they had had cost increases, an argument that the authorities would find difficult to disprove. Norman and Strandenes (1994) have calibrated the market equilibrium on the route Stockholm–Oslo prior to deregulation in 1993, and they conclude that '[i]nsofar as our calibrated coefficients seem "reasonable", the regulatory constraint cannot be severe' (ibid. p. 96).

3 This is shown in Lian (1996). He finds that the share of the discounted tickets increased by 2.5 per cent from 1992 to 1994–95. According to Lian (1996) this is no dramatic change: 'a 2–3 %-point increase in discount tickets in two–three years is in line with a long-term trend and implies no sudden change in this trend' (our translation) (ibid., p. 15). The increase in the share of discounted tickets are larger in the 'leisure' segment than in the business segment (Lian, 1996, Table 4.4).

4 For example, during the first year after deregulation, total capacity for routes to and from Oslo increased by 12.5 per cent (Lian 1996, Table 5.2).

5 As shown in Kreps and Scheinkman (1983), capacity setting followed by price setting may yield a Cournot outcome. Hence, what we label as competition is Cournot competition. Alternatively, we could assume Bertrand competition. This would not have changed the distinction between competition and collusion shown in Figure 10.2. The outcome in the semi-collusive regime follows from the model in Fershtman and Gandal (1994).

6 There are at least two reasons for a positive relationship between own share of total capacity and own share of total sale. First, the larger the capacity the larger the probability that the airline firm in question has a vacant seat. Second, the larger the capacity, the larger the number of flights, and thereby the larger the service frequency for the airline firm in question. More generally, when products and prices are identical, it is reasonable to assume that demand is distributed so that each firm's sale is related to its share of total supply in the market.

7 All theoretical studies of semi-collusion assume collusion in the product market (either on prices or quantity) and competition along other dimensions. Competition on capacity is analysed in Fershtman and Muller (1986), Osborne and Pitchik (1987), Davidson and Deneckere (1990), Matsui (1989) and Fershtman and Gandal (1994); competition on R&D is analysed in Katz (1986), D'Aspremont and Jacquemin (1987), Kamien et al. (1992) and Fershtman and Gandal (1994); competition on location is analysed in Friedman and Thisse (1993). For a survey of the literature, see Fershtman and Gandal (1994) or Phlips (1995), Chapters 9 and 10.

8 Price collusion led to intense rivalry for advertising in the American cigarette industry (Scherer, 1980, pp. 388–389), the installing of excess capacity in the German (Scherer, 1980, p. 370) as well as the US cement industry (Scherer and Ross, 1990, p. 674), and to excess capacity in ocean shipping (Scherer and Ross, 1990, p. 674). The existence of cartels in the domestic Japanese market, where quotas were allocated according to relative capacity, led to excess capacity in many Japanese industries during the 1950s and 1960s (Matsui, 1989). The price cartel in the Norwegian cement market led to the installment of excess capacity in the Norwegian cement industry in the 1950s and 1960s, which showed up as a large increase in exports (Steen and Sørgard, 1998).

9 Each firm's market share changed only modestly following deregulation; Braathens increased its market share from approximately 50 per cent in 1993 to 52 per cent in 1995 (Lorentzen et al., 1996).

10 The exception is the route Bodø–Tromsø, where each had two non-stop flights both before and after April 1994.

11 For an overview of the literature on location, see Eaton and Lipsey (1989) or Gabszewics and Thisse (1992).

12 Friedman and Thisse (1993) show that collusion on prices in a duopoly after location if chosen non-collusively results in clustering. This restores the classical result found in Hotelling (1929).

13 The example is from Eaton and Lipsey (1975). See also Gabszewicz and Thisse (1986).

14 Whether there is clustering or not in the equilibrium outcome depends on, *inter alia*, the structure of the transportation costs and the consumer heterogeneity. For example, d'Aspremont, Gabszewics and Thisse (1979) apply a model with quadratic transportation costs and find that maximum differentiation is obtained. On the other hand, De Palma *et al.* (1985) show that minimum differentiation is obtained if there is sufficient consumer heterogeneity.

15 See, for example, Tirole (1988) who concludes that one important insight from spatial models is that firms want to differentiate their products from their rivals' products to soften price competition (pp. 286–287). In Borenstein and Netz (1997), a study very much in the same spirit as ours, concerning flight departures, time schedules of flights in the United States before and after deregulation in 1978 are tested empirically. They found that price competition typically resulted in less clustering of flight departures.

16 As shown in Lian (1996), the prices of normal (non-rebated) tickets were not affected by deregulation. In addition, we have seen numerous examples of low price tickets tailored to the leisure segment. In September 1998, for example, Braathens offered a return ticket in Southern Norway for NOK 700 for two persons. Including taxes, the price per person is NOK 496. On the route Oslo–Bergen a full price return ticket, including taxes, amounts to NOK 2450. Then the price of the rebated ticket is 20 per cent of the price of the full price ticket.

17 It is, however, an open question whether this is of any large importance. Note that a monopoly has incentives to hold vacant seats as long as possible, in order to offer any person purchasing a full fare ticket very late a seat. Therefore, one could argue that flexibility is expected to be high even before deregulation.

18 In Sweden, in contrast, the two active firms SAS and Linjeflyg merged prior to the deregulation in 1992. New airlines challenged the merged incumbent firm, and we observed price competition (Randøy and Strandenes, 1997).

References

Borenstein, S. and Netz, J. (1997) 'Why do all flights leave at 8am? Competition and departure-time differentiation in airline markets', *International Journal of Industrial Organization*, forthcoming.

D'Aspremont, C., Gabszewicz, J.-J. and Thisse, J. (1979) 'On Hotelling's "Stability in competition"', *Econometrica* 47, 1145–1150.

D'Aspremont, C. and Jacquemin, A. (1987) 'Cooperative and noncooperative R&D in duopoly with spillovers', *American Economic Review* 78, 1133–1137.

Davidson, C. and Deneckere, R. (1986) 'Long-term competition in capacity, short-run competition in price, and the Cournot model', *Rand Journal of Economics* 17, 404–415.

Davidson, C. and Deneckere, R. (1990) 'Excess capacity and collusion', *International Economic Review* 31, 521–541.

DePalma, A., Ginsburg, V., Papageorgiou, Y. and Thisse, J.-F. (1985) 'The principle of minimum differentiation holds under sufficient heterogeneity', *Econometrica* 53, 767–781.

Eaton, B. C. and Lipsey, R. C. (1975) 'The principle of minimum differentiation reconsidered: some new developments in the theory of spatial competition', *Review of Economic Studies* 42, 27–49.

Eaton, B. C. and Lipsey, R. C. (1989) 'Product differentiation', in R. Schmalensee and R. Willig (eds), *Handbook of Industrial Organization*, vol I, Amsterdam: North-Holland.

Fershtman, C. and Gandal, N. (1994) 'Disadvantageous semicollusion', *International Journal of Industrial Organization* 12, 141–154.

Fershtman, C. and Muller, E. (1986) 'Capital investment and price agreement in semicollusive markets', *Rand Journal of Economics* 17, 214–226.

Friedman, J. M. and Thisse, J.-F. (1993) 'Partial collusion fosters minimum product differentiation', *Rand Journal of Economics* 24, 631–645.

Gabszewicz, J. and Thisse, J.-F. (1986) 'Spatial competition and the location of firms', in J. Gabszewicz, J.-F. Thisse, M. Fujiata and U. Schweizer (eds) *Location Theory*, London: Harwood Academic Press.

Gabszewicz, J. and Thisse, J.-F. (1992) 'Location', in R. Aumann and S. Hart (eds) *Handbook of Game Theory*, Amsterdam: North-Holland.

Hotelling, H. (1929) 'Stability in competition', *Economic Journal* 34, 41–57.

Kamien, M., Muller, E. and Zang, I. (1992) 'Research joint ventures and R&D Cartels', *American Economic Review* 82, 1293–1306.

Katz, M. (1986) 'An analysis of cooperative research and development', *Rand Journal of Economics* 17, 527–543.

Konkurransetilsynet (1998) *SAS' erverv av aksjer i Widerøe's flyveselskap ASA* (SAS' acquisition of shares in Widerøe's flyveselskap ASA), Konkurransetilsynets vedtak nr. 98/43 av 15.juni 1998 etter konkurranselovens § 3–11 i sak 97/1578.

Kreps, D. and Scheinkman, J. (1983) 'Quantity precommitment and Bertrand competition yield Cournot outcome', *Bell Journal of Economics* 14, 326–337.

Lian, J. I. (1996) *Økt luftfartskonkurranse?* (An increase in airline competition?), TØI-rapport nr. 322/1996, Transportøkonomisk Institutt, Oslo.

Lorentzen, I. C., Randøy, T. and Strandenes, S. P. (1996) *En samfunnsøkonomisk vurdering av SAS-samarbeidet* (An economic evaluation of the SAS-co-operation), SNF-report no. 48/96, SNF, Bergen.

Martines-Giralt, X. and Neven, D. J. (1988) 'Can price competition dominate market segmentation?', *Journal of Industrial Economics* 36, 431–442.

Matsui, A. (1989) 'Consumer-benefited cartels under strategic capital investment competition', *International Journal of Industrial Organization* 7, 451–470.

Norman, V. D. and Strandenes, S. P. (1994) 'Deregulation of Scandinavian airlines: a case study of the Oslo–Stockholm route', Chapter 4 in P. Krugman and A. Smith (eds) *Empirical Studies of Strategic Trade Policy*, Chicago: University of Chicago Press.

Osborne, M. and Pitchik, C. (1987) 'Cartels, profits and excess capacity', *International Economic Review* 28, 413–428.

Phlips, L. (1995) *Competition Policy: A Game-theoretic Perspective* London: Cambridge University Press.

Randøy, T. and Strandenes, S. P. (1997) 'The effect of public ownership and deregulation in the Scandinavian airline industry', *Journal of Air Transport Management* 3, 211–215.

Salop, S. (1986) 'Practices that (credibly) facilitate oligopoly co-ordination', in J. E. Stiglitz and G. F. Matthewson (eds) *New Developments in the Analysis of Market Structure*, London: Macmillan Press.

Salvanes, K.G., Steen, F. and Sørgard, L. (1998a) *Compete, Collude, or Both?*

Deregulation in the Norwegian Airline Industry, mimeo, Bergen: Norwegian School of Economics and Business Administration.

Salvanes, K.G., Steen, F. and Sørgard, L. (1998b) *Hotelling in the air? Flight departures in Norway*, mimeo, Bergen: Norwegian School of Economics and Business Administration.

Scherer, F. (1980) *Industrial Market Structure and Economic Performance*, Boston: Houghton-Mifflin.

Scherer, F. and Ross, D. (1990) *Industrial Market Structure and Economic Performance*, Boston: Houghton-Mifflin.

Steen, F. and Sørgard, L. (1998) 'Semicollusion in the Norwegian cement market', *European Economic Review*, forthcoming.

Strandenes, S. P. (1990) 'Regulering og konkurranse i skandinavisk luftfart' (Regulation and competition in the Scandinavian airline industry), in L. Sørgard (ed.) *Næringsøkonomi – 13 norske bransjestudier* (*Industrial Economics – 13 Norwegian Industry Studies*), Oslo: Bedriftsøkonomens Forlag.

Tirole, J. (1988) *The Theory of Industrial Organization*, Cambridge, MA: MIT Press.

Winston, C. (1993) 'Economic deregulation: days of reckoning for microeconomists', *Journal of Economic Literature* 31, 1263–1289.

11 Resource allocation by a competition authority

Stephen Martin

And when we deal with questions relating to principles of law and their applications, we do not suddenly rise into a stratosphere of icy certainty.

(Charles Evans Hughes)

Introduction

The workings of the law are uncertain. This is true in general and it is true for antitrust or competition law.

If firms are found to have violated competition policy, they open themselves up to the possibility of fines[1] – if the offending conduct is detected, if the enforcement agency decides to levy a fine or challenge the conduct in court, if a trial court sustains the enforcement agency, and, if all of these things come to pass, if the trial court is not overturned in the event of appeal to higher courts.

In some cases it is clear that a certain course of action violates competition policy. If a manufacturer has distributors in several EU member states, and forbids those distributors to sell across national boundaries, the manufacturer knows it is violating EU competition policy. Uncertainty is then limited to whether or not the conduct will be detected and the sizes of legal expenses and the eventual fine.

In other cases, whether a course of action violates competition law is far from clear in advance. For example, behavior that is found to constitute illegal collusion in one instance is often difficult to distinguish from behavior that is found to be legal conscious parallelism in another.[2]

Conscious parallelism decisions in both the European Union and the United States suggest that independent decisions independently arrived at will not be found to violate competition policy, even if those independent decisions lead to outcomes that generate economic profits over the long run. Some kinds of conduct will shift behavior from the legal category of 'independent' to the legal category of 'collusive', but exactly what kinds of conduct will have this effect sometimes seems idiosyncratic.[3,4]

In like manner, it seems fair to say that at this writing (September 1998), it is not clear whether the marketing practices that have been used by Microsoft Corporation for its operating systems and network browsers violate US antitrust law.

In this chapter, I develop a model of a competition authority that administers a deterrence-based competition policy regulating firm conduct[5] within a legal system that harbors an irreducible element of uncertainty. Firms and the competition authority take this uncertainty into account in deciding their actions.

The basic model, presented in the second section, considers a competition authority and two monopolized industries; this is used to examine the implications of changes in the competition authority's budget, in investigation cost, and in market size for enforcement decisions. Later sections consider oligopoly markets and discuss the impact of a deterrence-based competition policy on noncooperative collusion in repeated games.

The firm's problem

Demand

There are two monopolized industries. The markets serve final consumer demand, and the products of the two industries are independent in demand.[6] The demand curve for industry i is

$$p_i = p_i(q_i) + \varepsilon_i, \tag{1}$$

with $p'_i < 0$, $p''_i \geq 0$. ε_i, is a random element of demand, with well-behaved density function $f_i(\varepsilon_i)$, zero mean, and defined over the interval

$$\underline{\varepsilon} \leq \varepsilon_i \leq \overline{\varepsilon} \leq \infty. \tag{2}$$

The lower limit $\underline{\varepsilon}$ is such that price is not less than marginal cost if the quantity supplied is sufficiently small; that is,

$$p_i(0) + \underline{\varepsilon} \geq c_i, \tag{3}$$

where c_i is the firm's constant marginal cost of production. There is a random element to demand, but the random element is cannot be so negative that price would be less than marginal cost even at very low output levels.

The enforcement mechanism

In the real world, a competition authority will receive and monitor many signals about an industry's market performance. Such signals will include complaints from customers, from rivals, and information from trade sources about many aspects of market performance – prices, inventories, delivery times, and others.

In the model developed here, I collapse all these sources into a single signal, the realized price. I suppose that the competition agency sets a threshold price g_i for industry i. If the observed price rises above g_i, the agency investigates the industry. After investigation, it makes a decision about further action.

The probability that the realized price is above g_i, triggering an investigation, is

$$\tau_i = \Pr\left[p_i(q_i) + \varepsilon_i \geq g_i\right] \tag{4}$$
$$= \Pr\left[\varepsilon_i \geq g_i - p_i(q_i)\right]$$

If the firm is investigated, it is prosecuted and convicted with probability γ_i, with $0 < \gamma_i < 1$. If convicted, it pays a fine $F_i.^*$

The probability of prosecution and conviction γ_i is less than one. First, the competition authority may investigate the industry, conclude that the firm is not violating competition law, and close the matter without further action.

Second, an initial decision by the competition authority to prosecute or fine the firm may not survive eventual appeal to the courts. The legal system has its own mores, which are only imperfectly controlled by the legislature (and only indirectly influenced by economic considerations).

This is particularly true in common law systems; see Priest (1977) and Rubin (1977). The elaboration of the concepts of 'antitrust injury' and 'standing' in US antitrust law, which limit the ability of private plaintiffs to pursue private antitrust actions, are examples of endogenous judicial development of competition law.

For simplicity, I treat γ_i and F_i as parameters, with values that are known to firms and to the competition authority. It would be possible to examine an extended model in which the probability of conviction γ_i is positively influenced by spending of the competition authority to prosecute that case and negatively influenced by spending of the challenged firm in its own defense.[7] Similarly, F_i might modelled as depending on the nature of the offense.

Firm behavior

Firm i maximizes its expected profit,

$$E(\pi_i) = \left[p_i(q_i) - c_i\right]q_i - \tau_i\gamma_iF_i \tag{5}$$

The first-order condition is

$$\frac{\partial E(\pi_i)}{\partial q_i} = p_i - c_i + q_i\frac{dp_i}{dq_i} - \gamma_iF_i\frac{\partial \tau_i}{\partial q_i} \equiv 0. \tag{6}$$

This implies

$$p_i + q_i\frac{dp_i}{dq_i} = c_i + \gamma_iF_i\frac{\partial \tau_i}{\partial q_i} < c_i, \tag{7}$$

so that when the firm maximizes expected profit marginal revenue is less than marginal production cost. To reduce expected fines, the firm expands output above the level that makes marginal revenue equal to marginal production cost. This is the deterrence effect of competition policy.

Theorem 1, which is proven in the Appendix, gives some of the properties of equilibrium firm behavior.

Theorem 1

(a) The firm's profit-maximizing price is below the threshold price,

$$g_i - p_i > 0, \tag{8}$$

provided $\gamma_i F_i$ is sufficiently large;
(b) a lower threshold price increases equilibrium output, all else equal:

$$\frac{\partial q_i}{\partial g_i} < 0; \tag{9}$$

(c) greater expected fines increase equilibrium output, all else equal:

$$\frac{\partial q_i}{\partial(\gamma_i F_i)} > 0. \tag{10}$$

By (b), lowering the threshold price expands output and lowers expected price. To rule out destabilizing overreactions by the firm to changes in the threshold price, I assume that lowering the threshold price lowers the equilibrium threshold-price gap:

$$\frac{\partial(g_i - p_i)}{\partial g_i} = 1 - \frac{dp_i}{dq_i}\frac{\partial q_i}{\partial g_i} > 0. \tag{11}$$

If the government lowers g, the firm reacts by producing more, and price falls. But price does not fall so much that $g - p$ rises.[8]

Condition (11) means that when g falls, $g - p$ falls and the probability of investigation rises:

$$\frac{d\tau_i}{dg_i} = -f_i(g_i - p_i)\left(1 - \frac{\partial p_i}{\partial q_i}\right) = -f_i(g_i - p_i)\left(1 - \frac{\partial p_i}{\partial q_i}\frac{\partial q_i}{\partial g_i}\right) < 0 \tag{13}$$

I also assume that

$$\frac{d^2\tau_i}{dg_i^2} > 0, \tag{14}$$

implying that from the point of view of the competition authority, there are positive but decreasing returns to deterrence.

Example

Consider a market with linear inverse demand curve

$$p = 101 - \frac{1}{10}Q + \varepsilon \tag{15}$$

Let marginal cost be constant, 1 per unit, and suppose there are no fixed costs. If the industry were perfectly competitive, long-run equilibrium price would be 1.

Let the density of the random part of demand be exponential,

$$f(\varepsilon) = \frac{1}{10}\exp-\left(\frac{\varepsilon + 10}{10}\right) \tag{16}$$

This has range $(-10, \infty)$ (see Figure 11.1). ε has mean 0 and variance $\sigma^2 = 100$. For this density function, it is more likely that ε will fall in a range of modestly negative values than in a higher range of identical length.[9]

Table 11.1 reports the main characteristics of monopoly equilibrium for this example for threshold prices ranging from 70 to 10. The row labeled 'no CP' gives values for equilibrium without competition policy; the expected monopoly price is 51.[10] An investigation threshold $g = 70$ is almost two standard deviations above this; it results in a probability of investigation of 4.4 per cent, and an output of expansion of the same proportion. Profit falls, while consumers' surplus and the sum of profit and consumers' surplus rise.

As the investigation threshold falls, output and the probability of investigation rise. Profit falls continuously, and consumers' surplus rises continuously, as the

Table 11.1 Monopoly market performance: alternative investigation thresholds

g	q_m	p_m	τ	π_m	CS	$\pi_m + CS$	$\tau \gamma F$
No CP	500.00	51.0	na	25000	12500	37500	0
70	522.06	48.79	0.044	24510	13627	38137	441.31
65	532.71	47.73	0.065	24239	14189	38428	654.09
60	546.82	46.32	0.094	23844	14951	38795	936.49
55	564.62	44.54	0.129	23290	15940	39230	1292.3
50	586.01	42.40	0.172	22540	17170	39710	1720.0
45	610.74	39.93	0.221	21559	18650	40209	2214.9
40	638.43	37.16	0.277	20315	20380	40695	2768.4
35	668.67	34.13	0.337	18782	22356	41138	3373.3
30	701.09	30.89	0.402	16935	24576	41511	4021.6
25	735.35	27.47	0.471	14754	27037	41791	4707.2
20	771.18	23.88	0.542	1222	29736	41958	5423.7
15	808.34	20.17	0.617	9326	32671	41996	6166.8
10	846.63	16.34	0.693	6052	35839	41891	6932.9

Notes: $p = 101 - (1/10)q_m$, $c = 1$, $\gamma = 1/2$, $F = 20000$, $\sigma = 10$; p_m = expected monopoly price, q_m = monopoly output, τ = probability of investigation, π_m = expected monopoly profit, CS = expected consumers' surplus, $\tau \gamma F$ = expected antitrust fines.

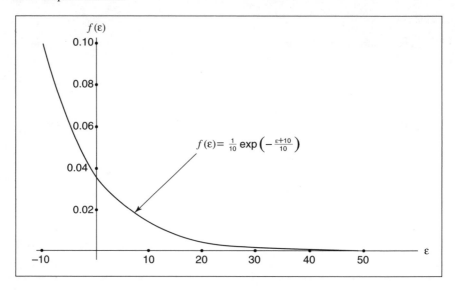

Figure 11.1 Exponential density function

investigation threshold falls. The sum of profit and consumers' surplus rises until the investigation threshold reaches a low level, $g = 15$, and then begins to fall. For $g = 15$, the improvement in profit plus consumers' surplus compared with the no competition policy case is about 12 per cent.

For very low threshold levels, expected fines become so great that private sector welfare falls with the investigation threshold. As shown in Figure 11.2, overall welfare – profit plus consumers' surplus plus expected fines – rises continuously as the investigation threshold falls.

For comparison purposes, Table 11.2 gives the duopoly outcomes for the parameters of Table 11.1.[11] The results for monopoly and duopoly are qualitatively similar. Profit plus consumers' surplus rises as the investigation threshold falls to 45, then declines. The improvement in profit plus consumers' surplus for $g = 45$, compared with the no-competition policy case, is negligible, about 1/10th of 1 per cent; this is also apparent from Figure 11.3.

To put this in perspective, duopoly welfare for $g = 45$ is about 11 per cent greater than monopoly welfare for $g = 45$. If markets converge on the noncooperative equilibrium of a one-shot game, actual competition yields greater static welfare gains than competition policy.[12]

The competition authority's problem

I model a competition authority that deals with two industries subject to a binding budget constraint.

Let I_i = cost of investigating industry i, for $i = 1, 2$.

I assume that the cost of investigation is industry specific, but do not model

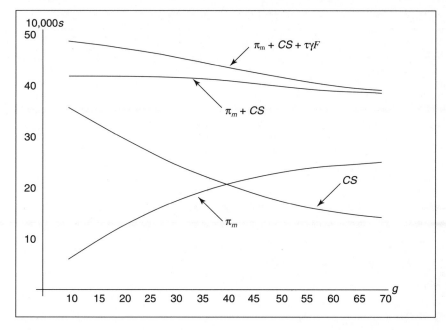

Figure 11.2 Monopoly investigation threshold–market performance relationship
Notes: $a = 101$, $c = 1$, $b = 1/10$, $\gamma = 1/2$, $F = 20000$, $\sigma = 10$

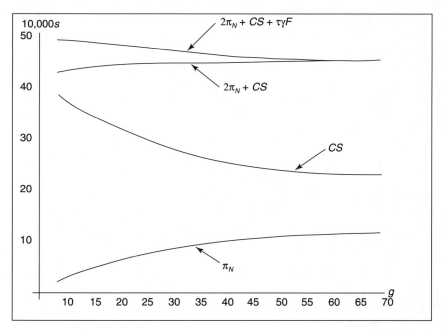

Figure 11.3 Duopoly investigation threshold–market performance relationship
Notes: $a = 101$, $c = 1$, $b = 1/10$, $\gamma = 1/2$, $F = 20000$, $\sigma = 10$

Table 11.2 Static duopoly market performance: alternative investigation thresholds

g	Q_N	p_N	τ	π_N	CS	$2\pi_N + CS$	$\tau \gamma F$
No CP	666.67	34.33	na	11111	22222	44444	0
70	670.02	34.00	0.010	11004	22446	44455	62.499
65	672.08	33.79	0.016	10938	22585	44461	162.32
60	675.30	33.47	0.026	10834	22802	44469	259.13
55	680.22	32.98	0.041	10673	23135	44480	406.73
50	687.46	32.25	0.062	10431	23630	44492	623.74
45	697.63	31.24	0.093	10083	24334	44500	928.94
40	711.23	29.88	0.134	9601	25292	44494	1336.8
35	728.49	28.15	0.185	8962	26535	44459	1854.6
30	749.38	26.06	0.248	8150	28079	44378	2481.3
25	773.65	23.64	0.321	7151	29927	44229	3209.4
20	800.93	20.91	0.403	5958	32074	43990	4028.1
15	830.83	17.92	0.492	4565	34514	43644	4924.8
10	862.96	14.70	0.589	2969	37235	43173	5888.4

Notes: $p = 101 - (1/10) Q_N$, $c = 1$, $\gamma = 1/2$, $F = 20000$, $\sigma = 10$; p_N = expected Nash equilibrium duopoly price, Q_N = expected duopoly equilibrium industry output, τ = probability of investigation, π_N = expected Nash equilibrium profit per firm, CS = expected consumers' surplus, $\tau \gamma F$ = expected antitrust fines.

the determinants of investigation cost. If the competition authority has had extensive experience with an industry, it may cost relatively little to investigate, even if the industry is large or complex in some objective sense. On the other hand, a small industry may be relatively costly to investigate if it is one with which the competition authority has not had prior contact. These considerations rule out any easy specification of the determinants of I_i, such as a positive relationship with market size.

The expected fine that follows investigation is $\gamma_i F_i$; the probability of investigation is τ_i. Overall, the expected fine is $\tau_i \gamma_i F_i$. This is an expected transfer from the firm to the government, and drops out of the expression for net social welfare.

The budget constraint is

$$\tau_1 I_1 + \tau_2 I_2 \leq B, \tag{17}$$

where B is the budget allocated by the legislature to the competition authority.[13]

I assume the budget constraint is binding: the competition authority does not have enough resources to investigate both industries with 100 per cent probability. Such an assumption is realistic,[14] and necessary to render the problem interesting.

This way of formulating the budget constraint implies that the competition authority has sufficient reserves to cover realized investigation costs. It may happen that both industries are investigated, and that realized investigation costs exceed B.

Net social welfare generated in industry i is the sum of consumers' and producers' surplus,

$$W_i(q_i) = \int_0^{q_i} \left[p_i(x_i) - c_i \right] dx_i. \tag{18}$$

The competition authority's problem to maximize social welfare, net of enforcement cost,[15]

$$\max_{g1,\, g2} W_1(q_1) + W_2(q_2) - \tau_1 I_1 - \tau_2 I_2 \tag{19}$$

subject to the budget constraint (17). Variations might weight consumers' and producers' surplus differently; for an example in the context of a model of competition policy, see Besanko and Spulber (1993).

To the extent that competition authorities act to maximize other goals, the analysis that follows from the assumption that (19) is the objective function is normative rather than positive.

A formal solution of the competition authority's problem is given in the Appendix. From an analytical point of view, the problem is like the standard analysis of consumer utility maximization. The equilibrium choice of investigation thresholds can be illustrated graphically in terms of a tangency in threshold- or (g_1, g_2)-space between an isobudget curve that

represents the competition authority's budget constraint and an isowelfare curve indicating the maximum attainable social welfare.

Isobudget curves

An isobudget curve shows all combinations of g_1 and g_2 that yield a given total expected investigation cost. The equation of the isobudget curve for budget level $\overline{B}$ is

$$\tau_1(g_1 - p_1)I_1 + \tau_2(g_2 - p_2)I_2 \equiv \overline{B}. \tag{20}$$

In this expression, prices are functions of the respective quantities supplied, via the demand curves. The quantities supplied are in turn functions of the investigation thresholds, functions that are defined by first-order conditions for the firms' expected profit maximization problems.

The slope of an isobudget curve is

$$\left. \frac{dg_2}{dg_1} \right|_{\overline{B}} = -\frac{I_1}{I_2} \frac{d\tau_1 / dg_1}{d\tau_2 / dg_2} < 0. \tag{21}$$

Greater values of B allow the agency to set lower values of one or both investigation thresholds. The map of budget curves therefore consists of downward-sloping lines, with values closer to the origin corresponding to higher budget levels (see Figure 11.1).

As shown in the Appendix, isobudget curves are convex. If I_1 rises, isobudget curves become steeper, all else equal; if I_2 rises, isobudget curves become flatter, all else equal.

Isowelfare curves

Isowelfare curves have equations of the form

$$W_1(q_1) + W_2(q_2) = \overline{W} \tag{22}$$

$$\int_0^{q_1} \left[p_1(x_1) - c_1 \right] \, dx_1 + \int_0^{q_2} \left[p_2(x_2) - c_2 \right] \, dx_2 = \overline{W} \tag{23}$$

where once again p_i is directly a function of q_i and indirectly a function of g_i.

The slope of an isowelfare curve is

$$\left. \frac{dg_2}{dg_1} \right|_{\overline{W}} = -\frac{dW_1 / dg_1}{dW_2 / dg_2} = -\frac{(p_1 - c_1) \dfrac{dq_1}{dg_1}}{(p_2 - c_2) \dfrac{dq_2}{dg_2}} < 0. \tag{24}$$

Isowelfare curves are downward sloping and convex (see Appendix), and isowelfare curves closer to the origin correspond to higher levels of welfare.

Tangency

It is shown in the Appendix that the second-order condition for the constrained optimization problem implies an equilibrium of the kind shown in Figure 11.4.

Isobudget curves and isowelfare curves are both downward sloping and convex. Isobudget curves are more sharply curved than isowelfare curves. The equilibrium investigation thresholds chosen by the competition authority are those at the point of tangency between the isobudget curve determined by the available budget, B, and the isowelfare curve that is closest to the origin, shown as E_A in 11.4. At the tangency point, the marginal increase in welfare per marginal increase in investigation cost is the same for both industries.

Comparative statics I

The comparative static behavior of optimal investigation thresholds with respect to changes in budget B and investigation costs I_1, I_2 is much the same as the comparative static behavior of individual consumption with respect to changes in income and in the prices of goods.

Comparative statics with respect to B

The 'normal markets' case is one in which an increase in the investigation budget induces lower investigation thresholds for both industries, is shown in Figure 11.5.

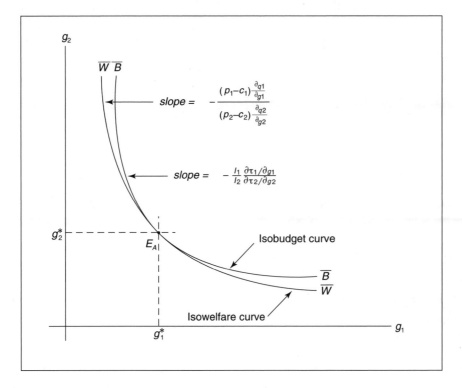

Figure 11.4 Competition authority's optimization problem
Notes: $\overline{W}$ indicates isowelfare curve; $\overline{B}$ indicates isobudget curve.

Just as there can be inferior goods, the consumption of which falls as income rises, so there can be 'inferior markets', which receive less attention from a competition authority as the competition authority's budget rises. We assume that markets are not inferior in this sense.

As shown in the Appendix, the condition for investigation thresholds to fall when the investigation budget increases is

$$\frac{1}{\partial W_i / \partial g_i} \frac{\partial^2 W_i}{\partial g_i^2} - \frac{1}{\partial \tau_i / \partial g_i} \frac{\partial^2 \tau_i}{\partial g_i^2} > 0 \qquad (25)$$

for all i.

Intuitively, an increase in the budget leads the competition authority to reduce investigation thresholds, which tends to lower $g_i - p_i$ and increase the investigation probability τ_i. Firms react to this by expanding output, which mitigates the direct effects of a lower threshold price. Condition (25) implies that the indirect effects of firms' reactions to lower threshold prices are not strong enough to reverse the direct effects of lower threshold prices.

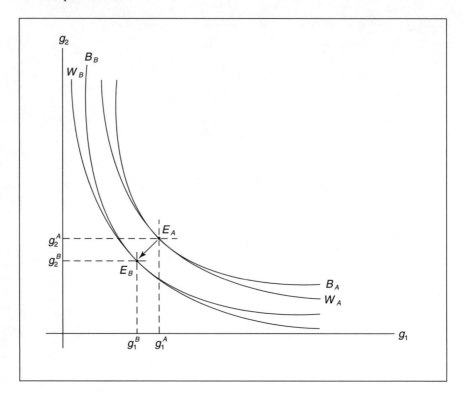

Figure 11.5 Comparative statics, budget increase
Notes: $B_B > B_A$, $W_B > W_A$

Example

Figure 11.6 shows the investigation threshold–budget relationship when the competition authority monitors two identical monopolized industries of the kind shown in Figure 11.2. Investigation costs are relatively low, 1000 per industry.

For this example, social welfare is maximized for a budget of 1,910, which makes the shadow cost of an additional dollar of investigation funds equal to one. Welfare (profit plus consumers' surplus minus the budget) is 49,020 per industry, compared with 37,500 in the no competition policy case (see Table 11.1). This is a welfare gain of nearly 31 per cent.

If the government as a whole allocates resources to equalize the marginal social value of funds devoted to alternative uses, the size of the budget allocated to enforcement of competition law would depend on the shadow value of funds to the government as a whole (and might therefore fall short of the level that would make the shadow value of funds allocated to enforcement of competition policy equal to one).

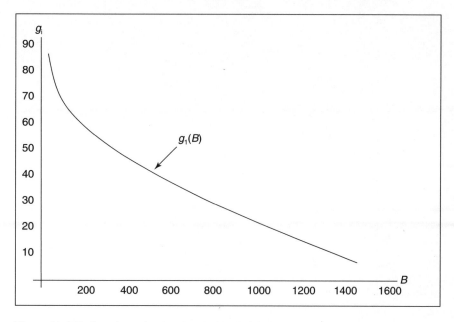

Figure 11.6 Budget–investigation threshold relationship 1

Notes: Two identical industries: $p = 101 - q_m$, $c = 1$, $b = 1/10$, $\gamma = 1/2$, $F = 20000$, $\sigma = 10$.

Comparative statics with respect to investigation costs

An increase in (say) I_1 has effects on the competition authority's problem that are like the effects of an increase in price on consumer behavior.

When I_1 increases, isobudget curves become steeper and the feasible set of thresholds (g_1, g_2) retreats away from the origin. If one compensates for this real budget effect by increasing the nominal budget so that the competition authority can remain on the original isowelfare curve, the increase in I_1 induces a pure substitution effect: g_1 rises, g_2 falls, the competition authority gives less attention to the industry that has become more expensive to investigate and more attention to the other industry. This is shown as the move from E_A to E_B in Figure 11.7.

The full effect of the investigation cost increase combines the substitution effect with a pure budget effect, leading from point E_B to point E_C. The case that is shown has a higher investigation threshold for the industry that has become more costly to investigate and a lower threshold for the other industry. If the budget effect is sufficiently strong, the investigation threshold for the other industry may rise as well.

It is shown in the Appendix that the condition for the comparative statics effects of an increase in I_1 to have the effects shown in Figure 11.7 is

$$\frac{1}{\partial W_1 / \partial g_1} \frac{d^2 W_1}{dg_1^2} - \frac{1}{\tau_1' / \tau_1} \frac{d}{dg_1} \left(\frac{\tau_1'}{\tau_1} \right) > 0. \tag{26}$$

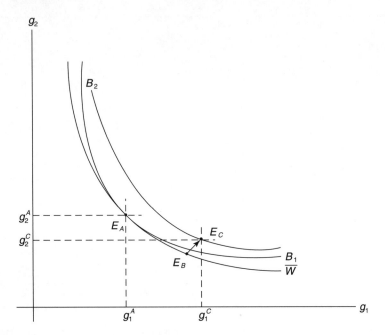

Figure 11.7 Comparative statics, increase in I_1

Similarly to (25), the implication of (26) is that the direct effects of the competition authority's reaction to an increase in I_1 are not reversed by the indirect effects of firm's reactions.

One can show that (26) implies (25). If the consequences of changes in investigation costs for investigation thresholds are what one would intuitively expect, then so are the consequences of an increase in the budget.

Example

Figure 11.8 shows the investigation threshold-budget relationships for the industries of the previous example, if the investigation cost for industry 2, I_2, is increased from 1000 to 2000. The dashed line in Figure 11.8 reproduces, from Figure 11.6, the threshold-budget relationship when the two industries have investigation costs equal to 1000.

For $B \leq 500$, the entire budget is devoted to investigating industry 1, the low-investigation-cost industry. For $B > 500$, g_2 is always greater than g_1: the investigation threshold is lower for the industry that costs less to investigate, all else equal. Comparing this example and the previous one, the investigation threshold for industry 2 when $I = 2000$ is always greater than the investigation threshold for industry 2 when $I = 1000$. When I_2 doubles, g_1 is less for B less than approximately 1333 (this is the kind of reaction shown in Figure 11.7), but is greater thereafter.

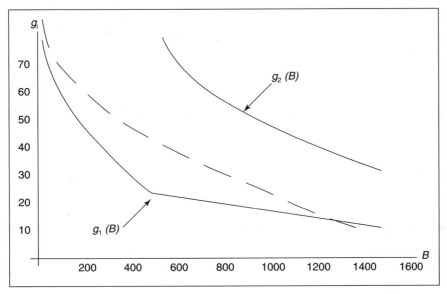

Figure 11.8 Budget–investigation threshold relationship 2
Notes: $n_i = 1$, $a_1 = 101$, $c_i = 1$, $b_i = 1/10$, $\gamma_i = 1/2$, $F_i = 20000$, $\sigma_i = 10$, $I_1 = 1000$, $I_2 = 2000$

Comparative statics with respect to market size

There are several alternative ways to measure market size, for example competitive equilibrium output or competitive equilibrium consumers' surplus. For a linear inverse demand curve,

$$p_i = a_i - b_i q_i,\tag{27}$$

market size in both these senses increases if a_i, the price-axis intercept, increases, holding the slope of the demand curve constant, or if b_i, the absolute value of the slope of the demand curve, declines, holding the price-axis intercept constant.

The effect of changes in a_i and b_i on equilibrium investigation thresholds is theoretically ambiguous. To give an indication of the nature of the results, I use the previous numerical examples to illustrate the effect of changes in the price axis intercept a_i on investigation thresholds. The impact of changes in b_i are qualitatively similar.

Figure 11.9 shows the equilibrium investigation thresholds as the intercept of the demand curve for good 1 varies from 51 to 191, for an investigation budget 1,100. The range for a_1 is chosen to ensure an interior solution for both industries.[16] All other parameter values are as in the basic example. Figure 11.10 shows the equilibrium threshold-expected price margin over the same range.

As the price-axis intercept increases, the maximum amount consumers are willing to pay for every unit of output goes up by the same amount. All else equal, equilibrium price rises as the demand curve shifts upward.

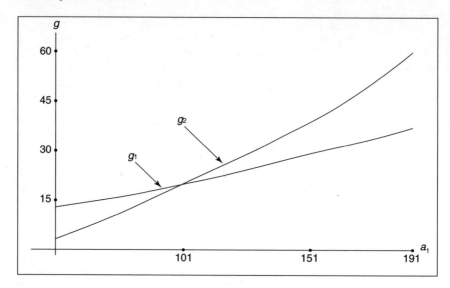

Figure 11.9 Threshold–a_1 relationship

Notes: $a_2 = 101$, $c_1 = c_2$ 1, $b_1 = b_2$ 1/10, $\gamma_1 F_1 = \gamma_2 F_2 = 20000$, $\sigma_1 = \sigma_2 = 10$, $n_1 = n_2 = 1$, $I_1 = I_2 = 1000$, $B = 1100$

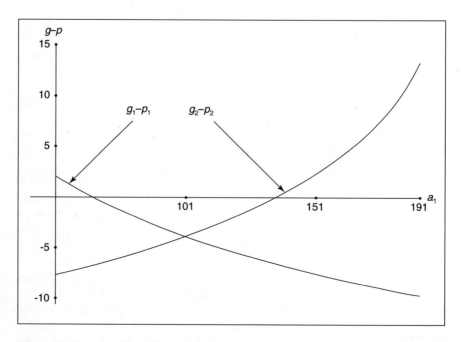

Figure 11.10 g–p relationship

Notes: $a_2 = 101$, $c_1 = c_2$ 1, $b_1 = b_2$ 1/10, $\gamma_1 F_1 = \gamma_2 F_2 = 10000$, $\sigma_1 = \sigma_2 = 10$, $n_1 = n_2 = 1$, $I_1 = I_2 = 1000$, $B = 1100$

When a_1 is smaller than a_2, g_1 is greater than g_2: a lower threshold is set for the larger industry. As a_1 rises, g_1 and g_2 both rise. As industry 1 becomes larger, competition policy is tightened for industry 1: $g_1 - p_1$ falls (Figure 11.12), and as resources are transferred (in an expected value sense) from industry 2 to industry 1, $g_2 - p_2$ rises. There is thus a general equilibrium effect as the greater potential consumers' surplus in industry 1 induces a reallocation of resources between the two industries.

The relationships shown in Figures 11.9 and 11.10 are typical. If both a_1 and B are small, there is a region in (B, a_1)-space over which g_1 falls as a_1 increases.

Summary

The results of this section may be summarized as

Theorem 2:

(a) An increase in the investigation budget leads the competition authority to reduce investigation thresholds, all else equal, if

$$\frac{1}{\partial W_i / \partial g_i} \frac{\partial^2 W_i}{\partial g_i^2} - \frac{1}{\partial \tau_i / \partial g_i} \frac{\partial^2 \tau_i}{\partial g_i^2} > 0, \tag{28}$$

for $i = 1, 2$;

(b) an increase in investigation cost I_i leads the competition authority to increase g_i and lower g_j, $j \neq i$, all else equal, if

$$\frac{1}{\partial W_1 / \partial g_1} \frac{d^2 W_1}{dg_1^2} - \frac{1}{\tau_1' / \tau_1} \frac{d}{dg_1} \left(\frac{\tau_1'}{\tau_1} \right) > 0, \tag{29}$$

(and (29) implies (28));

(c) for linear inverse demand curves, an increase in market size tends to lower $g - p$ for the larger industry and increase the investigation threshold for the other industry.

Comparative statics II: number of firms (Nash equilibrium)

To extend the model of competition policy from monopoly to oligopoly, suppose that there are n_i identical[17] firms in industry i, and that the expected profit of firm k in industry i is

$$\pi_{ik} = \left[p_i(Q_i) - c_i \right] q_{ik} - \frac{\gamma_i F_i}{n_i} \int_{g_i - p_i(Q_i)} f_i(\varepsilon_i) d\varepsilon_i. \tag{30}$$

q_{ik} is the output of firm ik, Q_i is industry output, c_i is unit cost for firms in industry i, and other notation is unchanged from the monopoly case.

If there is a successful prosecution, each firm expects to pay a fraction $1/n_i$ of the resulting fine. This specification is appropriate for joint offenses against competition policy, such as collusion to raise price or deter entry. It would not be appropriate for single-firm violations of competition policy, such as abuse of a dominant position.

The qualitative impact of competition policy on noncooperative equilibrium firm behavior is as in the monopoly case. In particular, a lower investigation threshold increases equilibrium output.

If the number of firms in industry 2 increases, market performance in industry 2 improves. This reduces the marginal social value of funds in the competition authority's budget. The improvement in market 2's performance permits the competition authority to toughen competition policy for industry 1: as n_2 rises, g_1 falls. The direct effect of an increase in n_2 is to increase output and lower price in industry 2; this permits the

competition authority to lower the investigation threshold without

increasing the expected probability of investigation of industry 2. But the reduction in g_1 and the consequent transfer of investigation resources to industry 1 works in the opposite direction, tending to induce the competition authority to raise g_2. The net impact of an increase in n_1 on g_1 is ambiguous. These results, which are derived in the Appendix, are summarized in

Theorem 3:

If tougher competition policy and more intense competition are substitutes in the sense that an increase in the number of firms reduces the magnitude of $\partial W_i/\partial g_i < 0$ and a reduction in the investigation threshold reduces $\partial W_i/\partial n_i > 0$, then

(a) an increase in n_i reduces the shadow value of funds in the competition authority's budget;
(b) an increase in n_i has an ambiguous effect on g_i;
(c) when there are two industries, n increase in n_i leads the competition authority to lower the investigation threshold for industry j (for $j \neq i$).

Example

Figure 11.11 shows the investigation thresholds for the basic example if n_2 is increased from 1 to 2, holding all other parameters fixed. The dashed line in Figure 11.8 reproduces the threshold-budget relationship from Figure 11.6, where both industries have a single supplier. For $B \leq 555.56$, all investigation resources are devoted to industry 1. For larger investigation budgets, g_1 is always lower than for $n_2 = 1$; g_2 is always greater than for $n_2 = 1$.

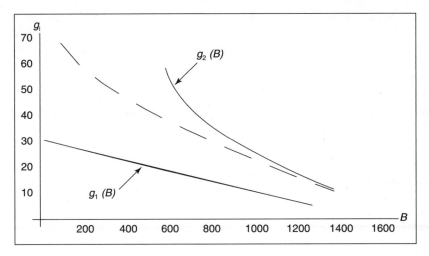

Figure 11.11 Budget–investigation threshold relationship 3
Notes: $n_1 = 1$, $n_2 = 1$, $a_i = 101$, $c = 1$, $b = 1/10$, $\gamma = 1/2$, $F = 20000$, $\sigma = 10$

Tacit collusion

Long before the emergence of game theory as the formal theoretical framework of industrial economics, Chamberlin (1933, p. 48) argued that if the number of firms in an industry were sufficiently small, suppliers would converge on the monopoly outcome simply through recognition of their own self-interest. The modern version of this argument is that the threat of a variety of punishment schemes can make tacit collusion on the joint-profit-maximizing output an equilibrium outcome of a repeated game, provided rates of time preference are sufficiently low.

For example (Friedman, 1971), a trigger strategy threatening reversion to Cournot outputs forever will make adherence to a joint-profit-maximizing output strategy an equilibrium if

$$\frac{1}{r} \geq R = \frac{\pi_D - \pi_m}{\pi_m - \pi_N}, \quad \text{or} \quad r \leq \frac{\pi_m - \pi_N}{\pi_D - \pi_m} = \frac{1}{R} \tag{31}$$

where r is the interest rate used to discount future income, π_N is Cournot equilibrium profit per firm, π_m is one firm's share of joint-profit-maximizing output, and π_D is a firm's single-period profit if it simply maximizes its own profit.

Each of the elements of the fraction on the right in (31) depends on the investigation threshold. Competition policy affects Cournot, joint-profit-maximizing, and defection payoffs, hence affects whether or not it will be an equilibrium for firms to follow a joint-profit-maximizing strategy.

The sign of

$$\frac{\partial}{\partial g}\left(\frac{\pi_D - \pi_m}{\pi_m - \pi_N}\right) \tag{32}$$

is in general ambiguous. For the case of linear demand, constant marginal cost, and exponential demand uncertainty, reductions in g from a high level at first reduce, then increase, the right-hand side of (31). This is shown in Table 11.3. Initial reductions in the investigation threshold make joint profit maximization more likely; further reductions make joint profit maximization less likely.

We know from p. 168 that reductions in the investigation threshold increase monopoly output. Over a certain range, at least, reductions in the investigation threshold can make tacit collusion more likely, although reducing the social cost of such behavior if it does emerge.

Conclusion

The research presented here is normative: it presents results about the way resources should be allocated to administer a deterrence-based competition policy that monitors joint exercise of market power if decisions are made to equalize the marginal benefit of competition policy across target industries when there is inherent uncertainty about the workings of the judicial system.

A deterrence-based competition policy improves market performance because it leads firms to expand output, thus reducing expected fines.

In a formal sense, the problem of resource allocation by a competition authority to maximize net social welfare has much in common with the problem of consumer welfare maximization. A greater enforcement budget allows a competition authority to monitor industries more intensely; if it is more costly to monitor a specific industry, that industry should normally be monitored less closely, others more closely, all else equal.

Competition policy significantly improves market performance if industries are monopolized or if firms tacitly collude on monopoly output. However, competition policy may make it more likely that such tacit collusion is an equilibrium

Table 11.3 Critical value for tacit duopoly collusion on joint profit-maximizing output

g	π_N	π_J	π_D	R	i/R
No CP	11111	12500	14063	1.1250	0.8889
70	11004	12255	13579	1.0584	0.9448
65	10938	12119	13340	1.0329	0.9681
60	10834	11922	13016	1.0052	0.9948
55	10673	11645	12596	0.9781	1.0224
50	10431	11270	12072	0.9555	1.0466
45	10083	10779	11434	0.9397	1.0642
40	9600.7	10158	10676	0.9314	1.0737
35	8962.3	9390.9	9789.5	0.9301	1.0752
30	8149.8	8467.3	8763.9	0.9340	1.0707
25	7151.1	7376.9	7589.6	0.9416	1.0620
20	5958.0	6111.2	6231.9	0.9511	1.0514
15	4565.2	4662.9	4756.8	0.9609	1.0407
10	2968.8	3025.9	3081.4	0.9711	1.0298

Notes: $p = 101 - Q$, $c = 1$, $b = 1/10$, $\gamma = 1/2$, $F = 20000$, $\sigma = 10$.

strategy. Competition policy has minimal impact on oligopoly market performance if markets settle on the noncooperative equilibrium of a one-shot game.

The models outlined here focus on the consequences of uncertainty about the working of the judicial system. They could be extended to explicitly allow for uncertainty on the part of the competition authority about elements of market structure (for example, market size) and firm structure (unit cost). They could also be extended to allow for the possibility of entry, mergers, and strategic behavior by single firms. These topics are the subject of ongoing research.

Appendix

Proof of Theorem 1

The first-order condition for the firm's profit-maximization is

$$\frac{\partial E(\pi_i)}{\partial q_i} = p_i - c_i + q_i \frac{dp_i}{dq_i} - \gamma_i F_i \frac{\partial \tau_i}{\partial q_i} = p_i - c_i + (q_i - \gamma_i F_i f_i) \frac{dp_i}{dq_i} \equiv 0. \tag{33}$$

This implies

$$q_i - \gamma_i F_i f_i > 0. \tag{34}$$

The second-order condition is

$$\frac{\partial^2 E(\pi_i)}{\partial q_i^2} = 2 \frac{dp_i}{dq_i} + q_i \frac{d^2 p_i}{dq_i^2} - \gamma_i F_i \frac{\partial \tau_i}{\partial q_i} < 0 \tag{35}$$

or equivalently

$$\frac{\partial^2 E(\pi_i)}{\partial q_i^2} = 2 \frac{dp_i}{dq_i} + \gamma_i F_i f'_i \left(\frac{dp_i}{dq_i}\right)^2 + (q_i - \gamma_i F_i f_i) \frac{d^2 p_i}{dq_i^2} < 0. \tag{36}$$

(a) Substituting $p_i = g_i - \varepsilon_i$, rewrite the first-order condition as

$$\frac{1}{\gamma_i F_i} \left(\frac{g_i - c_i - \varepsilon_i}{\frac{dp_i}{dq_i}} + q_i \right) = f_i(\varepsilon_i). \tag{37}$$

In the denominator on the left, q_i is evaluated at $g_i - \varepsilon_i^*$; $dp_i/dq_i < 0$ is evaluated at $q_i (g_i - \varepsilon_i^*)$.

Fix g_i and consider the left-hand and right-hand sides as separate functions of ε_i. The functions can be graphed, as in Figure 11.12;[18] the intersection of the two functions gives the equilibrium value ε_i^*.

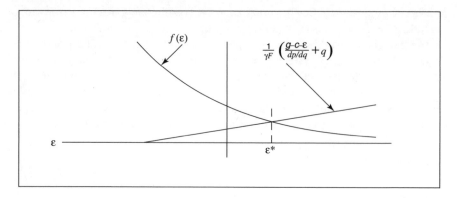

Figure 11.12 Equilibrium g–ε

Given that $f_i(\varepsilon_i)$ falls to the right of $\varepsilon_i = 0$, the first condition for $\varepsilon_i^* = g_i - p_p^*$ > 0 is that $\gamma_i F_i$ be sufficiently great that

$$\frac{1}{\gamma_i F_i} \left| \frac{g_i - c_i}{\dfrac{dp_i}{dq_i}} + q_i \right| < f_i(0) ; \tag{38}$$

then the left-hand side of (37) is below the right-hand side at $\varepsilon_i = 0$.

The second requirement for $\varepsilon_i^* = g_i - p_p^* > 0$ is that the function on the left slope upward. The slope of this function is

$$-\frac{1}{\gamma_i F_i} \left[2\frac{dq_i}{dp_i} + (p_i - c_i)\frac{d^2 q_i}{dp_i^2} \right]. \tag{39}$$

The second condition for $\varepsilon_i^* = g_i - p_p^* > 0$ is that the term in brackets be negative; this is satisfied for linear demand, and is assumed to hold.

(b) Differentiating the first-order condition with respect to g_i yields

$$\frac{\partial q_i}{\partial g_i} = \frac{1}{\left[-\dfrac{\partial^2 E(\pi_i)}{\partial q_i^2} \right]} \frac{\partial^2 E(\pi_i)}{\partial g_i \partial q_i} \tag{40}$$

The second-order condition implies that the term in brackets on the right is positive.

Differentiating the first-order condition gives

$$\frac{\partial^2 E(\pi_i)}{\partial g_i \partial q_i} = -\gamma_i F_i f_i' \frac{dp_i}{dq_i} < 0,$$

(41)

where the sign depends on $\varepsilon_i^* = g_i \cdot p_p^* > 0$ and the assumption that $f_i' < 0$ for $\varepsilon > 0$.

(c) Note that

$$\frac{\partial^2 E(\pi_i)}{\partial(\gamma_i F_i) \partial q_i} = -f_i \frac{dp_i}{dq_i} > 0;$$

(42)

then

$$\frac{\partial q_i}{\partial(\gamma_i F_i)} = \frac{1}{\left[-\dfrac{\partial^2 E(\pi_i)}{\partial q_i^2} \right]} \frac{\partial^2 E(\pi_i)}{\partial(\gamma_i F_i) \partial q_i} > 0.$$

The competition authority's problem: constrained optimization

We confine our attention to cases in which the budget constraint is binding: the competition authority does not have enough resources to investigate all industries for all realized prices. This allows us to reformulate the competition authority's problem as

$$\max_{g1, \, g2} W_1(q_1) + W_2(q_2) - B$$

(43)

such that

$$\tau_1 I_1 + \tau_2 I_2 \le B.$$

(44)

The first-order conditions for the solution to the competition authority's constrained optimization problem come from the Lagrangian

$$L = W_1(q_1) + W_2(q_2) - B + \lambda[B - \tau_1 I_1 - \tau_2 I_2].$$

(45)

First-order conditions

The first-order conditions are

$$\frac{\partial L}{\partial \lambda} = B - \tau_1 I_1 - \tau_2 I_2 \equiv 0,$$

(46)

$$\frac{\partial L}{\partial g_1} = \frac{dW_1}{dg_1} - \lambda I_1 \frac{d\tau_1}{dg_1} \equiv 0,$$

(47)

and

$$\frac{\partial L}{\partial g_2} = \frac{dW_2}{dg_2} - \lambda I_2 \frac{d\tau_2}{dg_2} \equiv 0, \tag{48}$$

(47) and (48) then imply

$$\lambda = \frac{W_1'}{I_1 \tau_1'} = \frac{W_2'}{I_2 \tau_2'} \tag{49}$$

(where $W_i' = \partial W/\partial g_i$).

Consider the expression for λ in terms of market 1 variables. The numerator

$$\frac{dW_1}{dg_1} \tag{50}$$

is negative: in absolute value, it gives the increase in welfare in market 1 if the enforcement agency lowers g_1 slightly.

The denominator,

$$I_1 \frac{d\tau_1}{dg_1} \tag{51}$$

is, in absolute value, the increase in expected investigation cost if g_1 is lowered slightly. The Lagrangian multiplier λ, the shadow value of the marginal budget allocation to the competition agency, is seen to be the marginal increase in welfare in market 1 per marginal increase in spending on enforcement in market 1. The enforcement agency's choice of threshold prices is optimal when this ratio is the same for all markets.

If (47) and (48) are rewritten breaking the total derivatives into their constituent parts, they become

$$\frac{\partial L}{\partial g_1} = \frac{\partial W_1}{\partial q_1} \frac{\partial q_1}{\partial g_1} - \lambda I_1 \tau_1' \left(1 - \frac{dp_1}{dq_1} \frac{\partial q_1}{\partial g_1}\right) \equiv 0 \tag{52}$$

and

$$\frac{\partial L}{\partial g_2} = \frac{\partial W_2}{\partial q_2} \frac{\partial q_2}{\partial g_2} - \lambda I_2 \tau_2' \left(1 - \frac{dp_2}{dq_2} \frac{\partial q_2}{\partial g_2}\right) \equiv 0 \tag{53}$$

respectively. (49) becomes

$$\lambda = \frac{\dfrac{\partial W_1}{\partial q_1} \dfrac{\partial q_1}{\partial g_1}}{I_1 \tau_1' \left(1 - \dfrac{dp_1}{dq_1} \dfrac{\partial q_1}{\partial g_1}\right)} = \frac{\dfrac{\partial W_2}{\partial q_2} \dfrac{\partial q_2}{\partial g_2}}{I_2 \tau_2' \left(1 - \dfrac{dp_2}{dq_2} \dfrac{\partial q_2}{\partial g_2}\right)} \tag{54}$$

This implies that where the first-order conditions are satisfied

$$-\frac{\dfrac{\partial W_1}{\partial q_1} \dfrac{\partial q_1}{\partial g_1}}{\dfrac{\partial W_2}{\partial q_2} \dfrac{\partial q_2}{\partial g_2}} = \frac{I_1 \tau_1' \left(1 - \dfrac{dp_1}{dq_1} \dfrac{\partial q_1}{\partial g_1}\right)}{I_2 \tau_2' \left(1 - \dfrac{dp_2}{dq_2} \dfrac{\partial q_2}{\partial g_2}\right)} < 0 \tag{55}$$

The expression on the left is the slope of an isowelfare curve; the expression on the right is the slope of an isobudget curve. The first-order conditions imply that the solution to the competition authority's problem occurs at the tangency of an isowelfare curve and the isobudget curve.

Second-order conditions

The second-order condition for a maximum requires that the determinant of the bordered Hessian

$$\begin{pmatrix} 0 & I_1 \tau_1' & I_2 \tau_2' \\ I_1 \tau_1' & L_{11} & 0 \\ I_2 \tau_2' & 0 & L_{22} \end{pmatrix} \tag{56}$$

be positive, where $L_{ii} = \partial^2 L / \partial g^2$. When written out, this condition is

$$-\left[\left(I_1 \tau_1'\right)^2 L_{22} + \left(I_2 \tau_2'\right)^2 L_{11}\right] > 0. \tag{57}$$

Sufficient conditions for this to be met are that $L_{ii} < 0$ for $i = 1, 2$. Using (47) to evaluate L_{11},

$$L_{11} = W_1'' - \lambda I_1 \tau_1' = W_1' \left(\frac{W_1''}{W_1'} - \frac{\tau_1''}{\tau_1'}\right). \tag{58}$$

Since $W_1' < 0$, $L_{11} < 0$ if the proportional impact of a change in g_1 on τ_1' is greater than its impact on a change in W_1'

$$-\frac{\tau_1''}{\tau_1'} > -\frac{W_1''}{W_1'} > 0. \tag{59}$$

We will henceforth assume $L_{ii} < 0$ for $i = 1, 2$.

We now show that the second-order condition implies the slope relationships (72).

Substitute

$$L_{ii} = W_i'' - \lambda I_i \tau_i'' ;$$

(60)

in

$$\left(I_1 \tau_1' \right)^2 L_{22} + \left(I_2 \tau_2' \right)^2 L_{11} < 0.$$

(61)

to obtain

$$\left(I_1 \tau_1' \right)^2 \left(W_2'' - \lambda \tau_2'' \right) + \left(I_2 \tau_2' \right)^2 \left(W_1'' - \lambda \tau_1'' \right) < 0.$$

(62)

Collect terms in λ:

$$\left(I_1 \tau_1' \right)^2 W_2'' + \left(I_2 \tau_2' \right)^2 W_1'' < \lambda \left[\left(I_1 \tau_1' \right)^2 \tau_2'' + \left(I_2 \tau_2' \right)^2 \tau_1'' \right]$$

(63)

The first-order conditions imply

$$I_i \tau_i' = \frac{1}{\lambda} W_i'.$$

(64)

Substitute these expressions on the left in (63):

$$\frac{1}{\lambda^2} \left[\left(W_1' \right)^2 W_2'' + \left(W_2' \right)^2 W_1'' \right] < \lambda \left[\left(I_1 \tau_1' \right)^2 \tau_2'' + \left(I_2 \tau_2' \right)^2 \tau_1'' \right]$$

(65)

λ is positive; dividing both sides of (65) by λ does not change the direction of the inequality:

$$\frac{1}{\lambda^3} \left[\left(W_1' \right)^2 W_2'' + \left(W_2' \right)^2 W_1'' \right] < \left(I_1 \frac{d\tau_1}{dg_1} \right)^2 \frac{d^2 \tau_2}{dg_2^2} + \left(I_2 \frac{d\tau_2}{dg_2} \right)^2 \frac{d^2 \tau_1}{dg_1^2}$$

(66)

Now substitute

$$\lambda = \frac{\dfrac{dW_2}{dq_2} \dfrac{dq_2}{dg_2}}{I_2 \dfrac{d\tau_2}{dg_2}}$$

(67)

to eliminate λ, and rearrange terms slightly to obtain

$$0 \leq \frac{\left(W_1' \right)^2 W_2'' + \left(W_2' \right)^2 W_1''}{\left(W_2' \right)^3} < \frac{\left(I_1 \tau_1' \right)^2 I_2 \tau_2'' + \left(I_2 \tau_2' \right)^2 I_1 \tau_1''}{\left(I_2 \tau_2' \right)^3},$$

(68)

Differentiating (21), the second derivative of an isobudget curve is

$$\frac{d^2 g_2}{dg_1^2}\bigg|_{\overline{B}} = -\frac{(I_1\tau_1')^2 I_2\tau_2'' + (I_2\tau_2')^2 I_1\tau_1''}{(I_2\tau_2')^3} > 0. \tag{69}$$

Differentiating (24), the second derivative of an isowelfare curve is

$$\frac{d^2 g_2}{dg_1^2}\bigg|_{\overline{W}} = -\frac{(W_1')^2 W_2'' + (W_2')^2 W_1''}{(W_2')^3} > 0, \tag{70}$$

where the sign depends on the assumption that there are decreasing returns to increasing welfare by lowering the investigation threshold,

$$W_i'' > 0. \tag{71}$$

Using (69) and (70), the transformed second-order condition (68) can be written

$$0 < \frac{d^2 g_2}{dg_1^2}\bigg|_{\overline{W}} < \frac{d^2 g_2}{dg_1^2}\bigg|_{\overline{B}} \tag{72}$$

This justifies the configuration shown in Figure 11.4.

Comparative statics with respect to **B**

Differentiate the first-order conditions (46), (47), and (48) with respect to B to obtain

$$-I_1\tau_1'\frac{\partial g_1}{\partial B} - I_2\tau_2'\frac{\partial g_2}{\partial B} = -1 \tag{73}$$

$$L_{11}\frac{\partial g_1}{\partial B} - I_1\tau_1'\frac{\partial \lambda}{\partial B} = 0, \tag{74}$$

and

$$L_{22}\frac{\partial g_2}{\partial B} - I_1\tau_2'\frac{\partial \lambda}{\partial B} = 0, \tag{75}$$

where

$$L_{ii} = W_i'' - \lambda l_i \tau_i'. \tag{76}$$

Write the system of equations in matrix form as

$$
\begin{pmatrix}
0 & -I_1\tau_1' & -I_2\tau_2' \\
-I_1\tau_1' & L_{11} & 0 \\
-I_2\tau_2' & 0 & L_{22}
\end{pmatrix}
\begin{pmatrix}
\dfrac{\partial\lambda}{\partial B} \\[4pt]
\dfrac{\partial g_1}{\partial B} \\[4pt]
\dfrac{\partial g_2}{\partial B}
\end{pmatrix}
=
\begin{pmatrix}
-1 \\
0 \\
0
\end{pmatrix}.
\tag{77}
$$

The second-order condition for a maximum, which we assume to be met, requires that the determinant of the bordered Hessian on the left be positive. Henceforth this determinant will be denoted as *DET*.

Inverting the matrix on the left,

$$
\begin{pmatrix}
\dfrac{\partial\lambda}{\partial B} \\[4pt]
\dfrac{\partial g_i}{\partial B} \\[4pt]
\dfrac{\partial g_2}{\partial B}
\end{pmatrix}
=
\frac{1}{DET}
\begin{bmatrix}
L_{11}L_{22} & I_1\tau_1'L_{22} & I_2\tau_2'L_{11} \\
I_1\tau_1'L_{22} & -(I_2\tau_2')^2 & I_1\tau_1'I_2\tau_2' \\
I_2\tau_2'L_{11} & I_1\tau_1'I_2\tau_2' & -(I_1\tau_1')^2
\end{bmatrix}
\begin{pmatrix}
-1 \\
0 \\
0
\end{pmatrix}.
\tag{78}
$$

$$
= -\frac{1}{DET}
\begin{pmatrix}
L_{11}L_{22} \\
I_1\tau_1'L_{22} \\
I_2\tau_2'L_{11}
\end{pmatrix}
\tag{79}
$$

so

$$\frac{\partial\lambda}{\partial B} = -\frac{L_{11}L_{22}}{DET} < 0 \tag{80}$$

$$\frac{\partial g_1}{\partial B} = -\frac{I_1\tau_1'L_{22}}{DET} < 0 \tag{81}$$

$$\frac{\partial g_2}{\partial B} = -\frac{I_1\tau_1'L_{11}}{DET} < 0. \tag{82}$$

DET > 0 and $\tau_1' < \tau_2' < 0$. The signs given for (81) and (82) hold for the normal market case, and imply $L_{11} < 0$, $L_{22} < 0$. These in turn imply the sign given in (80). For these cases, as B increases, g_1 and g_2 move down a positively-sloped 'budget expansion curve', and the shadow value of budget funds falls.

Comparative statics with respect to $\mathbf{I}_1$

Differentiating the first-order conditions (46), (47), and (48) with respect to I_1 gives

$$
\begin{pmatrix}
0 & -I_1\tau_1' & -I_2\tau_2' \\
-I_1\tau_1' & L_{11} & 0 \\
-I_2\tau_2' & 0 & L_{22}
\end{pmatrix}
\begin{pmatrix}
\dfrac{\partial\lambda}{\partial I_1} \\[2mm]
\dfrac{\partial g_1}{\partial I_1} \\[2mm]
\dfrac{\partial g_2}{\partial I_1}
\end{pmatrix}
=
\begin{pmatrix}
\tau_1 \\[2mm]
\lambda\dfrac{d\tau_1}{dg_1} \\[2mm]
0
\end{pmatrix},
\tag{83}
$$

from which

$$
\begin{pmatrix}
\dfrac{\partial\lambda}{\partial I_1} \\[2mm]
\dfrac{\partial g_1}{\partial I_1} \\[2mm]
\dfrac{\partial g_2}{\partial I_1}
\end{pmatrix}
=
\frac{1}{DET}
\begin{pmatrix}
L_{11}L_{22} & I_1\tau_1'L_{22} & I_2\tau_2'L_{11} \\
I_1\tau_1'L_{22} & -\left(I_2\tau_2'\right)^2 & I_1\tau_1'I_2\tau_2' \\
I_2\tau_2'L_{11} & I_1\tau_1'I_2\tau_2' & -\left(I_1\tau_1'\right)^2
\end{pmatrix}
\begin{pmatrix}
\tau_1 \\[2mm]
\lambda\dfrac{d\tau_1}{dg_1} \\[2mm]
0
\end{pmatrix}.
\tag{84}
$$

This leads to

$$
\frac{\partial\lambda}{\partial I_1} = \frac{L_{22}}{DET}\left[L_{11}\tau_1 + \lambda I_1\left(\tau_1'\right)^2\right]
\tag{85}
$$

$$
\frac{\partial g_1}{\partial I_1} = \frac{I_1\tau_1'L_{22}\tau_1 - \left(I_2\tau_2'\right)^2\lambda\tau_1'}{DET} > 0
\tag{86}
$$

$$
\frac{\partial g_2}{\partial I_1} = \frac{I_2\tau_2'}{DET}\left[L_{11}\tau_1 + \lambda I_1\left(\tau_1'\right)^2\right]
\tag{87}
$$

$\frac{\partial g_1}{\partial I_1} > 0$: if the cost of investigating industry 1 rises, the competition authority increases g_i.

The changes in g_1 and g_2 if I_1 rises can be broken down into a 'budget-compensated' change – a movement along a given isowelfare curve as the isobudget curve becomes steeper – and an outward move along a budget expansion curve.

To interpret the expression for $d\lambda/dI_1$, first differentiate

$$
I_2\lambda = \frac{W_2'}{\tau_2'}
\tag{88}
$$

with respect to I_1 to obtain

$$I_2 \frac{\partial \lambda}{\partial I_1} = \frac{W_2'}{\tau_2'} \left(\frac{W_1''}{W_1'} - \frac{\tau_1''}{\tau_1'} \right) \frac{\partial g_2}{\partial I_1}. \tag{89}$$

If the condition for $L_{11} < 0$, (59), is satisfied, the term in parentheses on the right is positive and $\frac{\partial \lambda}{\partial I_1}$ and $\frac{\partial g_2}{\partial I_1}$ have the same sign. This is also apparent directly from (85) and (87).

Second, differentiate the other expression for λ,

$$\lambda = \frac{W_1'/\tau_1'}{I_1}, \tag{90}$$

with respect to I_1 to obtain

$$\frac{\tau_1' I_1^2}{W_1'} \frac{\partial \lambda}{\partial I_1} = \frac{I_1}{W_1'/\tau_1'} \frac{d\left(W_1'/\tau_1'\right)}{dg_1} \frac{dg_1}{dI_1} - 1 \tag{91}$$

The coefficient of $\frac{\partial \lambda}{\partial I_1}$ on the left is positive. The first term on the right,

$$\frac{I_1}{W_1'/\tau_1'} \frac{d\left(W_1'/\tau_1'\right)}{dg_1} \frac{dg_1}{dI_1} = \frac{I_1}{\left(\tau_1'\right)^2} \left(\frac{W_1''}{W_1'} - \frac{\tau_1''}{\tau_1'} \right) \frac{dg_1}{dI_1}, \tag{92}$$

is positive, so long as $L_{11} < 0$.

It follows that $\frac{\partial \lambda}{\partial I_1}$ and $\frac{\partial g_2}{\partial I_1}$ are negative if the direct effect of an increase in I_1, the denominator of (90), in reducing λ, is greater in magnitude than the indirect effect of an increase in I_1, which is to increase W_1'/τ_1', the numerator of (90).

Directly from (85) and (87), if

$$L_{11}\tau_1 + \lambda I_1 \left(\tau_1'\right)^2 < 0, \tag{93}$$

then $\frac{\partial \lambda}{\partial I_1}$ and $\frac{\partial g_2}{\partial I_1}$ are negative. Evaluating (93), the condition for (93) is (compare (59))

$$-\frac{1}{\tau_1'/\tau_1} \frac{d}{dg_1} \left(\frac{\tau_1'}{\tau'} \right) > -\frac{W_1''}{W_1'} > 0. \tag{94}$$

Like (59), (94) is a condition which ensures that the direct effect of changes in investigation costs prevail over indirect effects. By expressing (59) and (94) in terms of their definitions, one can show that (94) implies (59).

If (94) is met, or equivalently if the right-hand side of (91) is positive, an increase in I_1 leads to a decrease in g_2, a decrease in the shadow value of budget funds λ, and, as follows from (86), an increase in g_1.

Comparative statics with respect to n_i

Industry output

Differentiate (30), the expression for firm ik's profit, with respect to q_{ik} to obtain firm ik's first-order condition:

$$\frac{\partial \pi_{ik}}{\partial g_{ik}} = p_i(Q_i) - c_i + q_{ik}\frac{dp_i}{dQ_i} - \frac{\gamma_i F_i}{n_i} f_i\big[g_i - p_1(Q_i)\big]\frac{dp_i}{dQ_i} = 0 \tag{95}$$

Adding (95) over all j gives

$$p_i(Q_i) - c_i + \frac{Q_i}{n_i}\frac{dp_i}{dQ_i} - \frac{\gamma_i F_i}{n_i} f_i\big[g_i - p_1(Q_i)\big]\frac{dp_i}{dQ_i} = 0. \tag{96}$$

As usual for Cournot oligopoly with constant marginal cost, industry output depends on unit cost and the number of firms.

Differentiating (96) with respect to g_i gives the comparative static derivative

$$\frac{\partial Q_i}{\partial g_i} = \frac{1}{D_i}\gamma_i F_i f_i'\frac{dp_i}{dQ_i} < 0, \tag{97}$$

where stability conditions imply that

$$D_i = (n_i - 1)\frac{dp_i}{dQ_i} + \frac{\gamma_i F_i f_i'}{n_i}\left(\frac{dp_i}{dQ_i}\right)^2 + \frac{1}{n_i}\frac{d^2 p_i}{dQ_i^2}(Q_i - \gamma_i F_i f_i) < 0. \tag{98}$$

A lower investigation threshold increases industry output.

Differentiating (96) with respect to n_i gives

$$\frac{\partial Q_i}{\partial n_i} = \frac{Q_i - \gamma_i F_i f_i}{n_i D_i}\frac{dp_i}{dQ_i} > 0. \tag{99}$$

Industry output rises with the number of firms in the industry.

The competition authority's problem

The investigation thresholds selected by the competition authority maximize

$$L = W_1(Q_1) + W_2(Q_2) - B + \lambda\big[B - \tau_1 I_1 - \tau_2 I_2\big] \tag{100}$$

where

$$W_i(Q_i) = \int_0^{Q_i}\big[p(x_i) - c_i\big]dx_i \tag{101}$$

and

$$\tau_i = \int_{g_i-p_i(Q_i)}^{\bar{\varepsilon}_i} f_i(\varepsilon_i)d\varepsilon_i. \tag{102}$$

The first-order conditions have the same form as (46)–(48). Differentiating the first-order conditions with respect to n_1 gives

$$
\begin{pmatrix}
0 & -I_1\tau_1' & -I_2\tau_2' \\
-I_1\tau_1' & L_{11} & 0 \\
-I_2\tau_2' & 0 & L_{22}
\end{pmatrix}
\begin{pmatrix}
\dfrac{\partial\lambda}{\partial n_1} \\[2mm]
\dfrac{\partial g_1}{\partial n_1} \\[2mm]
\dfrac{\partial g_2}{\partial n_1}
\end{pmatrix}
=
\begin{pmatrix}
-I_1\tau_1'\dfrac{dp_i}{dQ_i}\dfrac{\partial Q_1}{\partial n_1} \\[2mm]
-\dfrac{\partial^2 L}{\partial n_1 \partial g_1} \\[2mm]
0
\end{pmatrix},
\tag{103}
$$

Note that

$$\frac{\partial^2 L}{\partial n_1 \partial g_1} = \frac{\partial^2 W_1}{\partial n_1 \partial g_1} - \lambda I_1 \frac{\partial^2 \tau_1}{\partial n_1 \partial g_1} \tag{104}$$

$$= \frac{\partial W_1}{\partial g_1}\left(\frac{1}{\partial W_1/\partial g_1}\frac{\partial^2 W_1}{\partial n_1 \partial g_1} - \frac{1}{\partial \tau_1/\partial g_1}\frac{\partial^2 \tau_1}{\partial n_1 \partial g_1}\right) \tag{105}$$

To interpret the term in parentheses in (105), note that welfare in market 1 rises as the investigation threshold falls, holding the number of firms constant

$$\frac{\partial W_1}{\partial g_1} = \frac{\partial W_1}{\partial Q_1}\frac{\partial Q_1}{\partial g_1} < 0 \tag{106}$$

and as the number of firms increases, holding the investigation threshold constant:

$$\frac{\partial W_1}{\partial n_1} = \frac{\partial W_1}{\partial Q_1}\frac{\partial Q_1}{\partial n_1} > 0. \tag{107}$$

If

$$\frac{\partial^2 W_1}{\partial n_1 \partial g_1} > 0, \tag{108}$$

this means that from the point of view of market performance tougher competition policy and more intense competition are substitutes in the sense that an increase in the number of firms reduces the magnitude of $\partial W_1/\partial g_1 < 0$ and that a reduction in the investigation threshold reduces $\partial W_1 / \partial n_1 > 0$.

If the impacts of lower g_1 and greater n_1 on W_1 are related in this way, then

$$\frac{\partial^2 L}{\partial n_1 \partial g_1} = \frac{\partial W_1}{\partial g_1} \left(\frac{1}{\partial W_1 / \partial g_1} \frac{\partial^2 W_1}{\partial n_1 \partial g_1} - \frac{1}{\partial \tau_1 / \partial g_1} \frac{\partial^2 \tau_1}{\partial n_1 \partial g_1} \right) > 0 \tag{109}$$

Returning to and solving (103) gives

$$\frac{\partial \lambda}{\partial n_1} = -\frac{I_1 \tau_1' L_{22}}{DET} \left(L_{11} \frac{dp_1}{dQ_1} \frac{\partial Q_1}{\partial n_1} + \frac{\partial^2 L}{\partial n_1 \partial g_1} \right) < 0 \tag{110}$$

$$\frac{\partial g_1}{\partial n_1} = -\frac{1}{DET} \left[\left(I_2 \tau_2' \right)^2 \frac{\partial^2 L}{\partial n_1 \partial g_1} - \left(I_1 \tau_1' \right)^2 L_{22} \frac{dp_1}{dQ_1} \frac{\partial Q_1}{\partial n_1} \right] \tag{111}$$

$$\frac{\partial g_2}{\partial n_1} = -\frac{I_1 \tau_1' I_2 \tau_2'}{DET} \left(L_{11} \frac{dp_1}{dQ_1} \frac{\partial Q_1}{\partial n_1} + \frac{\partial^2 L}{\partial n_1 \partial g_1} \right) < 0 \tag{112}$$

An increase in n_1 improves market performance in market 1, all else equal, and reduces the shadow value of funds in the investigation budget. The improvement in market performance in market 1 leads the competition authority to lower the investigation threshold for industry 2.

The direct effect of an increase in n_1 is to raise output Q_1, permitting the competition authority to lower the investigation threshold for industry 1. The increase in g_2, which draws investigation resources away from industry 1, mitigates this. $\partial g_1 / \partial n_1$ is of ambiguous sign, although g_1 will fall if the direct effect of an increase in the number of firms dominates.[19]

Acknowledgement

I am grateful for comments received at Universitat Jaume I and the Copenhagen Business School. Responsibility for errors is my own.

Notes

1 In some legal regimes, employees of firms that violate antitrust law may be subject to criminal penalties. Such penalties are rare, and are not considered here.
2 See *U.S.* v. *Chas. Pfizer & Co., Inc.* 367 F. Supp. 91 (S.D.N.Y. 1973), where two firms were charged with collusion and conspiracy to monopolize following an agreement to settle certain patent disputes that was reached after discussions by the presidents of the two companies, and found not guilty when the court accepted their argument that the settlement reached after the discussions reflected the exercise of independent business judgment.
3 Competition policy typically frowns on the systematic exchange of price and/or quantity data referring to individual firms or transactions. Such a policy has a sound

basis in economic theory – detailed price reporting chills price rivalry by exposing price cutters to rapid retaliation – but detailed price reporting acts to enforce a 'collusive' set of strategies, once reached, not to facilitate initial convergence on such a set of strategies.

4 Nor is economic theory likely to be of much help in reducing this uncertainty. From the point of view of economic theory, *all* decisions by independent firms are independent if it is not possible for the firms involved to make binding commitments. If contracts to restrict output and raise price are not enforceable, all conduct that leads to outcomes in which firms exercise more market power than they would in the non-cooperative equilibrium of a one-shot game is non-cooperative, and in that sense independently arrived at.

5 Analysis of the administration of competition policy that regulates market structure is the subject of ongoing research.

6 Discussion of competition policy toward industries producing products related in demand would complicate expressions for net social welfare without changing fundamental aspects of the model. Discussion of competition policy toward industries producing intermediate goods (such as software) would require explicit analysis of input–output relationships throughout the economy.

7 This would be particularly important in a model including a separate stage of the game at which the firm would decide whether or not to settle and avoid litigation.

8 The condition is satisfied for a linear demand curve. It means that the output response to a change in the investigation threshold is less in magnitude than the slope of the demand curve,

$$-\frac{dq_i}{dp_i} > -\frac{\partial q_i}{\partial g_i} > 0. \tag{12}$$

9 The exponential distribution is convenient for examples because it always leads to interior solutions of the competition authority's problem. A uniform distribution would involve the possibility of corner solutions (for example, in which the probability of investigation is so high that the firm treats fines as a fixed cost and produces the no-competition policy monopoly output; see Martin (1998)).

10 In what follows, I will omit the adjective 'expected' unless clarity requires it.

11 Table 11.2 assumes that firms expect to evenly divide any fines; see p. 182.

12 In Martin (2000), I show that lower investigation thresholds generally stimulate private investment in cost-saving innovation. In this sense, stricter product-market competition policy promotes good dynamic market performance.

13 This formulation implies that expected fines are receipts to the government in general, not to the competition authority. In the contrary case, the budget constraint would be

$$\tau_1 I_1 + \tau_2 I_2 \leq B + \tau_1 \gamma_1 F_1 + \pi_2 \gamma_2 F_2.$$

14 In May 1998 the U.S. Department of Justice, prosecuting Microsoft and faced with the need to monitor a wave of mergers, requested an increase of 'several million dollars' in the Antitrust Division's annual budget of $95 million (Associated Press, 20 May 1998).

15 Variations might weight consumers' and producers' surplus differently; for an example in the context of a model of competition policy, see Besanko and Spulber (1993).

16 For any value of B, as the size of market 1 increases, holding the size of market 2 constant, it eventually becomes optimal to devote all investigation resources to industry 1.

17 The assumption that firms are identical can be relaxed without much difficulty. If unit costs are constant for each firm but differ across firms in the industry, then industry

outut depends on the number of firms and unweighted average output. To examine the impact of an additional firm on equilibrium investigation thresholds, one must specify the unit cost of the additional firm.

18 Figure 11.12 is drawn for an exponential density and linear demand.

19 Differentiating the budget constraint

$$I_2 \int_{g_1 - p_1(Q_1)}^{\bar{\varepsilon}_1} f_1(\varepsilon_1) d\varepsilon_1 + I_2 \int_{g_2 - p_2(Q_2)}^{\bar{\varepsilon}_2} f_2(\varepsilon_2) d\varepsilon_2 = B \qquad\qquad 113$$

with respect to n_1 gives

$$I_1 f_1 \left(\frac{\partial g_1}{\partial n_1} - \frac{dp_1}{dQ_1} \frac{\partial Q_1}{\partial n_1} \right) + I_2 f_2 \frac{\partial g_2}{\partial n_1} = 0 \qquad\qquad 114$$

$I_1 f_1$ and $I_2 f_2$ are both positive. By (112), $\partial g_2/\partial n_1 < 0$. It follows that

$$\frac{\partial g_1}{\partial n_1} - \frac{dp_1}{dQ_1} \frac{\partial Q_1}{\partial n_1} > 0 \qquad\qquad 115$$

This is certainly satisfied if $\partial g_1/\partial n_1 > 0$. It may be satisfied if $\partial g_1/\partial n_1$ is negative, if the second term on the left, which is negative, is sufficiently large in magnitude.

References

Besanko, D. and Spulber, D. F. (1993) 'Contested mergers and equilibrium antitrust policy', *Journal of Law, Economics and Organization* 9 (1), April, 1–29.

Chamberlin, E. H. (1933) *The Theory of Monopolistic Competition*, Cambridge, MA: Harvard University Press.

Friedman, J. W. (1971) 'A non-cooperative equilibrium for supergames', *Review of Economic Studies* 38 (1), January, 1–12, reprinted in Daughety, A. F. *Cournot Oligopoly: Characterization and Applications*, Cambridge: Cambridge University Press (1988) pp. 142-157.

Martin, S. (1998) 'Competition policy: publicity vs. prohibition and punishment', in S. Martin (ed.) *Competition Policies in Europe*, Amsterdam: Elsevier North Holland.

Martin, S. (2000) 'Product market competition policy and technological performance', in G. Norman and J. Thisse (eds) *Market Structure and Competition Policy*, Cambridge: Cambridge University Press.

Priest, G. (1977) 'The common law process and the selection of efficient rules', *Journal of Legal Studies* 6 (1) January, 65-82.

Rubin, P. H. (1977) 'Why is the common law efficient?', *Journal of Legal Studies* 6 (1), January, 51–63.

12 European state aid policy

An economic analysis

Timothy Besley and Paul Seabright

Introduction

When should action by an EU member state to assist the competitiveness of its own firms in world markets be of concern to other member states, and when is it a private matter between the government of that member state and its taxpayer/citizens? The use of state aids to industry by the governments of EU member states or by regional and local governments within those member states is probably the least well understood domain of competition policy, as well as raising some of the most difficult political questions of enforcement and the allocation of powers. In describing it as not well understood we mean that the fundamental principles for the economic analysis of the phenomenon remain unclear. As far as the magnitude of the phenomenon and its incidence among member states is concerned, we now know a great deal more than was known a few years ago, thanks in good measure to the European Commission's own efforts to improve the transparency and accuracy of statistical reporting. However, our ability to describe the phenomenon has moved far ahead of our capacity to analyse its effects and evaluate its implications for public policy. When exactly such aid should be viewed as a distortion of competition is something there are few agreed criteria for determining. This chapter should therefore be viewed as a preliminary account of a rudimentary and in many ways unsatisfactory academic debate, though one upon which we have sought to impose a degree of order.

The chapter is structured as follows. In the second section we review briefly the literature relevant to the state aids problem and summarize the reasons why the policy implications of this literature are so often conflicting and confused. This is a selective rather than an exhaustive review, to enable the issues to be brought out rather than drowned in a sea of references. In the third section we outline an analytical framework that in our view helps to reconcile the different approaches in the existing literature. We give an account of some of the main results that can be derived in this analytical framework. In the fourth section we draw out the implications for policy of these results, taking care to distinguish those issues where the policy implications are relatively clear from those that will require further research. In the fifth section we confront these implications with the actual practice of the European Commission as revealed in decisions of the last few years. In the conclusion we summarize the main unresolved questions and propose an agenda for future discussion.

We conclude this brief introduction by outlining the main reasons why the existing economic literature gives such unsatisfactory guidance, and why the question is nevertheless of primary importance for EU policy. Essentially, the relevant existing literature consists of not one but at least three families of models. Each provides a relatively clear and internally coherent view of the economic effects of state aids to industry, but based on different premises from, and therefore not coherent with, the view of the other models. Each has its own view of the fundamental determinants of the process by which governments compete to attract and support economic activity within their territories, a process we shall hereafter refer to as 'government competition' and which includes but is not restricted to the use of state aids to support firms. The first family of models consists of those comprising the literature on 'strategic trade policy'. In these models, countries compete with each other in a negative sum game of individually rational but collectively wasteful subsidies to industry, spurred by the prospect of poaching each other's profits in imperfectly competitive markets. All countries are therefore better off if they can reach and enforce an agreement to forgo such subsidies. However, in these models it makes no difference where firms choose to undertake their economic activity, so there is no purpose in governments' competing to attract economic activity, and no benefits from such competition to offset against its possible costs.

In a second class of models, however (namely those in the Tiebout tradition in public finance), part of the purpose of competition between governments is to induce an efficient allocation of local public goods. It does so by encouraging citizens and firms to migrate to those locations where the mix of public goods and tax rates most closely matches their preferences. Here competition between governments is broadly a welcome phenomenon, and the precise mechanisms by which it takes place are of secondary importance. There may be imperfections in such a competitive process (typically due to externalities between jurisdictions) but these rarely invalidate the view that some degree of competition to attract economic activity is desirable.

In a third class of models (namely, those in the literature on the new economic geography) competition between governments to attract economic activity has both potentially beneficial and potentially damaging consequences depending on circumstances. In these models the location and production decisions of firms may have important external effects on their host economies, so that government action to internalize these externalities (by taxes, subsidies or other means) is in principle justified. On the other hand, the systemic effect of some of these externalities means that we cannot be confident that unfettered competition between localities will produce efficient outcomes, so some collective agreements to restrain such competition may be appropriate.

To summarize, one set of models assumes no differences between either firms or locations and is broadly hostile to government competition. The second focuses upon differences between firms that induce endogenous differences between locations, and is broadly welcoming of government competition. The third focuses on differences between locations, and is ambivalent about the effects of government competition. Faced with these three very different perspectives it is tempting to conclude that since there is analytical confusion it is best to remain agnostic and to draw no policy conclusions. However, such an academic luxury is unjustifiable in the real world of international policy-making, for several distinct but related reasons. First, as Figure 12.1 shows, state aids to industry are a large and important phenomenon, but one that differs dramatically in magnitude between EU member states. It is hard to believe that expenditures such as these really represent optimal policy responses to differing circumstances across the EU. But if they do not it becomes important to ask: 'whose problem are they?' Are they properly a matter for the citizens of each state to determine with their governments but (in keeping with the principle of subsidiarity) of no concern to the rest of the EU? Or are they of concern precisely because they represent evidence of a collectively self-defeating struggle to gain industrial advantage?

Second, whatever economic analysis may say, state aids fall under the domain of international law, both the state aids provisions of the Treaty of Rome and the provisions of the General Agreement on Tariffs and Trade. International law does not proscribe government support of industry outright, but it does require such support not to distort competition. It therefore becomes inescapable to answer the question when distortion of competition is likely to result.

Third, competitors of firms receiving state aid are increasingly resorting to law to challenge them: Mederer (1996) reports that some 80 cases are pending before

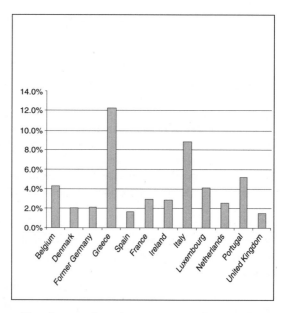

Figure 12.1 State aid to the manufacturing sector – % of value added 1990–2

the European courts. This does not, of course, imply that the Commission is being unduly lenient: competitors may be using the law strategically to harass other firms or simply to compensate for advantages they gain from state aid. But it does imply the increasing need to justify the Commission's policy before a skeptical and potentially litigious audience.

Fourth, the Commission's approach to state aids increasingly informs its approach to other aspects of EU economic policy. For example, moves to harmonize tax regimes within the EU have been growing in strength recently, partly because of a view that some forms of tax competition are 'a form of state aid', in the words of Commissioner Monti (*Financial Times*, 29 July 1997). Clearly, if these other policies are to be well founded it is important not only that the analogy with state aid be an appropriate one, but that state aid policy itself function in a way that can reasonably be taken as a normative model.

Finally, the proportion of all cases that give rise to negative decisions is very small, as Table 12.1 reveals. This proportion has fallen from between 2 per cent and 5 per cent in the late 1980s to under 1.5 per cent since 1991. Yet even these few cases have often given rise to major political difficulties for the Commission, since the firms receiving aid deemed incompatible with the common market usually have powerful political backers (which is often why they received the aid in the first place). In these circumstances the Commission needs to be able to explain convincingly what is special about the cases it has singled out for prohibition. It would be comforting if the economics literature provided a ready off-the-peg answer, but unfortunately it does not. Answers will need to be tailored more creatively from such material as the literature provides. This chapter is therefore aimed at discussing the principles according to which this can be done.

The literature relevant to state aids

Strategic trade policy

Three distinct and well-developed branches of the economics literature provide insights into the effects of state aids to industry. The first is the literature on strategic trade policy, for example, Brander and Spencer (1985). It has focused primarily on imperfectly competitive firms with fixed locations. Nationalistic governments can use various instruments to promote the interests of domestically located firms to shift rents to their home country. In general, world welfare suffers from such policies since they inflict a negative externality on other countries

Table 12.1 Trends in negative and conditional decisions

Year	Total cases	Negative decisions	Conditional decisions
1988	410	3.4%	2.2%
1991	597	1.2%	0.3%
1994	527	0.6%	0.4%
1997	502	1.8%	1.0%

which is not taken into account by the nationalistic governments. Importantly (as will be seen later) governments are assumed to be able to negotiate with their own domestic firms but not with those of other nations.

A recent literature has developed which recognises that the assumption of fixed firm locations can fruitfully be relaxed. Bond and Samuelson (1986) and Doyle and van Wijnbergen (1996) have studied the role of tax holidays in attracting firms to particular locations. Black and Hoyt (1989) study how provision of local public goods can pay by attracting firms who then contribute to the tax base. Keen and Marchand (1997) consider the impact of the composition of public spending (and particularly its division between public goods valued by citizen/taxpayers and those valued by firms) on the incentives for capital to migrate between jurisdictions.

In addition, recent contributions to this literature also emphasise the importance of dynamic considerations, and of examining the question whether governments are able to commit to future strategy (see especially Leahy and Neary (1996) and Karp and Perloff (1990)). These issues are of crucial importance in our framework below.

Whether firms can migrate does not really change the fundamental character of these models, since in either case there is no social benefit to their locating in one jurisdiction rather than another. Consequently action by one government to attract a firm from another jurisdiction produces no net benefit in terms of productive efficiency. It merely inflicts an externality (in terms of the lost rents) which is likely to have a negative overall impact on allocative efficiency. Interpreted in the context of state aids, this means that subsidies to firms will consequently be higher than would be efficient, and the subsidized activity will occur at a higher than efficient level. At least, this conclusion will be justified unless there are independent reasons for thinking that subsidies in the absence of the externality would have been below the efficient level. This might be because the activity in question was an international monopoly, potential entrants into which did not take account of the beneficial externality their entry would create for consumers. Nevertheless, such arguments (even if plausible in theory) may be difficult to justfy empirically. For example, Neven and Seabright (1995) estimate on the basis of a simulation model of the international aerospace industry that the positive consumer externalities from the entry of Airbus Industrie have been very much smaller than the negative profit externalities for the existing firms Boeing and McDonnell-Douglas. This implies that launch aid has been excessive from the point of view of the welfare of the world as a whole (though beneficial for Europe).

An alternative reason for thinking that the presence of negative externalities does not imply that state aids are excessive in strategic trade policy models might be that state aids merely return to firms some of the tax resources that have been inefficiently taken from them in the first place. Some have argued (like Brennan and Buchanan, 1980) that the normal processes of politics in the modern state are biased towards excessive taxation and the growth of a 'Leviathan' state. Competition between jurisdictions is therefore welcome, on this view, because it bids down overall taxation to more acceptable levels. Dye (1990, pp.1–3) gives the flavour of this point of view in a US context:

> All governments, even democratic governments, are dangerous ... Democratic political processes alone cannot restrain Leviathan ... Among the most important 'auxiliary precautions' the founders devised to control government is federalism [which] is not only competition between the national government and the states ... it is also competition between the states. Indeed it is also, by extension, competition among the nation's eighty-three thousand local governments.

Regardless of the general plausibility of this view, it is worth remarking that the selective distribution of state aids to a minority of enterprises seems like a very indirect and distortionary way to reduce the overall burden of taxation on firms.

It is important to appreciate that a central limitation of these models lies in their assuming that firms can negotiate only with their own governments. It is clear why this generates inefficiency: a firm can be induced to take account of the external benefits and costs of its own production decisions only in so far as these affect its 'own' patron government, but not in so far as they affect those of other countries. However, this is a seriously unrealistic assumption in a world of multinational corporations – and indeed of corporations that are potentially multinational in principle even if at any one time they are located in only one country in fact. In such a world their decisions will be influenced by the incentives they could receive from other governments than those that are currently their patrons. In the alternative analytical framework below we explore the consequences of making these assumptions more realistic, and show that the mere presence of externalities between countries alone is not sufficient to generate inefficient outcomes.

The implications of the models of strategic trade policy for policy towards state aids are reasonably clear in some dimensions though far from clear in others. Provided there are no other economic policy distortions, a binding agreement by all countries to reduce subsidy levels will increase world welfare. There is therefore a rationale for efforts by the European Commission and the World Trade Organization to reduce overall subsidy levels within their respective jurisdictions. However, the models give less clear guidance as to how it may be recognized what constitutes a subsidy. For example, it is quite possible for a government-guaranteed loan to a firm to be repaid in full at market rates of interest and still to constitute a subsidy without which the firm's entry into the industry (or expansion of output) would not have taken place. This is because the government guarantee works (in a way that an unguaranteed loan from a private bank could not) by dissuading the firm's competitors from responding aggressively. They know that in the event of their doing so the firm would stay in the industry and keep its output level, with its losses underwritten by the loan. They therefore respond by accommodating its presence and the loan guarantee is never required. Indeed, this is a specific example of a phenomenon that is of quite general validity in the strategic trade policy literature (see Brander and Spencer,

1985). This is that government support to industry works to change the way in which domestic firms *would* react to foreign competitors, seeking thereby to induce less aggressive behaviour on the part of such competitors. Because it changes hypothetical or anticipated behaviour it is not always possible to identify in a straightforward manner.

On this account, the main difference between government funds and private funds lies in the lower probability of repayment of the latter in bad circumstances. Since these circumstances may never be observed, government loans that are repaid in full may nevertheless constitute state aids and may significantly distort competition. It is therefore hard, within the context of these models, to resist the conclusion that state aids policy should simply forbid all payments by governments to firms other than for procurement purposes or to rectify an identifiable market failure. In particular, the Market Economy Investor Principle (hereafter MEIP) makes no sense in this context. If the payment to the firm was not made by a market economy investor, it is only reasonable to assume that the benefits it yielded would have been lower had the payment come from such an investor, and that the payment consequently constitutes a state aid that distorts competition.

Overall, therefore, the literature on strategic trade policy implies that a strict control of state aids is desirable, indeed one substantially stricter than is applied in the EU at present. However, it reaches these conclusions on the basis of a particular model that sees no point in the process of government competition in the first place. It is therefore in tension with that part of the public finance literature that stresses the virtues of decentralization as a means to encourage competition between jurisdictions. It also takes no account of the political and juridical tradition of subsidiarity, which has re-entered European politics in a powerful form through the Treaty of Maastricht.

Nevertheless, even if the framework of the strategic trade policy literature is restrictive, a number of lessons can be drawn from it with substantially wider applicability. First of all, even if (as we shall see) externalities between countries are not a sufficient condition for inefficient outcomes, they are at least likely to be necessary. In practical terms, this means that before diagnosing a significant distortion of competition it is important to demonstrate the existence of a substantial externality inflicted by the aid in question on the economy of some other member state. Furthermore, the models we have been considering show that such an externality will typically be due to imperfect competition in the markets concerned (usually output markets, but potentially also markets for inputs). Only if the market is imperfectly competitive will a subsidy to one firm make a significant difference to the reaction function of a competitor. Note that in the case of pure monopoly there is no problem, since there is no competitor to be harmed (indeed, subsidy to a monopoly may even enhance efficiency if it encourages pricing closer to marginal cost). Conversely, for competitive markets there is no problem, since a subsidy to one firm affects only its own profits, not the conditions faced by other firms.

Finally, note that for a firm to receive a subsidy at all implies that the price it pays for the public goods and services it receives lies below that paid by other comparable firms in its own jurisdiction, not necessarily one below that paid by competitor firms in other jurisdictions. A rent-shifting subsidy is one in which the patron government uses tax resources from elsewhere in the economy to make a commitment to altering the reaction function of the client firm. The models of strategic trade policy typically assume otherwise symmetric firms, but there is nothing inevitable about such an assumption. If two firms compete using production technologies that consume different levels of public goods, in the absence of subsidy they will pay different levels of taxes; while for them to pay the same levels of taxes would be quite consistent with one of them receiving a large subsidy. This reminds us that to identify a state aid at all requires us to compare a firm's tax payments with those of others in its jurisdiction, not with those of competitors in other jurisdictions.

Public finance

There are two main traditions in the literature on public finance dealing with the virtues of decentralization. One, given a classic statement by Oates (1969), supposes that there is spatial variation in the preferences of citizens for public goods (which may in turn be due partly to variations in local conditions). Decentralization allows different kinds and levels of public goods to be supplied in different localities. Centralized governments are supposed to be unable to practice such differentiation, either because they lack information about local preferences and conditions, or because they are constrained to make uniform provision for some other reason. However, they are able to exploit scale economies (important for such public goods as national defence), and to internalize externalities between localities (as when national highways benefit traffic between as well as within regions). For each type of public good, therefore, there will be some level of government that optimally balances these advantages and disadvantages. But for many types of good the presence of variations between localities is a positive benefit of decentralization. Not only will the playing field not be level (to adapt a much misused phrase), but it should not be.

A second tradition, due to Tiebout (1956), treats the spatial variation in preferences for public goods as partly the result rather than as purely the cause of the local differentiation of public good supply. Consumers cluster together with those who have similar preferences to themselves. The Tiebout literature therefore emphasises the benefits of decentralization in inducing jurisdictions to compete for sources of tax revenue by inducing citizens and firms to sort themselves into groups on the basis of their preferences for local public goods (Tiebout himself wrote about citizens, but others, such as Oates and Schwab (1991) have developed the analysis for firms). If citizens and firms are costlessly mobile between jurisdictions they can choose to locate in jurisdictions that offer their preferred combinations of local public goods, financed by lump-sum local taxes which can be thought of as the 'price' of purchasing a given combination. In effect local governments are like firms offering differentiated products.

Tiebout showed that competition between governments would lead to Pareto-efficient outcomes provided certain (stringent) conditions were met, notably that the number of jurisdictions was at least equal to the number of types of consumer and that there were no externalities between jurisdictions (see also Pestieau, 1977 and Bewley, 1981).

Neither of these two traditions answers the question why decentralization of power to local governments (which is surely necessary if they are to compete in any substantial sense) should be at all necessary for the local differentiation of public good supply. The Oates model simply assumes that central governments have no access to local preferences, whereas there is no reason why they could not – if they wished – implement mechanisms to induce revelation of these preferences as effectively as could local governments. Indeed, the Tiebout model shows how they could do so, since its central insight is available just as much to a centralized government as to a decentralized one. That is, a central government may realize that, although citizens have an incentive to distort their answers if asked to report their preferences for public goods, it can induce them to reveal these preferences truthfully by implementing a differentiated pattern of local public good supply, and watching citizens seek out their favourite combinations.

If central governments are indeed less responsive to local preferences than are local governments which have a genuine power of local decision-making, that must be because they have fewer incentives to be so responsive rather than because they are unable to be so. An important part of the explanation may lie in differences in the accountability of local and central governments to their respective populations. For example, one may ask why it makes sense for public transport in Toulouse to be run by an authority responsible to the Mayor and Council of Toulouse rather than by a subsidiary of the Parisian public transport authority. In either case the day-to-day running must be delegated to full-time employees who are located in Toulouse; it might be thought to make little difference who is the ultimate employer of these employees. In fact, since the citizens of Toulouse cannot specify in advance the right transport policy to implement in all possible circumstances, they need to be assured that ultimate authority to intervene in transport decisions rests in the hands of parties who are likely to have the right balance of interests at heart . These are more likely to be the Toulouse authorities than those in the capital who must balance many other conflicting priorities. One may say, in other words, that the advantages of decentralized governments lie in their potentially greater accountability to local interests. Furthermore, the importance of accountability arises in virtue of the incompleteness of the constitutional contract between citizens and their governments; citizens cannot commit their representatives to act in precise ways under all possible contingencies (Seabright, 1996, provides a formalization of this argument from the perspective of contract theory).

None of this implies that decentralized governments are always more responsive to their populations' preferences; indeed, 'capture' of local government by special interests is sometimes easier when these interests are locally concentrated and are therefore able to organize more effectively to influence local than central governments. Nevertheless, the notion of accountability provides an insight into the reasons why decentralized governments typically display more variation than do centralized ones in the pattern of public good provision. It thereby provides a rationale that is missing in the public finance literature for a preference in favour of decentralization in the absence of compelling arguments to the contrary.

Not only does this literature tend to imply that government competition brings many benefits; it also, and more subtly, provides a reason why pressures to centralize in the name of uniformity should be treated with suspicion. Some interest groups benefit from the uniform policies that a centralizing government would adopt. For example, the imposition of a constant minimum wage across economies with different overall income levels would benefit unskilled workers in rich countries by protecting them against competition from workers in poor countries. One can therefore expect to hear phrases such as 'a level playing-field' deployed by those interest groups as a means to advance their capture of the centralising jurisdiction.

Overall, therefore, the public finance literature provides a strong rationale for government competition, along with good reasons to treat with suspicion proposals to weaken the force of such competition by centralization. State aid control would appear on this account to be a policy of dubious merit and significant risk. Nevertheless, even within these models, it is far from clear that the provision of state aids is a particularly appropriate instrument for the pursuit of government competition, or that loss of the freedom to deploy them would matter very much. Within a given industry technologies are reasonably similar across firms. It is therefore unlikely that firms will have significantly different requirements in terms of industrial public goods as inputs to their production processes. Jurisdictions may specialize in attracting firms in particular industries, and these particular industries may require different levels of provision of local public goods. But there is no reason to expect different firms in the same industry to be given substantially different levels of public goods by their respective jurisdictions, and consequently not much to be feared from a policy that requires equal treatment of firms according to their jurisdiction of origin. That is not to say that such a policy is positively beneficial, and indeed it may be that the ability to set different prices provides the spur to government competition even if, in equilibrium, there is uniformity in pricing of the same public goods across jurisdictions. But these considerations do imply that spatial variation in the supply and pricing of local public goods may be of less importance within an industry than the simple Tiebout model suggests. A centrally enforced policy of equal treatment may therefore be more neutral than the argument originally appeared to imply.

More subtly, though, the Tiebout framework reminds us that in practice it may be hard to define precisely what constitutes a state aid. In the pure Tiebout model, purchasers of local public goods sort themselves by their preferences until each jurisdiction contains only a single type of consumer. This consumer pays a tax equal to the marginal cost of producing this bundle of goods (free entry implies this is also equal to the average cost of production). Furthermore, just as in Arrow–Debreu equilibrium, the process of competition itself defines what constitutes the 'market price' of such a bundle of public goods, and each consumer pays the common market price. Once we adopt a more realistic perspective, we shall accept that not all firms in a jurisdiction will pay the same taxes: does it follow therefore that all firms paying less than the average tax rate are thereby receiving subsidies? EU law on state aids requires firms to pay a market price for goods and services provided by the state, which is relatively easy to define when these consist of goods that are also privately traded, such as land. But when they consist of access to infrastructure services, for which no private market exists, what *is* a 'market price'? How can we calculate the appropriate level of tax liability for a firm using the services of publicly provided roads and airports, below which access to these facilities should be deemed a state aid? This is not to say that such definitional problems are insurmountable, or that rough-and-ready answers may not be accessible. But it does imply that caution should be exercised before seeking to use central policy in a jurisdiction such as the European Union to place a brake on the process of government competition.

To conclude, the public finance literature takes an altogether more benign view of the process of government competition. It does so by drawing attention to the benefits of diversity in the provision of local public goods. Although there are not many reasons to think these benefits important if the diversity is between different firms in the same industry (as opposed to between different industries), this literature highlights some of the risks of imposing uniformity and preventing government competition in the name of a 'level playing field'. It is difficult therefore to reconcile with the scepticism about government competition to emerge from the literature on strategic trade policy.

The 'new' economic geography

Many of the themes and preoccupations in the literature on the so-called new economic geography have a long tradition in economic analysis (Adam Smith's *The Wealth of Nations* devotes much space to considerations of economic geography, for instance). However, it is only recently that the policy implications of this analytical perspective have been incorporated into thinking about the process of government competition.

From the point of view of government competition, the central insight of the economic geography literature is that the location and production decisions of firms create external benefits and/or costs for the host economy. The magnitude of these externalities depends not just on the character of the activity but also on the place where it occurs. Thus a firm locating in an already overcrowded city may add to the congestion of the housing and transport infrastructure. Alternatively, the same firm moving to an area of unemployment may create beneficial externalities through its demand for labour. More subtly, a firm transferring its skilled workforce to an area where such skills already exist may deepen the pool of skilled labour and allow both firms and workers more effectively to cope with shocks in the demand for and supply of these skills.

These last externalities were first identified by Alfred Marshall and have been analysed in detail in Krugman (1991).

Why is this insight important? It provides a reason why the distribution of economic activity across geographical space has consequences for efficiency as well as for equity, and why the profit-seeking decisions of private firms will not necessarily realize efficient outcomes. If a way can be found to alter firms' incentives so that they internalize the externalities associated with their location and production decisions, the spatial distribution of economic activity will be more efficient than if they continue to ignore these externalities.

However, it is one thing to suggest that externalities should be internalized, another to discover an effective mechanism for doing so. A benevolent and omniscient government for the whole EU could in principle implement a pattern of locational taxes and subsidies designed to correct for geographical externalities. But the flaws in such an idea are the same as the flaws in the idea that a centralized government could use the insights of the Tiebout model to implement a spatially diverse pattern of local public goods. It could, but that does not mean it would. Its incentives to diversify local public good provision would depend on the kinds of pressure it faced to do so through the political process. In the public finance literature a degree of political decentralisation is seen as a necessary condition for diversity in public good provision. In the context of locational externalities it may also be a necessary condition for ensuring that the incentives faced by firms to locate and produce in particular regions accurately reflect the externalities created for the local economy in those regions.

To summarize, the literature on economic geography provides a reason for caring about providing locational incentives to firms. The insights of the public finance literature (and especially that portion of it concerned explicitly with the political economy of decentralization) provide a reason for supposing that some degree of government competition may be the only credible way to create these incentives. However, the economic geography literature also suggests ample reasons for caution about the way in which government competition might function. It has highlighted not only the externalities created within a region but the externalities between regions: the way in which activity locating in one region can draw resources away from others. It is sometimes hard even to be sure whether these externalities will be positive or negative. For example, improving the communications links to a certain region may either lead more activity to locate in that region or encourage activity already located there to migrate away. In the face of evidence about the complex character of such externalities between regions, is it possible to be confident that a process of unfettered competition between governments will lead to decisions that are efficient, or even superior to those that are left to the private choices of firms themselves?

These questions are ones that the existing literature relevant to state aids has yet to treat in a comprehensive and coherent fashion. The central aim of the present research has therefore been to provide a framework in which such an analysis can be conducted. Our task in the following section is to set out the essential components of such a framework.

An alternative analytical framework

General outline

The framework we outline consists of the following components:

- Firms make decisions about where to locate and how much output to produce. Firms do not intrinsically 'belong' to one country rather than another, though they may choose to produce in one country rather than another.
- These location and output decisions of firms create external costs and benefits for the economy of the country in which they take place. Benefits to governments include tax revenue, reduction of unemployment, generation of knowledge spillovers, Marshallian labour market externalities, and 'backward linkages'. More generally they may encompass any kind of 'market failure' about which governments care. Costs include congestion and pollution. It is reasonable to suppose that these costs and benefits can be different across possible locations and that firms' private decisions do not reflect these. For example, the same firm might in one place create beneficial backward linkages but in another place add to the burden on already congested infrastructure. But the firm itself would consider only its private profitability in each location.
- It is the fact that firms do not appropriate all the benefits of their location and production decisions that gives governments an incentive to compete to attract them. Governments can offer subsidies to firms contingent on their location and production decisions. For the time being we assume that these subsidies take the form of cash transfers and that there are no further restrictions on their nature. While a simplification, this assumption is not too unrealistic a representation of investment subsidies, tax holidays or employment subsidies. More generally, one could also imagine in-kind bidding in the form of infrastructure provision.

  Governments might also relax certain regulations such as those on environmental or employment standards to attract firms.
- In addition to externalities created for the economy in which production takes place, firms' decisions create externalities for other countries. These may be geographical (as when the decision of a firm to set up a plant in Belgium creates a demand for labour or components in nearby northern France). Alternatively, they may consist in an impact on the profits of rival firms, about which governments are assumed to care, either directly or because of their implications for tax revenue. So, for example, a decision by a Japanese firm to produce televisions in Wales may affect the profitability of a television producer located in France, paying French taxes and employing French workers.

This general framework allows us to draw a number of conclusions, based in part on the application of existing arguments and results in the literature, and in part on our own arguments and results. These conclusions depend on the precise circumstances of the process of competition between governments, which we distinguish along four dimensions. First, we distinguish between a static (one-period) framework and a dynamic (multi-period) framework. Second, we distinguish between a framework in which governments have an unrestricted ability to commit to a policy over time and one in which governments can reverse their earlier policies if it is in their interests to do so. Third, we distinguish between circumstances in which governments can negotiate unrestrictedly with all firms and those in which there are institutional limitations on their ability to do so. Finally, we distinguish between circumstances in which governments maximize national social welfare and those in which there is government failure at the national level.

The key insight that emerges from this analysis is that what causes inefficient outcomes under government competition is not solely the presence of externalities between governments. By themselves these are no obstacle to efficient allocations. What causes inefficiency is either a problem of time inconsistency due to governments' limited ability to commit to a policy over time, or some other institutional limitation on governments' ability to bid to attract the production of firms. This has important policy implications, notably that a blanket ban on state aids to firms is very unlikely to be beneficial (in contrast to the conclusions drawn from the strategic trade policy literature).

The reasoning behind this conclusion draws on the fact that the process of government competition can be modelled as a private-values auction. Governments are like bidders competing for the good that consists in a firm's location and production within their national territory. This good generates benefits (and costs) that typically vary between locations and in this sense are (in the terminology of auctions) 'private values'. In particular, governments are assumed to know what those values are to themselves and therefore to derive no new information from observing the bidding behaviour of others.

This bidding activity involves externalities between bidders. In the auction literature, such externalities were once thought to generate inefficiency. However, Bernheim and Whinston (1986) have shown that a menu auction (one in which bidders offer transfers to an auctioneer contingent on a full menu of allocations) can generate efficient outcomes even in the presence of externalities, provided that bidding strategies are 'truthful' in the sense that they reflect the bidders' true relative valuations of the various outcomes. Although this restriction on strategies might appear stringent, Bernheim and Whinston show that truthful bids are always (weak) best responses to other bids, even untruthful ones.

It is worth explaining in more detail precisely why the presence of externalities between bidders does not in itself result in inefficiency. Consider the following example. A few years ago in the East End of London a team of gardeners went from house to house offering to clear derelict gardens. They did this by tipping the rubbish from the cleared garden into the garden of the next door neighbour. This evidently created an externality ('environmental dumping', one might call it). However, it would be mistaken to think that the externality was not internalised in the process of bidding that went on between client and gardeners. The willingness to pay of any client for the services of garden clearance would depend not just on the value placed by the client on having a clear garden as opposed to having a garden in its original condition. It would also embody a component which is the value to the client of not having the garden next door cleared instead. The gardeners would visit that house whose inhabitant had the highest valuation of the difference between a cleared garden and one into which the neighbours' garden rubbish had been dumped. This would be the efficient house for them to visit.

More pertinently for the present argument, consider a process of negotiation between a government in one country (North) and a firm. Suppose that the net present value to the government of the benefits created by a decision by the firm to locate in the North is equal to ECU 100m. Suppose that, if instead the firm located in the South the South would gain benefits of ECU 120m but the North would suffer costs with a net present value of ECU 50m. (To simplify assume there are no externalities in the other direction.) The Northern government's willingness to bid to attract the firm is not ECU 100m but ECU 150m, since that is the difference between its overall benefits if it wins the bid and its benefits if the bid is won instead by the South. And the North would indeed win the bid since ECU 150m exceeds ECU 120m. Furthermore, it would be efficient for it to do so since the overall benefits that result (namely ECU 100m) exceed those of a decision to locate in the South (namely ECU 120m less the externality of ECU 50m).

This simple example shows why externalities alone do not result in inefficiency. There is indeed much inefficiency in the process of government competition, but its roots lie elsewhere. To see this, we outline the principal findings of this analytical framework.

The static (one-period) model

In a one-period framework with no restrictions on the form of governments' bidding strategies, the menu auction model of Bernheim and Whinston (1986) can be straightforwardly applied. Provided governments bid their true willingness to pay for firms' location and production decisions, government competition will result in efficient outcomes. In addition (and equivalently, in a world in which transfers between parties can be costlessly undertaken), firms' location and production decisions are those that maximize the sum of private profits and the net external benefits to the host economies. Where one-time locational subsidies are concerned (for instance when a firm is considering in which country to locate a greenfield plant of given size), firms receive transfers from governments equal to the net benefits that would have been created in the country with the second highest willingness to pay. The idea is the same as in an English auction where the successful bidder pays an amount equal to the willingness to pay of the second highest bidder. Where subsidies dependent on production levels are involved, the equilibrium transfers are more complex, but the marginal subsidies (the transfers for each extra unit of output) are equal to the net marginal external benefits while the absolute levels of transfer once again reflect the willingness to pay of the most serious rival bidder.

What would be the effects of controlling state aids in a world corresponding to the assumptions of this model? Since outcomes are efficient such a policy could not result in better location and production decisions by firms. At best it might be able to yield the same outcomes as under government competition, but at lower levels of transfers to firms. This might be a desirable policy if governments' overall ability to raise taxes is constrained below the efficient level (otherwise the payment of subsidies to firms can simply be covered from tax revenue raised elsewhere, albeit at some cost in tax distortions elsewhere in the economy). The costs of such a policy would depend upon whether in the absence of government competition there were other mechanisms for inducing firms to take account of externalities to the host economies in their location and production decisions. So, overall, the rationale for state aids policy would be like that of any policy for limiting public expenditure, and the costs of such limitation would depend on the effectiveness with which the benefits otherwise yielded by public expenditure could be achieved by other means. In the present post-Maastricht climate for public finance in the European Union, such an argument may carry considerable weight.

In practice, though, it is far from clear what those 'other means' might be. A supra-national authority (such as the European Commission) that knew the value of the external costs and benefits at all possible locations could simply implement a system of taxes and subsidies that gave the right fiscal incentives to firms. Quite apart from the question whether a supra-national authority could in practice know the value of these externalities as well as a national government or would have as strong incentives to reflect them in its tax system, it is evident that in the European Union as it exists today such supra-national fiscal powers do not exist. Alternatively, it could act as broker in an agreement between member states to restrict the levels of their state aids to firms. But such an agreement would have to ensure that incentives for production and location at the margin remained undistorted relative to those that would result from unfettered government competition, and it is hard to see how this could be achieved, since this would require knowing what firms would have bid in the absence of the policy.

Overall, it is hard to avoid the conclusion that there would be no credible role for EU state aids policy as such if the assumptions of this simple framework adequately described the real world. Or rather, state aids policy would merely be a form of collusion among governments to help each other keep down levels of public expenditure in general.

The dynamic (multi-period) model with commitment

In practice, of course, a single-period model does not adequately describe a world in which decisions about industrial location and production are made repeatedly over time. In particular, the magnitude of externalities to firms' decisions depends on the decisions made by those firms and by others in earlier and in later periods. There are both snowball and congestion effects, whereby the growth of economic activity in one particular location either increases the benefits of attracting further economic activity or raises the costs of doing so.

On its own this interdependence of the benefits of firms' decisions in time does not prevent efficient allocations, any more than their interdependence in space was seen to do in the single-period model. Indeed, if governments can commit to a single policy over time, then interdependence in time is exactly analogous to interdependence in space. A simple application of the Bernheim–Whinston argument shows that the auction process will lead to efficient allocations. All the arguments of the single-period model continue to apply.

However, there are good reasons for thinking that this analogy between spatial and temporal interdependence is misleading. In practice, governments (like any decision-maker) will find themselves tempted to do what is in their interests at the time, even if (when earlier decisions were in question) they would have preferred to be able to commit themselves to a different policy. This problem (known as the problem of time-consistency) bedevils many kinds of economic policy-making, of both a macro and a micro kind. Here it may yield inefficient results when governments compete with each other in the provision of state aids to firms.

The dynamic model without commitment

In this framework it is assumed that governments can make transfers to firms conditional on their present and past location and output decisions. But it cannot commit to making transfers conditional on future decisions; it can promise to do so, but it cannot prevent itself from changing its mind in the future when these decisions are realized.

Here the relevant results are those of Besley and Seabright (1998). They show that in a multi-period model without commitment, competition between governments can result in Pareto-inefficient outcomes. It does so because of a variant of what has come to be known as the 'hold-up problem'. The hold-up problem applies to situations in which parties entering an agreement fear that subsequent bargaining will oblige them to hand over to others a large share of the fruits of that agreement. Because they cannot commit not to engage in such bargaining they avoid entering into the agreement, even though (had such a commitment been possible) all parties would have been better off under the terms of the agreement. For example, workers may be deterred from undertaking firm-specific investments in human capital by the inability of the firm to commit to giving them an adequate return on these investments.

In the context of government competition the problem arises because governments competing to attract economic activity cannot commit themselves to avoid competing in the future. They therefore know that some decisions taken today will oblige them to pay out sums of money to firms in the future. Their inability to commit themselves not to do so may distort their current bidding, leading inefficient outcomes to be chosen. The circumstances under which this will occur are the following: the payoffs received by governments as a consequence of firms' decisions in later periods must depend on the outcome of earlier decisions. They must do so in a way that makes a significant difference to the sums of money that governments expect to pay out in future periods, so that some current decisions make it likely that there will be significantly higher transfers to firms than do others. For example, consider a high-technology industry in which the location decision of the first firm to set up substantially affects the external-ities generated by the decisions of later firms. Subsequent firms bringing a skilled workforce to an area may generate much higher benefits if there is already an industry employing those kinds of skill. Then the bidding for the first firm may be distorted, not by the induced impact on future external costs and benefits but by the induced impact on the price paid to firms by governments (which is a pure transfer and should not influence the present decision). For instance, it might be efficient for the North to allow the first firm to locate in the South, but the knowledge that this will induce the South to bid more keenly for subsequent firms (and therefore increase the price that the North has to pay) may make the North bid inefficiently high in the first period.

Typically, the efficient outcomes that are hard to attain in the Besley–Seabright model are those in which the earlier decisions make the bidding in later stages more intense. They will tend to lose to outcomes in which the earlier decisions lessen the intensity of bidding in later rounds and therefore lower the transfers that countries have to pay to attract firms. Even though the overall benefits generated may be lower, fewer of those benefits will be transferred to firms, and governments will consequently tend to prefer the result. This can be true even if governments attach some value to the profits of firms, provided this value is not as great as the value they attach to tax revenue.

To summarize, the circumstances in which state aids are most likely to be inef-ficient are those in which there is substantial interdependence between decisions over time, either because of locational 'clustering' effects or because of the effect of later decisions on the distribution of rents to existing firms. Governments' bids to attract firms are not just affected by the induced effect of current location decisions on the returns to future decisions (which it is reasonable and desirable for them to take into account). They are also affected by the induced impact on future bid payments, which are pure transfers from governments to firms with no real allocative consequences.

It is worth noting that although this interdependence between decisions over time requires firms to be in some sense 'large', imperfect competition in product markets is only one way in which this may occur. A firm can have large effects on the returns to future decisions through locational clustering effects even if it faces relatively competitive output markets. In effect, monopsony power in factor or input markets is as likely a source of distortion as monopoly power in output markets.

In such a model what would be the effect of a state aids policy? One possi-bility is to consider ceilings on allowable levels of subsidy (a complete ban on state aids would be a special case of such a policy, with the ceiling set at zero). After all, the inefficiency arises because governments are unable to commit not to compete against each other in the future. They therefore know that they will find themselves paying out subsidies to firms in the future, and their willingness to pay for location decisions today is distorted by their expectation of the likely subsidy burden in the future. For example, a government bidding for a firm in a high-technology industry today is likely to expect many competitor firms to come along in the future. It therefore knows that bids from rival countries will be high since there is a reasonable expectation that this industry will generate large rents, and that therefore it will find itself in the future likely to be obliged to pay large subsidies to attract firms that would otherwise have been wooed away to the detriment of the domestic industry. This likely future burden makes it unwilling to bid its true intrinsic willingness to pay today. In these circumstances it is tempting to conclude that an assurance of a cap on future subsidies tomorrow would make today's bids reflect more accurately the true strengths of benefit yielded by today's location decisions, besides ensuring that less of the resources of domestic taxpayers disappeared into the pockets of the firm.

However, this argument is seriously misleading. Why? It is true that the bidding today will be more likely to yield efficient outcomes if there is an assurance that there will be a ceiling on the bidding tomorrow. However, the bidding tomorrow is the mechanism by which firms' location and production decisions are induced to take account of the external costs and benefits to the host economy. Therefore a ceiling on the bidding tomorrow can only lower the expected value of state aids actually paid by distorting tomorrow's decisions.

Once again, as in the single-period model, the question arises whether there might exist a realistic alternative to a bidding mechanism as a way of internalizing the external effects of location and production decisions. In the absence of such a plausible alternative it must be concluded that restrictions on state aids have a significant cost which must be set against any benefits of avoiding the hold-up problem.

Finally, there is one other application of the multi-period model that might suggest a more active role for state aids policy. This is where the different periods of the model are interpreted not as stages in a sequence of location and production decisions by different firms in the same industry, but as different stages in the life of a given industrial project. Period 1 is the decision to build a plant. Period 2 is a decision whether to keep the plant in operation or to close it down and transfer production to another site, perhaps in a country with lower wage costs. Here there is a very good reason for the interdependence between the returns to decisions in the two periods, namely that the costs of setting up a greenfield site are very different from those of continuing production in an existing plant. In typical circumstances the former costs are higher, which is why production is not shifted continually to and fro between sites (and why therefore no new state aids are typically required to induce firms to keep production going in existing sites). But there are some circumstances in which greenfield production is cheaper. This may be because of a shift in costs at the new location (due for example to exchange rate movements). Alternatively, commitments at the existing plants may have become more expensive than foreseen, perhaps because of wage rises negotiated by existing employees or because of regulatory circumstances such as more stringent environmental legislation. These changes may make it credible that a firm might shift location without having yielded all the external benefits that were anticipated a the time of its original location; to prevent this from happening, a host government might then find itself paying a second time for the same benefits. The fear of doing so in the future might then distort original location decisions.

What would the role of state aids policy be in such circumstances? Presumably such a policy would treat asymmetrically aid to new investment from aid to existing plants, restricting the latter much more tightly. At least, it might try to do so, though the difficulties would be formidable since aid is given to firms rather than to plants, and aid may be fungible in practice even if it is tied in theory. The restriction of aid to existing plants could be seen as a kind of commitment device enabling the host government credibly to insist on paying once and only once for the external benefits yielded by the plant's initial location. The costs of such a restriction would be twofold: first, the inability of the aid policy to respond with adequate flexibility to changes in the external costs and benefits of a firm's production and location; and second, it would tend to distort investment decisions in favour of greenfield investment and away from development of existing plants. This second cost in particular might be severe. Of course, one conclusion might be that aid to greenfield investment should be similarly restricted, but this would return to the problem of preventing governments from acting to internalize the external benefits of the original location decision.

Alternatively, this predicament might provide some kind of rationale for the existing European policy of distinguishing between 'generic' and '*ad hoc*' state aids, the latter being those directed to specific firms while the former are available to all firms that meet general criteria. Such a distinction can be seen as obliging aid to existing plants to be justified by objective evidence about changes in the external costs and benefits, and as ruling out aids that arise purely from an increase in the firm's bargaining position relative to its host government.

It may indeed be true that a distinction of this kind is a valuable means of strengthening the hand of national governments against firms that seek state aids with the explicit or implicit threat that without such aids they will move their operations elsewhere. However, there is nothing that requires such a distinction to be applied at an international level: it does not help governments to restrict their competition against each other but rather to implement a more consistent policy with respect to their domestic firms. It therefore falls into the category of mechanisms to cope with national government failure, an issue to be discussed more fully below.

To summarize the conclusions of the multi-period analysis, there are indeed grounds for thinking that competition between governments may result in inefficient outcomes. This is particularly likely where imperfect competition or 'clustering' effects of locational decisions make the returns to later decisions in an industry heavily dependent on the results of earlier decisions. It is much less clear, however, that restrictions on the level of state aids are an appropriate response to the problem, since they alleviate the hold-up problem in current decisions at the costs of preventing future decisions from internalizing the external costs and benefits of industrial production to the host economy. The enforcement of a distinction between generic and ad hoc aids is, however, a more promising policy. But its primary benefit is to prevent a firm from using the threat of relocation to make governments pay more than once for the same external benefits, and should therefore be seen as a mechanism to solve a national market failure rather than one that solves a problem of genuinely international dimension.

Before moving to discuss national market failure we should consider a different set of conclusions which emerge once we take seriously the idea that institutional restrictions limit the applicability of the menu auction model of the process of government competition.

The model with institutional restrictions on bidding

In the case of a firm deciding where to locate a new plant it makes sense to suppose that it is free to bargain with all the governments that are affected by its decision. The assumptions of the menu auction model do not seem unrealistic in such a context. However, where the issue concerns a firm deciding levels of output in existing plants (and seeking state aid to do so), such an assertion is less clear-cut. Increases in its output may well impose costs on the economies of other countries that exceed the benefits to the host economy. What means do these other countries have to ensure the firm internalizes the costs?

In the case of a multinational firm the most convincing answer is via 'aid linkage'. Consider a car firm negotiating with government A about support for its existing operations in that country. At the same time, however, it is also being supported by government B for producing output in country B. If this output imposes external costs on country A – perhaps through reducing employment in country A – then the willingness of government A to pay it state aid will be reduced. Consequently, the external effects of any negotiation with country B will be internalized because the firm has other relations with country A.

Since many of the firms that are large enough for state aid to have a distortionary impact are also large enough to be multinational, in principle there is a mechanism for the internalization of the most important international externalities even when the aid does not concern investment in new plants. However, in practice this mechanism may work only imperfectly. For one thing, firms may not actually be in receipt of state aid in the second country that is damaged by their receipt of state aid in the first country. In theory so long as they pay taxes there is scope for negotiations over their tax liabilities, but most countries have rules requiring uniformity of tax treatment between firms. These rules could be changed (indeed, a special tax schedule requiring firms to pay a surcharge related to their receipt of state aid in other countries might do more to lower state aid levels than any amount of supra-national enforcement). But in their presence it seems reasonable to conclude that international externalities may be internalized only imperfectly. Second, some large firms may be intrinsically limited by regulatory or other factors from freely operating across national boundaries (banks or airlines, for example), even if the market within which they operate is clearly international. It may therefore be difficult for the governments of other countries to find a means to oblige the firm to take account of the costs it imposes upon them.

It is important not to overdramatize these costs. Output increases in country A will cause some loss of rents to country B but some gain to the consumers of country B. The only circumstance in which the consumer surplus change reinforces rather than offsetting the rent-shifting effect is when the state aid is used to finance predation designed to force rival firms out of the market, causing a long-run rise in the price of the product as well as a shift in rents. However, in the European Union predation is already illegal under Article 86, and there is no justification for using state aids policy as a means to enforce Article 86 by the back door.

Nevertheless, there are almost certainly cases in which the international externalities are large, are inadequately internalised by existing mechanisms of negotiation between firms and governments, and cannot be considered subject to the terms of Article 86. Aerospace may be one such industry (see Neven and Seabright, 1995). Semiconductors may be another. In both cases the presence of learning economies in production (the dependence of variable costs on scale) make the externalities of one firm's production decisions on another very large. The benefits of some kind of restraint on state aid at the supra-national level may be significant. Whether they warrant a state aid regime of the type currently in place in the EU is a more complex question, which we shall consider below.

The model with national government failure

The models so far considered all examine ways in which state aids that are in the interests of individual national governments may nevertheless lead to outcomes that are collectively inefficient. However, some arguments for the control of state aids at a supra-national level appeal to a different rationale. State aids, it is sometimes argued, frequently damage the interests even of those countries that undertake them. It would be in those countries' own interests to cut down their incidence. Supra-national state aid control is merely a collectively agreed mechanism for enabling them to do so.

Three versions of this argument need to be distinguished, of which the third is much the strongest. The first version points out that state aid damages the interests of the countries that undertake it, and then offers supra-national control as a form of medicine which countries should take for their own good even if at the time they find it unpalatable. In the context of the European Union this is clearly an unfortunate argument to deploy, particularly in the post-Maastricht era when member states are rightly concerned that the institutions of the EU should respect subsidiarity. It may be true (and often is) that subsidies to a particular firm are a waste of taxpayers' money. It is much less obvious that this waste is any business of the European Union.

Similar points have been made in the context of competition between states in the United States. For example, Netzer (1991) concludes a review of studies of inter-state competition for economic development in the following terms:

> Economic development incentives are, for the most part, neither very good nor very bad from the standpoint of efficient resource allocation in the economy. With all the imperfections, the offering of incentives does not represent a fall from grace, but neither does competition in this form operate in ways that truly parallel the efficiency-creating operations of private competitive markets. Given the low cost-effectiveness of lost instruments, there is little national impact, only a waste of local resources in most instances.

A second version of the argument says that state aid control is a form of pre-commitment device that is only credible when it is enforced at a supranational level. Governments would like to be able to commit themselves not to give state aids (particularly of the kind that enables firms with existing plants to extract further aid by threatening to move their operations elsewhere). Domestic mechanisms do not have the credibility that attaches to international mechanisms. So, for example, it would be possible for domestic aid policy or even domestic legislation to enshrine a distinction between generic aid and *ad hoc* aid, and refuse to give *ad hoc* aid, thereby obliging firms to demonstrate a credible source of market failure before they may have access to aid. But domestic firms with sufficiently political influence will find ways round such policies, which are therefore better enforced supranationally.

A difficulty with this argument is that it fails to explain why state aid control is a better candidate for internationalisation than is any other branch of competition policy. Competition policy in general involves exactly such issues of credibility and enforceability at the national level. Internationalization is normally justified only when there are identifiable international externalities, and not merely as a means to enhance domestic credibility, unless this is specifically requested by the member state concerned (see the discussion of the 'Dutch clause' in Neven *et al.*, 1993). By analogy therefore, the use of EU state aid control on credibility grounds should be something that individual member states should be free to sign up to, not something that should be imposed upon them.

The third version of the argument from national government failure focuses more precisely on identifiable international externalities. In preliminary work we are developing a model in which state aid decisions reflect not just the national interests of the host countries but may also reflect the private interests of lobbies. This is a two-period model in which, prior to taking state aid decisions, governments may choose whether or not to pre-commit themselves, at a cost, to a mechanism for ensuring rigour in state aid decisions (it is not specified how such a mechanism would be implemented). This choice can be made in a way that reflects national and not sectional interests. If there were no international externalities, countries would do so if the national benefits of increased rigour outweighed the costs of the commitment mechanism. But if state aid decisions in the second period involve significant negative international externalities, then it may be in individual countries' national interest to free ride on each other. In effect, if a significant proportion of the net costs of a country's government failure is borne by other countries, it may have a less than optimal incentive to pre-commit itself to a mechanism restricting the power of its lobbies.

The conclusion therefore appears to be that the justification for compulsory state aid control at the EU levels has to be based on the identification of international externalities that existing mechanisms of government competition are unable to internalize. Furthermore, these externalities must lead to consequences which state aid control can realistically ameliorate without losing the advantages of state aids in redressing market failures and internalizing the various costs and benefits to the host economy created by the location and production decisions of firms. Considering what such a policy might look like is the task of the section, Policy implications.

First, however, it is important to emphasize that the argument from national government failure depends upon there being some assurance that government failure at the international level is less serious than it is at the national level. In particular, the vulnerability of the state aid process to capture by lobbying interests must be less severe at the international level. Given that international externalities may affect consumers as well as firms, this is by no means a foregone conclusion: firms could easily come to use the process of state aid control (much as they have come to use the anti-dumping procedures) as a means of strategic harassment of competitors in which the interests of consumers are inadequately represented.

Policy implications

General implications

One sobering implication of our review of the literature has been that a state aids policy cannot simply be based on an attempt to distinguish between those aids to industry that rectify market failures and those that impose externalities on other countries. Because of the complex nature of interdependencies between the location and production decisions of firms, aids that do the former will typically also do the latter. What matters is whether the processes of government competition are able to internalize these externalities, and if not, whether a coordinated international policy of state aid control is able to improve the outcome.

Certainly, a policy which sought to outlaw all state aids that might impose externalities on other countries would be quite unrealistic. It would founder first on the inability even to define state aids as distinct from legitimate state activity. The state is involved in supplying all kinds of public goods, at prices which are not 'market prices' in any meaningful sense of the term, since the private sector cannot efficiently supply them, otherwise they would not be public goods. But even if some acceptable definition of state aids could be found, the only way to ensure that no such aids imposed externalities on other countries would be to outlaw state aids altogether. This is indeed the implication of the main contributions to the strategic trade policy literature, which draw on a model in which the location of economic activity makes essentially no difference except in distributional terms. But although the official rationale for state aid control often appears to draw on the intuitions of this literature, in practice, EU state aid control shrinks from so radical a conclusion, outlawing only a tiny proportion of those policy actions classified as state aid. It is right to do so, because the world is not like the models of strategic trade policy. Location makes a major difference, and there are major market failures which the location and production decisions of firms may either exacerbate or alleviate. It is right and legitimate that governments intervene to alleviate such market failures, and the test of the legitimacy of these interventions cannot be whether there are cross-border effects.

In practice, EU policy in recent years has rested heavily on the distinction between generic and *ad hoc* aids, where the former are understood as those aids that are available to all firms that meet suitably broad qualifying criteria, while the latter are those that are granted to particular named firms.[1] Normally speaking, there is more of a presumption of acceptability for generic schemes, while *ad hoc* aids are treated as presumptively suspect. (Policy has not been consistent on this point, however.) In principle this distinction is based on a reasonable idea, namely that generic aids are more likely to be targeted at genuine market failures rather than to be motivated purely by the desire to shift rents strategically from other countries. The reason for this is that, in markets that are imperfectly competitive and in which a struggle for rent-shifting takes place, the amount of subsidy that is optimal from the individual government's point of view will vary very much according to the strategic conditions in the industry concerned and the characteristics of the firm taking up the subsidy. A generic scheme which enables all firms to access a given level of subsidy according to pre-set conditions will be both a relatively ineffective and a relatively expensive way to engage in rent-shifting. It is relatively ineffective since it sets common subsidy levels whether these are the appropriate ones or not. It is relatively expensive since it grants subsidies to many firms that do not thereby gain increased rents in order to shift rents to the few that do.

The reflection that *ad hoc* aids may also give rise to *ex post* bargaining between firms and governments in which firms use the threat of relocation to induce governments to pay more than once for the same external benefits (as was discussed on pp. 220–221 above) also implies that a greater suspicion of *ad hoc* aids may be appropriate. Nevertheless it should be recognized that state aid control of this kind would be essentially a device to enable governments to overcome their own bargaining weaknesses rather than a means to prevent them from inflicting damage on each other. The grounds for making such a policy compulsory (as opposed to inviting governments to sign up on an individual basis to a code of conduct) are therefore somewhat weak.

However, although there are grounds for distinguishing between aid according to this criterion, the conclusion that all and only *ad hoc* aids should be outlawed is not really tenable. Many imperfectly competitive industries may have only one or a very few firms that can realistically benefit from a generic scheme. This has two implications: first, that it is relatively easy to devise a scheme that looks generic but is in fact designed to benefit a particular named firm. Second, that the market failures that arise in imperfectly competitive industries will often need to be addressed by measures that in fact benefit particular firms, and to prevent all ad hoc aids would be to leave such market failures unaddressed.

So the important policy question becomes two questions: is it possible to find criteria for identifying, first, generic aids that do distort competition, and second, *ad hoc* aids that are acceptable?

The first question is quite hard to answer. On the face of it, generic aid schemes would seem to be unlikely to distort competition provided significant numbers of firms are eligible, and the criteria for eligibility do not arbitrarily exclude certain firms that otherwise meet the purpose of the scheme. Schemes that in fact are taken up by very few firms are more problematic, and in these circumstances it seems appropriate to consider whether the fact of there being few eligible firms is the result of the market failure in question being of very localized applicability, or whether the generic aid is in fact an *ad hoc* aid in disguise.

However, it is important to stress that there is no reason whatever to expect generic aids to lead to a uniformity of competitive conditions between countries. Only in a world in which geography were irrelevant would this be so. There is no distortion of competition implicit in, say, one country's choosing to subsidize environmentally-friendly investment at a higher level than another. The importance of geography implies that we should expect the levels of taxes and subsidies that compensate for externalities to vary significantly between different locations – as indeed they need to do if they are to correct for the inefficiencies of location and production decisions taken solely on the basis of private profitability.

The second question is not much easier to answer. But some initial pointers can be made. First of all, *ad hoc* aids to firms that do not have significant market power are not likely to lead to rent-shifting on an important scale. Note that this market power need not be confined to output markets: a firm with little market power in output markets but with substantial market power in markets for a specialized input (say, skilled labour) could still use state aids to gain rents in this way (e.g. by poaching research scientists from other countries). However, given the similarity of technological processes across firms it is likely that market power in input markets will usually be exercised by firm also enjoying market power in output markets. A good beginning therefore would be to allow all *ad hoc* aids to firms with less than some threshold level of market power (which could in principle be analysed in the same way as is done for mergers or other anti-trust investigations). In effect, this conclusion reflects the fact that what matters is not whether the aid is intrinsically generic or intrinsically *ad hoc*, but whether the decision to grant it imposes a significant international externality. The *ad hoc*/generic distinction captures somewhat imperfectly the difference between aid that does and aid that does not create this type of externality.

The analysis of Besley and Seabright (1998) also suggests that for multinational firms undertaking greenfield investment, where it is realistic to suppose that they can negotiate with several governments, there is no case for compulsory state aid control. This is not to say that the outcome of such competition will always be efficient, but there is no reason to suppose that preventing state aids would improve matters, and it would remove from governments one of the principal means of internalizing locational externalities.

Matters are different where there are significant barriers to firms moving their operations between countries, and where output decisions in one country may therefore impose significant externalities between countries that cannot easily be internalized in the negotiation process. In such circumstances it makes sense to suppose that state aids may cause production and location decisions that internalize only one set of externalities (those in the home country) while failing to internalise those on other countries. But there are good grounds for requiring the case to be made with some care. It needs to be established: first, that the aid enables production to be at a level significantly different from what it would otherwise be; second, that this production affects the prices at which other firms in the EU can sell their output, or the amount of output they can sell; and third, that the cost of this externality more than outweighs any benefit to the host economy in terms of the alleviation of local market failures.

In making an evaluation along these lines it is important to note that it should not be the function of state aids policy to determine whether each and every instance of state aid is an appropriate response to a particular market failure. A great many cases are not, but those who bear the cost of inappropriately devised policies are overwhelmingly the citizens and taxpayers of the country granting the aid. The evaluation is appropriate only when it has been established that the aid creates an international externality that cannot be internalized by other means.

Nevertheless, if such an evaluation is to be performed it is important for it to be performed rigorously. Current EU policy contains a very significant flaw as far as the market failure evaluation is concerned. The Commission has sought to ensure that the regions eligible for aid under Article 92(3) are the same as those eligible for Structural Funds.[2] This policy has no justification, for it ignores the fact that state aids are those granted by member states (and therefore represent transfers between different regions of the same country), while the Structural Funds to a considerable extent represent transfers between member states. To put it another way, the fiscal resources required to pay for state aid have to come from within the country. If it is a rich country then it may be a legitimate use of resources to support other regions within that country even if these do not qualify for EU Structural Funds. If it is a poor country then transfers to a region eligible for Structural Funds may not resolve any market failures if they come from taxation levied upon other even poorer regions.

Finally, it is important to note that the most important cases in which *ad hoc* aids impose major externalities are those in which the presence of the aid enables predatory behaviour on the part of the aid recipient. In such circumstances Article 86 proceedings should be an adequate remedy.

To sum up, at a pragmatic level there is something to be said for the distinction between generic aids and *ad hoc* aids, and for treating the former as presumptively legal even though it must be recognized that some apparently generic aids may really be *ad hoc* aids in disguise. It should be emphasized that it is perfectly legitimate for the terms of generic aids to differ between countries. For countries that suffer badly from acid rain to subsidize environmental investment more than others is no more a distortion of competition that for countries with relatively scarce labour to have higher wages: both represent an appropriate response of the price mechanism to relative scarcity even if the good in question is in the former case a public good.

Ad hoc aids to multinational firms undertaking greenfield investment are also hard to justify prohibiting. Only when the firm in question is genuinely a national firm facing significant barriers to operating in other member states, and when the aid imposes externalities on other member states the cost of which outweighs any alleviation of domestic market failures, is there a defensible case for prohibition. Even here the most flagrant cases are ones for which Article 86 proceedings are likely to be an adequate remedy.

This is not to say that most state aids are desirable policy mechanisms. On the contrary, a great many of them are inefficient, a waste of taxpayers' resources. But those who suffer from them are the taxpayers of the member states that grant them. Those member states that wish to sign up to a collective code of practice on state aids, backed by the resources of the Commission in making the aid-granting process more transparent, may find that collective action improves their ability to reduce the incidence of wasteful aid. But the application of EU state aids policy to recalcitrant and unwilling member states, in the absence of a clear identification of the damage they cause to other countries, has very little rationale in economic analysis, and risks stifling the legitimate and healthy process of competition between governments.

A proposed policy rule

The considerations we have discussed above argue in favour of a policy rule that distinguishes between the compulsory elements of state aid control (those that should be binding on all member states) and those where member states may voluntarily sign up for a more rigorous form of monitoring and control. We begin with the compulsory component. We propose this in the form of a series of questions that the competition authority can pose, and a presumptive allocation of the burden of proof in response to these questions. We begin by presuming that the authority has identified a particular measure as constituting aid, on the grounds that a firm or group of firms is treated more favourably than other firms in the same jurisidiction:

1   Is the aid in question directed towards a named firm or to any firm that meets a number of generic criteria?

2   Is the actual beneficiary of the aid (in the case of *ad hoc* aids) or any of the likely beneficiaries (in the case of generic schemes) in a position to exert significant market power in either output or input markets? If not, the aid can be declared legal.

3   If the answer to question 2 is 'yes', would this market power, in conjunction with the granting of the aid, create a significant net negative cross-border externality? If not, the aid can be declared legal.

4   If the answer to question 3 is 'yes', is the rationale for the aid grounded in the alleviation of a domestic market failure (and is the aid an appropriate instrument, in quality and quantity, for that end)?

5   If the answer to question 4 is 'yes', and the aid is for greenfield investment, it can be declared legal.

6   If the answer to question 4 is 'yes', and it is aid to an existing firm or firms, have the firm or firms concerned already received aid in respect of the claimed market failure in question? If not, the aid can be declared legal. If they have already received such aid, the aid is illegal.

7   If the answer to question 4 is 'no', the aid can be declared illegal unless it can be shown that there are significant benefits from permitting it that would outweigh the cross-border costs (the burden of proof lying on the country granting aid to show that such benefits exist).

In question 3, note the importance of identifying a *net* negative cross-border externality. It should not be enough merely to show that some third party (such as a competitor) might be damaged by the state aid in question, for there may be others (such as consumers) who would benefit. Given the bias of lobbying procedures towards the interests of firms, failure to emphasize that the net externality be substantial might easily lead to an unduly restrictive policy.

What purpose might be served by a more rigorous form of supra-national monitoring and control? Countries might wish to sign up to this for one of two reasons: first, to enable a more credible commitment to more rigorous evaluation of the market failure rationale for state aid in the first place than they feel capable of undertaking on their own. One could imagine a code of practice or set of Brussels (or Geneva) Principles to which countries could choose to subscribe, and for the monitoring of which they might wish to draw on supra-national expertise. This could operate even in circumstances where clear cross-border externalities had not been identified. Second, countries might wish to undertake supra-national coordination of their bidding strategies in seeking to attract foreign direct investment. This may be either for the purpose of reducing the (explicit or implicit) subsidies paid to firms to locate in given areas, or to take account of the fact that initial location decisions are likely to change the economic benefits from location decisions in the future.

The appropriate form and institutional embodiment of this more rigorous form of monitoring and control are beyond the scope of this chapter. But we hope to have clarified the boundary between those forms of supranational action that can be justified by a clear appeal to international cross-border effects and those than cannot.

The Commission's procedure in its analysis of cases

General issues

Cases that have been found difficult by the Commission fall naturally into two types:

1 Cases of aid to firms in difficulty, which may be private sector firms at risk of bankruptcy, state-owned firms making losses or state-owned firms the government wishes to privatize.
2 Investment aid to ordinary profitable firms, usually under the umbrella of general schemes of aid in sectors or regions.

In practice, most of the difficult issues arise in respect of the first type of case. Before considering these types of aid in turn, it is important to note a number of issues that arise across all types of case (even though they are not always raised in the decisions). These issues fall into three main categories:

1 The 'asymmetry' question: does an alleged aid enable some firm or firms to enjoy cost or other advantages that are not enjoyed by its competitors?
2 The 'cross-border' question: does an aid to firms in one member state impose significant costs on the economy of another member state?
3 The 'market failure' question: does an aid contribute effectively to solving a real market failure in the member state concerned?

Logically, there is a natural link between the questions, in that only if the asymmetry question is answered affirmatively is there any need to ask the cross-border question. If the answer to the cross-border question is negative, then the market failure question is relevant only in so far as it reveals whether the member state concerned has been using its funds wisely. If the answer to the cross-border question is positive, then the market failure question becomes important, for if the aid concerned is not genuinely and effectively directed at solving a market failure, the suspicion must be that it succeeds in shifting resources to the domestic firm at the expense of firms in other member states.

The asymmetry question appears in several guises. It is used to establish whether an alleged aid should actually count as state aid in the first place. As a number of cases involving land sales have demonstrated (*Toyota*, *FMC*, *Fresenius*), this is often a difficult exercise to perform, since costs and other conditions of production vary in any case across locations. In the case of land sales the question asked is whether the firms concerned received the land more cheaply than the appropriate market price for that location. This is equivalent to asking whether it received the land at a cheaper price than another purchaser would have been willing to pay (and therefore whether it was privileged by comparison with this other hypothetical purchaser). This question is typically answered not by looking for another purchaser but by asking for a professional valuation; it provokes the question what is the use of a professional valuation if no other purchaser can be found. Bizarrely, in the *FMC* case (C41/96) the Commission arbitrarily decided that 'le prix evalué par l'expert peut être réduit de 10%, compte tenu de l'absence d'intérêt de tout candidat-acheteur' (p.11). A more useful way of determining whether an asymmetrical advantage has been conferred would be to examine whether the procedure for sale of the land or other asset was sufficiently open and transparent, and accepting whatever price had been offered by the highest bidder in an open transaction.

The asymmetry question also appears in establishing whether aid schemes for whole sectors or types of enterprises are in some sense discriminatory. For example, the aid scheme for the Greek pharmaceutical sector was disallowed on the grounds that, while its beneficiaries were only Greek firms, it was financed by a levy on the sales of all pharmaceutical products including imports. Foreign producers were therefore disadvantaged by being made to pay a levy for a scheme from which they were not entitled to benefit. Similarly, tax concessions in the Basque country were disallowed since they were granted only for locally established firms; foreign firms or even local subsidiaries of foreign firms were not entitled to benefit.

However, the asymmetry question is sometimes used in a subtly but importantly different sense, namely to establish whether firms in one location have advantages not enjoyed by firms in another location. Thus in *Ford-VW* (N 186/91) the Commission argues that locating in Setubal in Portugal will be highly disadvantageous to the firms concerned and that

> the resulting net cost disadvantages to the promoters of locating the plant at Setubal and the need to give an additional incentive to attract investment to this region justify the level and intensity of aid proposed and do not confer an unfair competitive advantage to the promoters in the market segment concerned.
>
> (p.7)

The judgment is that firms may justifiably receive aid up to the point at which their costs are no lower than those of other producers in other locations.[3] Implicit in this judgment is the claim that a 'reasonable' level of aid is on that equalizes costs and conditions of production in different locations. As our discussion has already made clear, there is no basis in economic logic for such a judgment. There will always be different conditions of competition in different locations, and their presence is what gives rise to gains from economic integration. For such differences to constitute 'distortions' of competition it is necessary that there be different conditions for firms at the same location (essentially in the same tax jurisdiction), whereby certain firms are assisted by being levied lower taxes or higher subsidies than otherwise similar firms in the same jurisdiction.

The reference to 'fairness' in the quoted sentence nevertheless reveals that the Commission feels itself under powerful pressure to reassure competitors that the recipients of aid are not thereby enjoying an 'unfair' or undeserved advantage. In our view the Commission should be very wary of accepting a role as an adjudicator of fairness, and even if it does should certainly avoid construing fairness as meaning that costs of production do not differ between locations.

The 'cross-border' question is crucial for establishing whether the existence of an asymmetry can be said to constitute a distortion of competition. As was pointed out in our discussion of the strategic trade policy literature above, the incentives for governments to engage in rent-shifting depend on the possibility that governments enjoy a first mover advantage over foreign firms, and can therefore commit to subsidy regimes that shift the reaction function of those foreign firms. For this to be true it is a necessary condition that there exist significant imperfect competition in the markets concerned, and that therefore the subsidy regime results in higher profits for the domestic industry not just by the amount of the subsidy but because foreign producers thereby lose profits themselves. The mere fact that domestic producers make a profit because of a subsidy may not make much difference to the profit opportunities for their foreign competitors.

The practice as revealed by the decisions is not at all consistent. Sometimes the presence of a distortion of competition is inferred merely from a large volume of intra-Community trade in the sector in question (see C20/91 on *Aid to the Italian electronics sector*, and C62/91 *Volkswagen* where it is stated that 'As there is considerable intra-Community trade in cars, the direct and indirect aid measures . . . clearly threaten to distort competition among vehicle manufacturers in the Community'). This is not a defensible procedure, since the magnitude of trade is no indication of the size of the externality imposed on other member states by one particular aid measure. The *Leyland-DAF Vans* case (N309/93) is based on more careful reasoning, for it is pointed out that since the firm's share of the overall EC van market is small (2.7 per cent falling to below 2 per cent), 'the effect of the restructuring aid . . . on other EC van producers will be negligible' (p. 6). Unfortunately this reasoning is directly contradicted in some other cases, such as *CNP* chemicals case (C47/91). Here it is stated (p. 7) that

> The Community market in chemical products is characterised by intense competition, and a large volume of intra-Community trade . . . the share of Portugal in the ethylene trade was 2.1% in value . . . and in the propylene trade 4.28% in value . . . in view of the foregoing considerations, the aid . . . is likely to affect trade between the member states and distort competition.

This is not an isolated case: in *Imepiel* (92/318/EEC), to take just one more example, the Community footwear market is described as 'highly competitive', and the aid is deemed to distort competition even though the firm in question produces less than a third of 1 per cent of the Community footwear market. As we have emphasized, if the sector is truly characterised by intense competition, then the only impact of state aid is (at worst) a waste of the member state's own tax resources, not any cross-border effect on the competitive situation faced by firms in other member states. Only if some important degree of imperfect competition can be identified (which may exist in factor markets and not only in product markets) should it be concluded that support for one firm creates a significant externality for those in other member states. However, as the *Micro Compact Car* case (N933/95) makes clear, in the case of an innovation that creates its own distinct sub-market, the fact of imperfect competition need not imply an adverse externality, because the product in question is a *de facto* monopoly, aid to which is not disadvantaging a competitor unless such a competitor already at least potentially exists.

The *LG electronics* case (N907/96) illustrates some difficulties in identifying the relevant cross-border effects. On the one hand, the Commission argues (p. 8) that 'The monitor market is a global market', which if correct implies that the projected output from the project (of about 2 per cent of world output) is too small to constitute a distortion of competition. However, it also cites two irrelevant considerations, first, that the major part of the projected output of computer monitors 'will be to replace products currently imported from the Far East to the EU'. This is irrelevant because other EU producers could be harmed just as easily by the presence of LG preventing them from displacing Far Eastern production themselves. Second, the Commission cites as a mitigating factor the fact that 94 per cent of output of television receivers will be supplied to LG's own television plant in the North East of England. This is similarly irrelevant since the output can just as much replace that which the LG plant would otherwise have to buy in from other suppliers. Overall, the conclusion should be that if the market is a world market there will be little distortion of competition, whereas if it is not, the precise destination of output will not prevent the aid from imposing an externality on other EU producers.

The 'market failure' question is one that is often asked indirectly and in a roundabout fashion when it could usefully be asked much more directly. Again, the precision in the Commission documents varies considerably. In *LG electronics* there is a section on 'the impact on the region' which mentions in a reasonably persuasive way some of the main market failures the project could be expected to alleviate (though without mentioning the term explicitly and without quantitative corroboration). In the *Micro Compact Car* case, however, the market failure issues are more sketchily addressed, the innovative character of the project being considered a reason for support in itself (without consideration as to whether there already exist adequate incentives for private sector firms to undertake such innovations without state support). Other considerations cited in mitigation include the high labour costs due to the 'jours fériés supplémentaires' in the Hambach region! In the *Ford-VW* case (186/91), high unemployment in the region of the plant is considered a reason to justify the aid (which makes sense) but no consideration is given to whether this is a good or cost-effective way to tackle the problem. Indeed, in these two decisions the Commission comes close to arguing that the adverse costs of operating in such an area constitute *ipso facto* justifications for the project, which is a perverse way of reasoning (so would siting a project in the Sahara desert). Overall, the question is never directly asked whether the aid concerned represents the best way of alleviating a given market failure. Measures such as the level of subsidy per job created, for example, might help to make this analysis more persuasive.

The careful posing of these three questions ought, therefore, to underlie the reasoning in all of the Commission's decisions. The practice of the Commission tends to vary significantly according to the type of case under consideration. We turn to the three main types of case.

Aid to firms in difficulty

Aid to a firm in difficulty has the effect at least of allowing the firm to continue its activities at a higher level than would otherwise occur. It may even be what allows the firm to continue in business at all rather than to exit the industry altogether, perhaps via bankruptcy. In more complex cases (such as *DAF* – 96/75/EC) the aid may allow assets from a bankrupt firm to be transferred to another company in ways the latter to keep them in production at a higher level than would otherwise be possible. If such a firm has significant market power, the aid may indeed shift rents from its competitors. However, this does not mean that in the absence of aid the firm's decisions would be efficient from the point of view of the market as a whole. As is well known, firms may exit an industry either too early (because senior creditors force bankruptcy without regard to the interests of other stakeholders in the firm, including workers) or too late, because they fail to internalize the beneficial externality created for other firms by their reduction of output. Although the incentive issues are complex (not least because there may be a conflict between what is efficient in a given case and the need to maintain credible incentives for other firms in the future), there are certainly good reasons why a government might wish to intervene to help firms in particular difficulties. This is not to imply that their intervention is always motivated by such good reasons: existing firms usually have much more political influence than do the potential firms that might exist in their absence.

In practice, the Commission has relied on a number of rules of thumb. The first is that aid should not consist of subsidies to operating losses. The second is that where aid takes the form of a capital injection or debt write-off to compensate for past losses, it must be linked to a credible restructuring plan whose purpose is to enable the firm to avoid making losses in the future. The third is that, in industries characterized by excess capacity, this plan should involve significant capacity reductions.

Although the Commission is not explicit on this point, the rationale for these rules of thumb is not that aid which observes these rules is less distortive of competition than the absence of aid altogether. After all, even the requirement that a restructuring plan involve capacity reductions implies that capacity will be lower than it was previously, not that capacity will be lower than it would have been in the absence of aid. Instead, the rules of thumb are best seen as a way of ensuring that, if the fact of aid is accepted as something which the Commission cannot realistically do much to prevent, it should at least be implemented in such a way as to minimise its distorting impact on competition. This is often admirable *realpolitik*, though it does not amount to a prohibition on competition-distorting aid. One way in which this makes a difference is in the arguments deployed in some controversial decisions in favour of allowing aid rather than insisting on liquidation of the firms concerned. In the *GAN* case, for example (C20/97), there is a lengthy discussion (pp. 11–14) of the comparison of the costs of the aid and restructuring compared to alternative solutions, notably that of liquidation. During the course of this discussion the Commission rejects the French government claim that the full social costs of liquidation should be considered, rather than merely the financial costs. The Commission argues that only the private costs are relevant to the question whether the French government acted as a private investor would have done, and consequently on the basis of this comparison deems the proposed capital injection to constitute state aid. But in subsequently determining compatibility of this aid with the common market, the Commission never poses the question whether, from a social point of view, the restructuring plan is better than the alternative of liquidation; for this comparison the full social costs of the two alternatives would have been relevant. Instead, the Commission takes the support for GAN as a *fait accompli*, and concentrates on two questions, namely, whether the restructuring plan is credible as a means of returning the group to viability, and whether a reduction in the group's presence on overseas markets would help to diminish the effect of the operation on competition in other member states. It may be that, if a full social comparison had been undertaken, liquidation would have seemed less costly overall, but the Commission would have been unable to insist upon this. Similar reasoning is followed in the case of *Almagrera*, a state-owned Spanish firm engaged in mineral production (N131/97).

Given that in many cases the granting of some aid is seen as a *fait accompli*, the requirement that aid should not consist of subsidies to operating losses makes sense principally as a form of commitment mechanism (see *VW Sachsen* C62/91). Repeated capital injections involve no less a subsidy to a firm's production than do operating subsidies. The Commission's intention, even if not always its effect, has been to make capital injections 'once and for all' measures which are easier to enforce than the ending of a continuing subsidy regime.

The requirement of a credible restructuring plan is likewise best understood as a means of reducing the likelihood of further aid rather than as a way of determining whether the current aid distorts competition. A number of cases of aid have been refused almost entirely on the grounds of the inadequacy of the restructuring plan (*Imepiel* – 92/318/EEC – *Intelhorce* – 92/321/EEC – and *Hytasa* – 92/317/EEC). Paradoxically, these firms operate in such competitive markets that, even with no restructuring at all, it is inconceivable that the aid would create anything like the distortion caused by *GAN* or *Thomson* (C62/96) even under the optimistic assumption that the restructuring plans proposed by the latter were entirely successful.

That said, the comments of the Commission on the plans proposed by companies often inject a note of highly welcome skepticism into what can otherwise read like exercises in bureaucratic wish-fulfilment on the part of the member state governments. *Thomson* is a good example of this, where the Commission's analysis reveals a large number of flaws in the hypotheses on which the restructuring plan is based, and also shows that these imply an expansion of Thomson's presence on European markets that would certainly have important cross-border effects on competitors. Nevertheless, the Commission's analysis, sharp though it is, never questions the judgment that the viability of Thomson multimedia (the part of the group in question that is in difficulty) should be assured if possible.

Investment aid to profitable firms

Aid of this kind is often justified in Commission decisions either on regional grounds or by specific reference to the need to create employment in the area concerned. Approval of the aid in question usually follows the routine application of certain rules of thumb concerning aid intensity (the aid may not constitute more than a certain percentage of the overall investment, the percentage depending on the region and the type of aid). In addition there is also a requirement, in industries characterized by excess capacity, that the aid not contribute to additional capacity. The routine application of this criterion can sometimes lead to illogical results. In *Technofibres* (44/91), for instance, the Commission concludes that there is no distortion of competition because the aid in question (for a new facility) will not increase capacity. However, the aid is intended to upgrade the quality of production, which is in principle no less likely to influence the behaviour of other competitors than an augmentation of the quantity of production.

Most of the negative decisions under this heading arise because the Commission deems a particular aid not to follow the rules on aid intensity or capacity. One or two (such as *Hoffman–LaRoche* 6/96) arise because the aid in question is deemed not to fall under the category of the appropriate scheme. The aid to Hoffman–LaRoche was (rightly) deemed by the Commission not to fall under the headings of basic or pre-competitive research and therefore not to qualify for the aid appropriate to such categories of research.

There is no doubt that the relatively routine application of such rules of thumb is a necessary approach to avoid the Commission becoming swamped by the workload that would be necessary to evaluate the individual merits of each case. However, particularly in the case of regional aid, this can mean that the Commission never really poses the question whether the aid concerned is an effective way of meeting the presumed market failure, or whether it distorts competition less than other ways of tackling the market failure in question. There is no easy way of resolving the question what is the appropriate balance between rules and discretion in such matters. But it should be noted that the effective scrutiny given by the Commission to regional aid is very much weaker than the scrutiny it gives to other forms of aid, and that this asymmetry by itself may give rise to potential distortions. To the extent that Commission scrutiny may be seen as a way of strengthening member states' own procedures for making aid decisions, it is far from obvious that it is less important to do so in assisted regions than in the rest of the Union.

Conclusion

It will be evident from our discussion above that the practice of the Commission in analysing cases is subject to a number of important strengths and weaknesses. Among its strengths are that the Commission can cast a skeptical eye over the often unrealistic judgments made by member states when deciding how to use public funds for the benefit of firms. Such a scrutiny may be of very great assistance to the member states concerned. The Commission is on weaker ground, however, in identifying the circumstances that constitute genuinely defensible grounds for compulsory state aid control. These ought properly to involve the identification of a clear cross border externality resulting from the aid in question. A necessary condition in most circumstances is that there be significantly imperfect competition in the product or factor markets in which the firm operates. The Commission's actual procedure fails to observe this, frequently diagnosing a distortion of competition where there is merely a pointless waste of resources for the member state concerned. We have also identified a number of other issues raised by the Commission's procedures.

The arguments of this chapter have yielded a number of conclusions that are significantly at variance with the mainstream of current policy analysis with regard to state aids. Nevertheless, the research remains preliminary. Many issues remain unresolved, and further investigation is necessary in order to assess the robustness of these conclusions. Here we mention briefly one or two such issues.

The first issue on which not enough is known is the process by which firms and governments negotiate over aid. In particular, it would be valuable to know more about the process according to which local and national governments plan their efforts to attract economic activity, and the way in which firms plan their negotiating strategies when seeking to extract benefits from governments. Evidence of this kind would be valuable in casting light on the extent to which the menu auction model is an adequate representation of the negotiating process, as well as highlighting the various dynamic problems (including failures of commitment) to which the negotiating process may give rise.

Second, we need to know more about how to identify empirically the circumstances in which state aids give rise to inefficiency. The work we have described above has shown through stylized examples how and why inefficiencies may arise. But it is one thing to use stylized examples, and quite another to diagnose the real-world circumstances to which these examples correspond.

Third, we need better empirical evidence about the effects of location decisions on the overall efficiency of production. The economic geography literature has argued, and we have assumed, that location decisions matter enough to make a quantitatively important difference to the overall efficiency of production. This assertion needs to be tested more rigorously: under what circumstances does location matter, and by how much?

These questions alone (and we could cite others) provide a formidable agenda for future work. But we hope we have already done enough to indicate that fundamental examination of the rationale for state aid control is both justified and necessary.

Notes

1 This statement needs to be qualified in two main ways. First, to qualify as state aid a measure must favour certain undertakings or the production of certain goods (fully general measures which do neither are addressed separately by Articles 101 and 102 of the Treaty). Second, early state aid decisions often argued that the granting of aid automatically implied a distortion of competition (see C-47/69 *France* v. *Commission*, where the latter argued that the imposition of a low tax on textile products was sure to distort trade and that 'the extent to which such . . . effects are translated into reality is . . . irrelevant'). Policy analysis in recent years has become more sophisticated!
2 See *Competition Policy Newsletter* summer 1995, p. 46.
3 This does not imply that it is wrong to compensate firms for undertaking public service obligations, nor that the appropriate level of compensation in such cases should be other than that which precisely offsets the disadvantage to the firm of supplying the service (see the discussion in *TAP* – 94/666/EC). But a public service obligation implies the provision of a (by definition non-tradable) service that would not otherwise have been provided. Here what is at issue is the production of a good that *would* otherwise have been produced, only at a different location.

References

Bernheim, D. and Whinston, M. (1986) 'Menu auctions, resource allocation and economic influence', *Quarterly Journal of Economics* 101, 1–31.

Besley, T. and Seabright, P. (1998): *Does Intergovernmental Competition Result in Efficient Investments in the Presence of Locational Externalities?*, London: London School of Economics, mimeo.

Bewley, T. (1981) 'A Critique of Tiebout's theory of local public expenditures', *Econometrica* 49, 713–740.

Black, D. and Hoyt, W. (1989) 'Bidding for firms', *American Economic Review* 79, 1249–1256.

Bond, E. and Samuelson, L. (1986) 'Tax holidays as signals', *American Economic Review* 76, 820–826.

Brander, J. and Spencer, B. (1985) 'Export subsidies and international market share rivalry', *Journal of International Economics* 18, 83–100.

Brennan, G. and Buchanan, J. (1980) *The Power to Tax: Analytical Foundations of a Fiscal Constitution*, Cambridge: Cambridge University Press.

Dye, T. (1990) *American Federalism: Competition among Governments*, Lexington, MA: D.C. Heath.

Haaparanta, P. (1996) 'Competition for foreign direct investments', *Journal of Public Economics* 63, 141–53.

Karp, L. and Perloff, J. (1990) *Why Industrial Policies Fail: Limited Commitment* discussion paper no. 450, London: Centre for Economic Policy Research.

Keen, M. and Marchand, M. (1997) *Fiscal Competition and the Pattern of Public Spending*, University of Essex, mimeo.

Kenyon, D. and Kincaid, J. (1991) *Competition among States and Local Governments*, Washington DC: The Urban Institute.

King, I. and Welling, L. (1992): 'Commitment, efficiency and footloose firms', *Economica* 59, 63–73.

King, I., McAfee, P. and Welling, L. (1993) 'Industrial blackmail: dynamic tax competition and public investment', *Canadian Journal of Economics* 26, 590–608.

Krugman, P. (1991) *Geography and Trade*, Cambridge, MA: MIT Press.

Leahy, D. and Neary, P. (1996): 'International R&D rivalry and industrial strategy without government commitment', *Review of International Economics* 4, 322–338.

Mederer, W. (1996) 'The future of state aid control', *Competition Policy Newsletter* 3(2), 12–14.

Netzer, R. (1991) 'An evaluation of interjurisdictional competition through economic development incentives', in D. Kenyon and J. Kincaid (eds) *Competition among States and Local Governments*, Washington DC: The Urban Institute.

Neven, D. and Seabright, P. (1995) 'European industrial policy: the Airbus case', *Economic Policy* 21.

Neven, D., Nuttall, R. and Seabright, P. (1993) *Merger in Daylight*, London: Centre for Economic Policy Research.

Oates, W. (1969) 'The effects of property taxes and local public spending on property values: an empirical study of tax capitalization and the Tiebout hypothesis', *Journal of Political Economy* 77, 957–971.

Oates, W. and Schwab, R. (1991) 'The allocative and distributive implications of local fiscal competition', in D. Kenyon and J. Kincaid (eds) *Competition among States and Local Governments*, Washington, DC: The Urban Institute.

Pestieau, P. (1977) 'The optimality limits of the Tiebout model', in W. Oates (ed.) *The Political Economy of Fiscal Federalism*, Lexington, MA: Lexington Books.

Seabright, P. (1996) 'Accountability and decentralisation in government: an incomplete contracts model', *European Economic Review*.

Tiebout, W. (1956) 'A pure theory of local expenditures', *Journal of Political Economy* 6, 416–424.

Index

DATE DUE